Earliest Christianity

MARTIN HENGEL

Earliest Christianity

Containing

Acts and the History of
Earliest Christianity

Property and Riches
in the Early Church

SCM PRESS LTD

Translated by John Bowden from the German.

Acts and the History of Earliest Christianity,
first published 1979 by SCM Press Ltd, is a
translation of *Zur urchristlichen
Geschichtsschreibung*, and *Property and Riches
in the Early Church*, first published 1974 by
SCM Press Ltd, is a translation of *Eigentum
und Reichtum in der frühen Kirche*, both
originally published by Calwer Verlag,
Stuttgart, 1979, 1973.

British Library Cataloguing-in-Publication Data available

334 00346 6
This collection first published 1986
by SCM Press Ltd,
26–30 Tottenham Road, London N1
Printed in Great Britain by
Richard Clay (The Chaucer Press) plc
Bungay, Suffolk

CONTENTS

PROPERTY AND RICHES IN THE EARLY CHURCH

Acts and the History of Earliest Christianity

I

History Writing in Antiquity and in Earliest Christianity

I

The Sources of the History of Earliest Christianity in the Context of Ancient Historiography and Biography

1.1 The basic problem in writing a history of early Christianity lies in the fragmentariness of the sources and the haphazard way in which they have survived. However, this situation hampers not only research into the origins of our faith, but also the study of ancient history generally, in both the political and the cultural and religious spheres. In contrast to modern historiography, the particular difficulty here is not the over-abundance of source material, but the chronic shortage of it. Only seldom do we have a full supply, and often it is a question of working, like a detective, with sparse clues, all of which we have to examine very carefully (to some degree with a magnifying glass) without reading too much into them. It is not always easy to find the right level here.

In other words, the absence or the sparseness of the sources vitiates our knowledge of large areas of the ancient world. Furthermore, what we do know is largely dependent on often quite chance circumstances. Thus, for example, our knowledge about events in the Hellenistic states after the time of Alexander the Great in the third and second centuries BC, or about the Roman principate in the second and third centuries AD, is as fragmentary and inadequate as that about the development of contemporary philosophical schools, say the Academy after Plato, the early Stoa, or so-called Middle Platonism in the first and second centuries AD.

Our knowledge is even more fragmentary when it comes to the fortunes of individual areas and provinces. How very little we really know about Syria in the first century BC and the first century AD, above all about the religious atmosphere prevailing there in that period, or about Judaea under the Roman prefects between AD 6 and AD 41 (which is even closer to the heart of the New Testament scholar)! Our knowledge of the Roman province of Judaea (which in the meantime had become independent) in the period between the Jewish War of AD 66–74 and the Bar Kochba revolt (AD 132–135) is even slimmer. Ancient secular sources only give it quite passing mentions. True, we have a relatively large number of Talmudic reports from that period, but they are disjointed in the extreme, uninterested in historical connections, and for the most part a mishmash of legends and historical anecdotes which it is virtually impossible to sort out. All one can do here, with a great deal of hard work and considerable caution, is to attempt to reconstruct individual events. What I have said here also applies to other areas or places. One need only read once through the relevant chapter in Downey's great history of Antioch to see how much our knowledge of the fortunes of the Syrian metropolis in the first century AD consists of fragments and conjectures. The accounts which have come down to us are far from being adequate for the reconstruction of a continuous history of the city which became the first cosmopolitan centre of Christianity, even if we resign ourselves to the inevitability of a number of gaps. What is true of Syria can be said to be even more true of tiny Palestine. The Bar Kochba rebellion, mentioned above, is a good instance of that. It is only as a result of the numerous new discoveries from the caves in the wilderness of Judaea that we gain a more vivid picture of the desperate revolt under the leadership of the pseudo-messianic 'Son of the stars', which ended in a war of total annihilation and drove the Jews out of Judaea for about 1700 years. Now we suddenly have a view of the fortunes of some individuals, like the Jewess Babatha and her family. Unfortunately, however, that remains the exception.

All too often we are left only with traces: names of people without specific details, isolated events, sporadic accounts or obscure legends – as from the Talmudic literature, except where suddenly larger fragments emerge, resting on individual, lucky discoveries. We constantly come up against gaps and white patches on the map; our sources are uncertain and we have to content ourselves with more or less hypothetical reconstructions. All this is true of ancient history in general and even more of the history of early Christianity in particular, above all during its first 150 years. Whether they like it or not, scholars find that narrow limits are set to their quest for knowledge here. This may be a stumbling block to us, but we must recognize that for the truth's sake. The situation is not altered much by the fact that our knowledge has constantly been enlarged since the middle of the last century by a wealth of new discoveries. Their fragmentary character remains. There are great expanses where we can no longer obtain a really comprehensive view of individual events and epochs in the ancient world, and earliest Christianity is no exception here. New discoveries which seem to answer old questions always at the same time pose new problems and call for new hypotheses. Thus for example the few specific messianic texts from Qumran, which are most interesting for Jewish religious history, have been preserved only in a very fragmentary condition. Here our knowledge is essentially based on what rats and worms happen to have left of the scrolls in the caves in the wilderness of Judaea. Each fragment enlarges our knowledge, but also poses still more new riddles. The situation is often the same with Egyptian papyri, which are significant from a literary or historical point of view, or with inscriptions. How often the fragment of a text breaks off at the most important point! That is why the historian is asked to show self-critical modesty, if not scepticism – which here would be no more than a form of all too convenient resignation. He needs to see the limits to the possibilities of his knowledge, while at the same time pressing on within these limits and carefully attempting to extend them step by step. In doing this he must clearly differentiate between the various degrees of probability in his knowledge.

1.2 We have already seen that our lack of sources is often due to fortuitous and apparently external circumstances. Another factor is the whole complex of problems associated with the nature of books in antiquity and the transmission of ancient texts. The writing and reproduction of books was a much more wearisome business than it is today. As a rule, for technical reasons alone, an

author was compelled to keep his material within strict limits.
He had to make careful plans in advance so that his work would
be the right length, since there was comparatively little room on
papyrus scrolls and they were very expensive indeed, given the
wages earned by the majority of the population. By and large, only
rich people could afford a large number of books, i.e. a real library.
So, for example, it is very doubtful whether the early Christian
churches always owned the texts of all the books of the Old
Testament; indeed, we cannot even take it for granted that in the
early period everyone had access to the writings which were
collected together towards the end of the second century to form
the New Testament canon. For this reason people were fond of
using collections of testimonies and extracts, or often simply
quoted from memory – which at that time still tended to be very
good. For instance, Luke does not seem to have known the letters
of Paul (see p. 66 below), and they are not referred to by Papias
or even by Justin. On the other hand, the letters of Paul appear
round about AD 180, in a Latin translation, in the African church
of Scili, where they were confiscated by the Roman authorities.
By contrast, the source which gives us this information does not
make any clear reference to the gospels.

A further problem is the copying and handing down of earlier
historical works, where chance, external difficulties of transmission
and various questions of content have all contributed to the destruction and reduction of sources. Hardly any of the great historical
works of the Hellenistic and Roman period have come down to us
unabbreviated. Extensive gaps in the text and abbreviation in the
form of summaries are the rule here. I need mention only the three
most important Greek historians of the Hellenistic and Roman
period in this connection. These were Polybius and Diodore, each
of whom wrote a history of the world in forty volumes (the first was
a contemporary of Scipio the Younger in the second century BC and
the second a contemporary of Caesar in the first century BC), and
Dio Cassius, who wrote in the time of Septimius Severus at the end
of the second and beginning of the third century AD, and whose
History of Rome extended to eighty books. We have only about a
third of Polybius' work, with the first five books in their entirety;

sixteen books of Diodore, and some very fragmentary excerpts; while from Dio Cassius we have books 36–60, fragments of books 78 and 79, and some very abbreviated summaries from the Byzantine period. The 144-volume history of the world written by Nicolaus of Damascus, a friend of king Herod, who composed his work in Jerusalem, has been lost completely – presumably, like most ancient histories, because of its excessive length. However, even smaller works did not escape unscathed. Of the sixteen books of Tacitus' *Annals*, which are fundamental to our knowledge of Roman history in the first century AD, books 7–10 are missing. They are important for the history of the New Testament period as they covered the years 37–47 and also dealt with the situation in Judaea under Tiberius and Caligula. Of the sixteen books of his *Histories*, about the period from the death of Nero to Nerva, we have only books 1–4 and the beginning of 5 with its notorious antisemitic account of the Jews and the conquest of Jerusalem. Compared with the great histories of the world, the twenty books of Josephus' *Jewish Antiquities*, our main source for Jewish history after the exile and up to the beginning of the Jewish War in AD 66, make quite a modest impression. Here the priest and historian who lived in Jerusalem assiduously transcribed the great work of Nicolaus of Damascus. The same thing is even more true of the seven books of his first work, the *Jewish War*. It is a special gift of providence that the works of Josephus have survived when those of his Jewish competitor and opponent, Justus of Tiberias, have been lost. By far the greater part of our knowledge about Jewish history in the Hellenistic period from the time of the conquest of Palestine by Alexander the Great comes from Josephus. A whole series of names and narratives from the gospels and Acts only become really comprehensible in the light of the more detailed report by the Jewish historian. Presumably his works continued to be handed down because of their relevance for early Christian history writing. By contrast, apart from a very few allusions, the work of Justus, who is said to have composed a chronicle of the Jewish kings in addition to a history of the Jewish war, has disappeared completely. The Patriarch Photius (*c.* AD 820–886) still had extracts from it read aloud to him, but it made a very bad impression on him, as it said nothing about 'the appearance of Christ, his history and his miracles'. Since then it has disappeared completely.

1.3 In the last resort, the length of the four gospels and Acts is also determined by the fact that they are deliberately limited to one scroll. The earliest Christian communities were poor, and did not have large libraries at their disposal; furthermore, too long a book presented problems for liturgical readings. Its content had to be restricted to the most important details, and other less essential features were omitted. Scrolls were inconvenient to use in worship, and the Christian church tended to differ markedly from the Jewish community from which it had arisen; presumably round about the beginning of the second century these factors led to a transition from the scroll to the codex, which had the form of a modern book. The codex derived from the notebook, and as the poet Martial already pointed out, was much more practical than the traditional, more conservative papyrus scroll. The need to keep to the length of one scroll themselves is presumably the chief reason why both Matthew and Luke restricted their use of the material in Mark, which served as their model. Matthew abbreviated Mark by a radical reduction of Mark's miracle stories; Luke avoided doublets and simply omitted a complete section of the Second Gospel (Mark 6.45–8.10). Thus the reasons for the self-restraint of the earliest Christian historians were predominantly external and do not go back, say, to deficiencies in the tradition about Jesus or a concern for theological purity. One of their chief problems was to make an acceptable selection from the wider and still abundant tradition at their disposal. So the evidence of Luke 1.1 and John 20.30 is more than exaggerated literary convention. The Fourth Evangelist could certainly have told of further signs which Jesus performed in the presence of his disciples. Papias indicated as much in his *Exposition of the Oracles of the Lord*, written round about AD 130 (Eusebius, HE 3.39.1). This was a five-volume work in which (as far as we can tell from the surviving fragments) he neatly combined the extravagances of the tradition with sound and authentic material. Luke already departed from the rule that works should occupy a single scroll when he continued the history which he had begun by adding a second volume to his 'first book' (cf. Acts 1.1, *protos logos*). This represents the first step towards a multi-volume history. He will have been prompted to do this not so much by the extensive histories current in the Hellenistic Roman world, which ran to a far greater number of volumes, as by the histories in the Old Testament. There the five books of Moses, the Pentateuch, were followed by the 'prophetic' historical books of Joshua, Judges and Samuel, which continue the history of the people of God called into being by God's revelation to Moses (see p. 31 below).

It is easy to see how later revision led to the loss of an original source. This is already clear in earliest Christianity from the way in which Matthew and Luke transcribed a sayings source (Q), which then disappeared. At this point we need not concern ourselves further with the fact that the evangelists presumably had different forms of this writing, the existence of which is disputed by a number of scholars. It is a piece of good fortune that the Gospel of Mark did not suffer the same fate; possibly the authority of Peter, which was supposed to stand behind the work, presented the Second Gospel for posterity (see pp. 92f. below). It is quite likely that we would have lost further sources had Tatian succeeded in his purpose of replacing the four 'different' gospels with his harmony of the gospels, the so-called *Diatessaron*. This work, composed in Syriac or Greek after AD 170, arranged the synoptic material within the framework of the Gospel of John, while omitting the obvious parallel traditions. It was only the fact that the four gospels already had a firm place in the church at the time when Tatian produced his Harmony which saved them from extinction. The *Diatessaron* continued to play a significant part in the church in Syria for a long time to come, but the canonization of 'individual' gospels contributed to its suppression, and we no longer possess it in its original language. The fact that it was translated into numerous languages shows how great was the need for a comprehensive harmony of this kind which did away with the contradictions between the four gospels. As well as the five-volume work by Papias, which has already been mentioned, we have also lost the 'church history' which followed Luke's work, namely the 'historical apologetic' (von Weizsäcker) of the Jewish Christian Hegesippus. This ran to five books and was written at about the same time as the *Diatessaron*. It contained information from the earliest period, for example about the martyrdom of James the brother of the Lord and the fate of the Lord's kinsfolk (Eusebius, HE 2.23; 3.20). Manuscripts of this work, which could add considerably to our knowledge of early Christianity in the second half of the first and the first half of the second century AD, are said to have survived in Greek monasteries down to the sixteenth and seventeenth centuries. Nevertheless, they shared the fate of the greater part of the flourishing Christian literature of the second century AD, and are no longer available to us.

1.4 Generally speaking, it is the case that our lack of information begins with the fact that ancient authors were compelled to set quite strict limits to the narrative material which came down to them from oral tradition or from written sources, and this reduction in the extent of the tradition continued constantly even in works which had become 'literature'. This abbreviation of the source material is due to later authors of summaries, and those who produced excerpts. Much – it would be better to say most – has been lost either because the style and content were displeasing to later generations or because of numerous strokes of fate in an all too long history of tradition. For example, the only extant manuscript of the Epistle of Diognetus (end of the second century) was burnt during the bombardment of Strasbourg in the siege of 1870. Fortunately, there had been numerous editions of this epistle in the meantime. It was largely unknown in antiquity and during the Middle Ages, and was ascribed to Justin Martyr; the first edition was produced by the printer and philologist Henri Stephanus in 1592. The most recent discoveries of manuscripts on Sinai show the enormous amount of early Christian literature which was destroyed or forgotten in eastern monasteries and was therefore lost. In other words, down to the nineteenth century the handing on of tradition was accompanied by a constant loss of tradition. In essentials this begins when the first work was committed to writing, since we must reckon with the fact that from the beginning the earliest Christian writers and their successors tended to reduce their narrative material much more often than they expanded and elaborated it. Thus even in the case of the gospels and Acts, we should not put too much emphasis on the narrative expansion of the material; we should be much more concerned to begin from the reduction and concentration of a tradition that was originally much richer. In oral tradition, a broad, detailed narrative which could be longer or shorter as occasion demanded may have been the rule; however, as soon as it was put down in writing, it tended to be abbreviated. Where we still come across it, for example in Mark or Acts, its content and character are significant or normative and represent an exception. There is abundant evidence of this from the treatment of rabbinic anecdotes in the Mishnah and the Talmudim, in the Gospels and elsewhere in ancient historiography – for example in Josephus. The same is true of the presentation of teaching. The lectures of the Stoic Epictetus were put into good Attic and collected together in eight books by his favourite pupil Arrian. However, the quintessence of them was recorded yet again in a single 'handbook'. Thus we have no more of the 'original' Epictetus than we do of the original Socrates or Jesus. We may assume that Paul's letters, for example Romans and certain passages of the two letters to the Corinthians, contain brief summaries of lectures and to some extent the much reduced quintessence of what Paul taught in public over a period of two or three years in the 'school of Tyrannus' in Ephesus (Acts 19.9), albeit directed towards the situation of the recipients of the letter.

We have an excellent example of the deliberate literary abbreviation of a historical work in the account of the Hellenistic reform in Jerusalem and the victorious struggle of Judas Maccabaeus. Jason of Cyrene, a Diaspora Jew, wrote a history in five volumes which in the first century BC was compressed into one volume, known to us as II Maccabees, by an unknown epitomator. The epitomator did this to provide the reader with better entertainment by making the work easier to read, for 'wine mixed with water is sweet and delicious and enhances one's enjoyment. So also the style of the story delights the ears of those who read the summary account' (II Macc. 15.39). The works of the Roman jurists suffered a similar fate of abbreviation and compression. At the time of Justinian they were concentrated in the *Digests*. The rigour of this procedure emerges from the fact that at that time two thousand books of three million lines are said to have been reduced to fifty 'books' of one hundred and fifty thousand lines.

By contrast, we find an untrammelled and open 'delight in storytelling', which is contrary to real history writing, in the romance; in early Christianity, the romance took the form of 'acts' of apostles. In the ancient world, however, assessments differed from those of modern times, and the romance in particular was seen as a more second-rate literary genre, a form of entertainment for the semi-literate. No writer of any pretensions bothered with it. We may frame all kinds of hypotheses about the literary genre of the gospels and Luke's Acts, but they certainly did not set out to be religious romances. Though they are set in the context of antiquity and do not come up to modern standards in this respect, they claim to be accounts of what really happened, and not literary fictions. People did not look to them for edifying entertainment which bore no relation to the truth. A passage in Tertullian shows that people in antiquity were well aware of the problem of pious fiction and were critical of it in at least some respects. Tertullian reports that the presbyter who in Asia Minor during the second half of the second century related the acts of Paul and Thecla 'as though he could make his own contribution to Paul's reputation, was removed from office after he had been found guilty and had confessed that he had done this out of love for Paul'.

The modern historian has to keep making new critical investigations of the question how far the reports of the earliest Christian writers are based on historical reality. He cannot give either a prompt and over-hasty 'yes' or an emphatic 'no' to the question whether a particular narrative has historical value. Even legends with a miraculous character may well have a valuable historical nucleus, whereas allegedly eye-witness accounts and original documents could well be forgeries. Accounts of miracles keep cropping up in 'secular' historiography from ancient times, since the way in which reality was understood in this period by the

narrator, who often not only handed on his report but also interpreted it, was substantially different from our own. Even when we
doubt the historicity of a particular account, we must look for its
historical nucleus, or ask why it was produced in the first place.

1.5 There are also intrinsic reasons for the lack of ancient sources
which makes the work of modern exegetes and historians so
difficult. This lack is connected with the one-sided methodology of
ancient narrators and historians, whose methods are poles apart
from their modern counterparts. One typical feature of their way of
going about things is the concentration of their accounts on what
happens in the world of the great figures; they take account of
relatively few centres or focal points. At least in those works which
have come down to us, ancient history writing was concerned with
what seemed to be the most important events, with leading figures
and with select, characteristic evidence. They simply presented
what interested them and their readers, because they depended
on the good will of their readers and wanted to instruct them,
admonish them and – also – entertain them. In the ancient world,
the abundance of information from all sides, which we take for
granted, was simply not there. Reports were still in short
supply.

Lucian of Samosata, the Voltaire of the ancient world, drew up a
set of rules for the budding historian in his book *How to Write
History*. In it, he counselled the historian against having an eye for
his own advantage and the favour of his reader, as this would
destroy his freedom and veracity (9, 61, 63), but he did promise
him success with his readers if he attracted their attention and
curiosity as early as the foreword: 'If he shows that what he is
going to say will be important, essential, personal, or useful' (53).
On the other hand, all inessential and minor matters ought to be
left on one side, since those who entertain their friends with an
opulent meal do not produce salt fish and pea soup at the same
time (56). So from this perspective, too, there was pressure towards
a strict limitation and selection of material. Lucian was concerned
to enjoin this narrow perspective on the historian. The chief
interest of historiography was political history, which was concen-

trated in the great cities and seats of government, and the description of warlike events, disturbances and strokes of fate. The deeds and misdeeds of rulers and usurpers had a special role – the way in which they were assessed depended on the degree of their success; other important features were the fates of important members of the upper classes, individual generals, politicians and artists. There was also some interest in the inclusion of geographical, ethnographic and religious information. In addition there were also historical monographs, i.e. specialist histories on quite limited themes: individual provinces, cities, nations and sanctuaries, or even 'notable' features. However, for the most part we have only the title, or excerpts and fragments, as quoted in other historical works. Thus the way in which the ancient historian went about his work called for a degree of eclecticism. Great importance was attached to typical episodes and programme-like speeches, which were composed in a relatively free way; there was no concern to avoid tendentiousness or powerful value judgments. True, Lucian (7) warns against confusing historiography and panegyric, but for all his strict rules he has to concede the right to praise and to blame. However, value judgments must be applied 'sparingly and with due consideration', and there must be real reasons for them (59). All this was, of course, easier said than done. Probably no ancient historian really did justice to Cicero's requirement of the orator that he should 'avoid any suspicion of favour or hostility' (*De oratore* 2.15, 62), or Tacitus' ideal that 'no one should be mentioned out of favour or hate' (*Hist.* 1.1.4; see p. 22 below).

What was neglected tended to be everyday life, things that were taken for granted because they were uninteresting. For the most part, the historian could leave on one side the situation of the ordinary population, the manual workers and the slaves, the proletariat in the city and the peasants and tax farmers in the country, in short, everything that is of particular interest today under the heading of 'social history'. When it came to this kind of thing, the ancient historian at best raised the question in connection with slave rebellions and other social unrest, with famines and severe natural catastrophes.

1.6 Biography is a case by itself. A wide variety of biographies have come down to us from antiquity. Because they concentrated on the fortunes of one person, they differed from history writing proper and had laws of their own. We may see them as a typical product of the early-Hellenistic period, the era in which the individual was discovered. Classic historians, like Thucydides, who was interested in public politics and the waging of war, still had no feeling for the individual. The roots of biography lie in panegyric of rulers and generals on the one hand, and in the oriental novel on the other. Herodotus already made use of the novel, and it then came to be utilized above all to portray the philosophical teacher and his pupils, say Pythagoras and Socrates. It reached a first golden age in the narrative of the deeds of Alexander. Auto-biography was one by-product of this development, emerging above all from accounts of journeys and campaigns. Nicolaus of Damascus, Herod's friend, whom we have already come across, spent a good deal of his life in Jerusalem. In addition to his great 144-volume history, he wrote not only a biography of Augustus but also a very conceited autobiography. In it, he boasts that he taught Herod rhetoric and history writing (FGrHist 90 F 135). At the very beginning of our era, Greek education was firmly established even in Jerusalem. Of course, ancient biography was very different from modern biography in the scientific sense. It did not even have a unitary form, thanks to its very different roots. It ranged from a loose collection of anecdotes and sayings of the kind that we find in Lucian's *Demonax* or Diogenes Laertius' *Lives and Opinions of Famous Philosophers*, to romance-like portrayals dressed up in all the trappings of oratory. It even included the romance-like 'popular book', enriched with fables, anecdotes, wisdom sayings and travel adventures, like the *Vita Aesopis*. The aim of the ancient biography was not to depict the psychological development of a hero against a clearly defined chronological background, nor to trace the changes in his personality produced by his career; the biography served, rather, to work out the already established character of the hero and his predetermined fate. It was concerned with his *aretē* and his *tychē*. People were more interested in the typical and permanent features of a person, which could serve as models, rather than in his development and the way in which he changed. The literary enjoyment of *Metamorphoses* was concentrated on adventures of gods or satirical romances. There was little interest in the psychological metamorphoses of a historical hero. Thus the ancient biography cannot in any way be measured by the laws of modern biography. The boundaries between biography and the romance were more blurred than those between the romance and historiography; indeed, there is such a genre as the romantic biography. The development of the history of Alexander is a typical instance of the way in which historical biography can turn into romance. In the course of time, romantic fiction almost completely suppressed the historical report, finally resulting during the Christian era in the fantastic romance with its numerous popular offshoots, which extend into Talmudic literature and the medieval poetry of chivalry. After the Bible, the history of Alexander in its countless versions was the most-read book of the early Middle Ages. Here we have a parallel to the later development of the apocryphal gospels. But the development of the biography of Alexander and the Jesus biographies of the gospels begins from a relatively trustworthy historical report; it was not free invention. Of course, partisan hate and favour often led to biographies which were written very much in black and white, and to exaggerated value judgments in one direction or another. Furthermore, chronological sequence, which is indispensable for us, played a secondary role in ancient biography: as Diogenes Laertius' lives of the philosophers or Suetonius' lives of the emperors show, chronology could be largely dispensed with; or, as in the case of Plutarch, it could be treated in a fairly cavalier fashion. In biography in particular, the tendency was less towards a continuous and consecutive account; authors were quite content to string together a series of typical anecdotes with virtually no connection between them.

1.7 Even in a number of the larger historical works, however, the author limited himself to linking individual events and scenes loosely together; he would even jump over long intervals of time in a few sentences, after which he would once again describe particular incidents in very great detail. This loose form was often a result of the source material which happened to be at the author's disposal or of the particular bias of his work. A good example of this is the account of the last seventy years before the Jewish War in books 18–20 of Josephus' *Jewish Antiquities*. We should also note that the larger historical works in turn contained detailed 'biographical' passages; once again Josephus' *Antiquities* are a good illustration. In books 14–17 Josephus has incorporated a valuable portrait of Herod deriving from two opposed sources, Nicolaus of Damascus and an anti-Herodian priestly source. The exact chronological order of the material, which we take for granted, was certainly preserved to some extent in annals and historical works in the form of chronicles, but chronology was not the basis for every historical account, far less for a biographical work. Lucian's admonition that the narrative should progress 'steadily and evenly, without bumps or gaps', applied less to the chronological course of events than to the stylistic skill of the author, and this, as Lucian himself concedes, was largely a question of education. Not everyone had learnt the art of joining together individual episodes in a convincing way so as 'to make a firm chain', as Lucian requires. Lucian's warning against gaps and a disjointed accumulation of individual narratives shows that a tabu form of historiography along these lines was by no means uncommon (55). We find this anecdotal pattern of narration even more often in biographies than in history writing in the strict sense. The anecdote is the biographical form of reminiscence, since in a particular way it expresses what is typical or characteristic of its hero by means of an individual incident – one might even say by an 'ideal scene'. In some circumstances the character and destiny of the hero can be presented in a more illuminating way by means of a juxtaposition of typical sayings and actions than in an account of the fortuitous events of a human life arranged in chronological order. At all events, ancient authors knew nothing of the modern psychological-type approach, which gives a detailed analysis of a character and explores the factors in a person's make-up. Specific actions, apt remarks, captured in a pointed anecdote, made psychological explanations superfluous. From the beginning the hero appeared as a rounded personality, and the deeds and events of his youth illuminated his later destiny. It was not the hero himself, or his character, which changed, but at best the world around him. He could only become what he always had been. Luke's presentation of Paul before he became a Christian as a 'zealot for God' (Acts 22.3) – albeit in agreement with Paul's own comments (Gal. 1.14; Phil. 3.6) – is simply the reverse side of his portrayal of the missionary as a figure who is driven by zeal for Christ's cause in all that he says and does, even if Luke no longer uses the word 'zeal' in this connection (cf. Acts 9.15). II Corinthians 11.2, 'I burn for you with a divine zeal', shows that this was Paul's own estimation of himself. A cool, unemotional approach may have been regarded as a Stoic virtue, but it was not a Christian one. Accordingly, for Luke, Paul's conversion is not the result of an inner psychological development; it is a sudden miraculous event coming from outside, the work of Christ himself, the 'objectivity' of which is not altered in the threefold account of it, which differs from one telling to another. We learn nothing of a lengthy inner transformation within the heart of Saul the Pharisee before his conversion, which would interest us moderns so much and which has been the object of so much scholarly hypothesis. Even as a Christian, Paul remains for Luke the zealot for God's cause which he was from the start, though now of course he is the right kind of zealot (cf. Rom. 10.3); indeed, he even remains faithful to Pharisaic principles (Acts 23.6; cf. 26.5). However, even Paul himself does not speak of an inner development, but only of God's miraculous intervention (Gal. 1.15f.), which was a radical turning point in his life. The psychology of human development is a modern invention.

1.8 Accordingly, early Christian historical accounts, which are of a predominantly 'biographical' character, do not form any notable exception. It would be a gross error were we to regard them as quite self-contained islands within the world of ancient literature and culture. To presuppose the existence of an isolated 'salvation history' which could be demonstrated by historical means, a 'sacred' literature which has escaped the influence of its environment because it derives from the direct inspiration of God, distorts any genuine understanding of early Christianity and with it the origins of our faith. The first Christians in Jerusalem, Antioch, Corinth and Rome, used the 'religious *koine*', the current religious language of their immediate environment, as it was shaped by Jewish synagogues in Palestine and the Hellenistic world, and they used the literary forms of their time. The first Christian authors did not claim to be inspired writers, like the prophets of the Old Testament. Their authority did not rest on a theory of inspiration, but on the truth-claim contained in the eschatological saving event which they presented (see pp. 44ff. below). So for all their indisputable uniqueness (which is connected with their particular claim), their theological concerns, the level of education of their narrators and the sociological context of their communities and schools, the earliest Christian writings cannot be considered in isolation from contemporary Jewish or Hellenistic and Roman biography and historiography.

A study by Karl Ludwig Schmidt, 'The Place of the Gospels in the History of Literature generally' ('Die Stellung der Evangelien in der allgemeinen Literaturgeschichte'), published in *Eucharisterion*, the *Gestschrift* presented to Hermann Gunkel on his sixtieth birthday (II, 50–134), has acquired almost canonical status. However, it probably made too sharp a distinction between ancient biography and histories on the one hand and the gospels and Acts on the other. All the gospels – even the Gospel of John, which differs substantially from the synoptic gospels – tell of selected 'words and deeds' (Papias, in Eusebius, HE 3.39.15) of the divinely sent 'founder' or 'revealer', who in his divine status is identical with the man Jesus of Nazareth, a simple Jewish craftsman. In other words, for all their religious concern, they set out to depict the activity and the suffering of a real man and not a phantom figure. All the gospels follow a geographical and chronological order, which contains fundamental historical features common in essentials to all the gospels, even if there are differences between the synoptic gospels and John. The author of the Fourth Gospel, who knew the Gospel of Mark, deliberately kept to his different chronological order, because he thought that it was the right one. In other words, he applied not only theological but also

historical criticism to the Markan tradition, which had been followed by Matthew and Luke. Nevertheless, we should not mini-
mize the essential features which the four gospels have in common;
Jesus comes from a Jewish family from Nazareth in Galilee, and
we also hear of his mother and brothers, with whom he is to some
degree at odds (Mark 1.9; John 1.45; Mark 3.21f., 31ff., 6.3;
John 2.1ff., 12; 7.3ff.). His public ministry followed the appearance of John the Baptist, by whom he allowed himself to be
baptized in the Jordan, an incident which the Fourth Evangelist
of course merely paraphrases and does not relate in so many words,
since he does not want to put in question the difference in status
between Jesus and John the Baptist. Geographically speaking, the
focal point of Jesus' activity lay in a very remote corner of the
ancient world, in Jewish Galilee, more precisely, in the region of the
fishing village of K^ephar Nahum, on the north shore of Lake
Genessaret. Leaving aside Jerusalem, the place of his death, he
hardly ever came into contact with cities. There on the lake shore
he spoke to crowds of people who came to him from different parts
of the country; there he healed the sick and gathered the first
disciples round him. While Judaea and Samaria are more prominent in the Fourth Gospel than in the synoptics, the Fourth Gospel
too does not deny the significance of the out-of-the-way region
around K^ephar Nahum (2.12; 4.46; 6.17ff.). It is one of those
features of the gospels which could not have been invented.
Finally, the dominant goal of all four evangelists is the account of
Jesus' arrest, condemnation and execution on the cross in Jerusalem
and the subsequent Easter events, the discovery of the empty tomb
or the appearance of the risen Christ.

K. L. Schmidt has forced scholarly research too much in one
direction with his rejection of analogies from history and biography
in antiquity and his reference to medieval legends and popular
works like Thomas of Celano's Life of St Francis or the popular
account of Dr Faustus. The ancient world, too, was familiar with
popular biographies, like that of Homer, which was current in a
number of versions, and above all the life of Aesop, the tradition of
which has undergone a long history. With his wisdom, Aesop the
slave puts to shame his master the philosopher Xanthus, and as a

result gains his freedom. He surpasses kings and wise men at the royal courts of Egypt and Babylon by virtue of his wisdom. Here the *Vita* is strongly influenced by the Aramaic Ahikar romance, which was also known in Jewish circles (Tobit 1.21f.; 2.10; 11.19; 14.10ff.). Finally Aesop is lured to his death by the inhabitants of Delphi because of his boldness and his wisdom. Another possible analogy is the collection of anecdotes about the sharp-tongued philosopher Demonax, which comes from the pen of Lucian. By contrast, the legends about St Francis have already been influenced by the Gospels, and the popular book about Dr Faustus is essentially a dramatic patchwork which is better compared with the lowest form of the ancient romance as we find it now in, say, the papyrus fragments of the *Phoinikika* of Lollian, which is a lurid mixture of 'crime, sex and religion'. Under the influence of the rabid criticism of Overbeck, K. L. Schmidt allows himself to be guided too much by the standards of modern historiography or the great solitary representatives of ancient history-writing like Thucydides, Polybius and Tacitus, when on the one hand he concedes that the prologue to Luke has 'the format of a document of contemporary world literature' and yet on the other hand censures Luke 'because intention and ability fail in some strange way to relate to one another'. By contrast, in his polemical writing, Lucian points out that historical works differed widely in style, construction and literary level. Some contained only a 'bare narration of events', of the kind that if need be could have been produced by a soldier, artisan (*tekton*, cf. Mark 6.3) or pedlar who had kept a diary. As a deterrent, he cites a regimental doctor who was a budding historian and who wrote about a Parthian expedition in honour of Asclepius (16). Why should Luke, the Christian doctor (Col. 4.13), not have written about Paul's missionary 'expedition' from Jerusalem to Rome in honour of Christ (see pp. 125ff. below)? Even the disproportion between a 'brilliant foreword' and a weaker, indeed childish, composition of the historical work proper is a butt for the scorn of the famous satirist; in contrast to such bungling Lucian requires the whole work to be a harmonious unity (23). Here, too, we could refer to the contrast in style between the prologue, Luke 1.1–4, and the further continuation of the double work. Lucian's polemic suggests that historiography of this kind, deficient when measured by the strictest standards, was the rule, and that exemplary large-scale works were rare. What the satirist from Samosata in Syria has to offer the reader, even in his polemical 'biographies' of Alexander the false prophet or Peregrinus Proteus the cheat, should in no way be measured against his own strict verdict on the absolute love of truth and his warning against exaggerated polemic. In the heat of literary battles people were fond of writing in sharp black and white and were in no way punctilious or sensitive. This is demonstrated equally by the anti-Pharisaic polemic in Matt. 23. Celsus' work against the Christians or the anecdotal Talmudic tradition about Jesus, which goes down as far as the later novellistic *Toledot Jeshu*. Even Tacitus never really kept to his much-quoted motto *sine ira et studio*, 'without hate and zeal' (*Ann.*1.1). This is shown not only by his hate-filled portrayal of Tiberius which comes immediately after this remark, but also by his account of the Jews in the fifth book of his *Histories*, in which he assembles a confused conglomeration of antisemitic calumnies. Individual New Testament writings are by no means unaffected by these 'polemical sins', and it says much for Luke that in this respect he shows what might be termed an admirable degree of restraint.

1.9 The qualification which K. L. Schmidt makes to his unduly harsh judgment on Luke in a subsequent sentence is emphatically to be welcomed. It was 'the material' which 'proved a limitation for him' (132). As far as his Gospel is concerned, we may be grateful that the third evangelist did not remould and 'harmonize' his sources in rhetorical fashion as Lucian required, but for the most part preserved the individual pieces of tradition, anecdotes, parables and sayings as 'small units', like Mark before him, the sayings source (Q), the rabbinic Pirqe Aboth and Aboth de Rabbi Natan, and even like Lucian himself in his *Demonax*. We cannot go into the problems of oral tradition and its rules (the word 'laws' is better avoided in this connection) in any detail here; however, after a history of fifty years it must be pointed out that 'form criticism' has not lived up to its promising beginnings in the early 1920s.

Unfortunately, it has all too quickly become ossified in a form of scholasticism; this state of stagnation has been reached because there has been too long a delay in analysing and making a comparative evaluation of the most important parallels from the same milieu and the same period, namely the rich rabbinic tradition of anecdotes and sayings. This material could provide scholars with an inexhaustibly rich source of material for form-critical and traditio-critical research, for which countless parallel traditions provide a control. Far too little attention has been paid, especially in Germany, to the work of contemporary American scholars, for example Jacob Neusner. We still need a thorough form-critical study of the rabbinic miracle stories and biographical anecdotes, and a comparison of them with the gospel tradition. The soothing comfort offered to New Testament scholars by Strack-Billerbeck's great commentary has hindered rather than helped a real investigation of rabbinic material. Perhaps a thoroughgoing analysis of the Talmudic material would shown that it is not as easy to determine and establish the 'laws' of oral tradition as the founders of form criticism supposed in the first flush of their new discovery; here, too, chance plays a considerable part, and it would be better not to have talked in terms of fixed 'laws' 'which govern popular tradition' or – even more unfortunately – of a 'biology of the saga' (Dibelius, *Die Formgeschichte des Evangeliums*[2], 1: the sentence does not appear in the English translation). Even the reconstruction of the so-called *Sitz im Leben* remains for the most part a highly questionable business. It was always a plausible assumption, and therefore essentially a truism, that an anecdote or a logion was used and shaped in communal worship. Thus the 'formation' of the gospel material would need to be investigated in the first place in terms of the arrangement ot the text, independently of the hypothesis of a *Sitz im Leben* which would need to be defined in more detail.

One of the chief reasons why historical events, i.e. history, are for the most part primarily expressed in stories, i.e. anecdotes, and teaching in poetic form is narrated in individual sayings or groups of sayings, is that our memory is structured in a particular way. This is the way in which it retains the typical, easily repeatable elements in events and forms of teaching. Our memory finds it much more difficult to reconstruct the chronological sequence of events. Unless one makes entries on a calendar or keeps a diary – and that was certainly not the case with Jesus' disciples – it is often almost impossible to reconstruct the wider context. As paradigmatic events and sayings were the principal ingredients of the tradition, the chronological sequence of events was no longer of decisive interest, and people were quite happy with a schematic arrangement. On the other hand, the construction of a narrative framework presupposes fixed reminiscences or a fixed tradition. This is demonstrated both by the summary in Acts 10.36–40 and above all by the evangelist Mark himself, who did not simply invent the framework of his Gospel from scratch. It is highly probable that Jesus worked not only in Galilee, but at times – possibly after the death of John the Baptist – in neighbouring Gentile territory like the regions round the cities of Tyre, Sidon, Caesarea Philippi, Philip's territory or the Decapolis.

We can hardly doubt that Jesus' activity in Galilee and Judaea caused an elemental chain reaction and in the relatively short span of one or two years provided a wealth of firmly fixed and permanent impressions. Because of the overwhelming impression which he made, from the beginning it was difficult to arrange individual events and sayings chronologically and geographically within a fixed framework, and before long that became impossible. The last days in Jerusalem are an exception here; even Paul himself has exact information in this respect (I Cor. 11.23ff.; see p. 46 below).

In the meantime it has become a commonplace, reiterated by almost everyone, that we can no longer write a 'biography of Jesus' which could stand up to the demands of modern historiography. In return, we ought to ask: is there any person in antiquity about whom we could write a 'biography' which would be at all comparable with modern works in its wealth of documentation and information? Leaving aside Cicero and Caesar, for whom we have an extraordinarily large amount of autobiographical material, there are only a few figures from antiquity for whom this would be the case. The very fact that countless books about Jesus continue to be written, of which at least some need to be taken seriously as historical studies, despite the general view mentioned above, is indication enough that we perhaps know more about him than those with a hypercritical attitude tend to assume. One might almost speak of an Indian summer of this genre of theological literature.

1.10 The idea cherished by form critics for decades, of individual traditions completely detached and in 'free circulation' as isolated units, is just as unrealistic as the attempt to write a life of Jesus. It is based on a very schematic conception of oral tradition. The earliest stage was not the isolated individual tradition, but the elemental wealth of impressions called forth by the meteoric appearance of Jesus. Then, still during Jesus' life-time, there began a process of collection which at the same time meant selection and restriction. It should also be noted that in terms of antiquity the period of time between the start of the tradition and the composition of our gospels was relatively short, and lasted only between thirty and sixty years. Considerably greater periods had to be bridged in the rabbinic and Talmudic traditions. There is also the fact that oral tradition in primitive Christianity was not at everyone's disposal in the same way; still less was it the result of the anonymous, creative productive force of some 'Palestinian' or 'Hellenistic' communities which cannot be defined more closely than that, and which shaped these traditions in accordance with their particular 'needs'. It is in fact amazing how few signs the synoptic gospels show of the 'needs' of the communities as we know them from the letters of the New Testament. Often we are virtually forced to read these needs into the synoptic texts. The term 'community construction' which is used so readily today, usually without further explanation, can seldom elucidate actual historical circumstances; more frequently, it tends to obscure them. It is probable that by far the majority of narratives and sayings in the gospels will have had a historical basis in the activity of Jesus, though perhaps in a different form. Here the commonplace axiom 'Nothing comes out of nothing' applies. The basic stimulus towards the rise of the Jesus tradition was the man Jesus, in his proclamation, his behaviour and his actions. Anyone who posits a 'community construction' must go on to give time, place and reasons. However, in essentials we know far less about the 'communities' which are said to have given rise to such traditions in an unbridled way than we do about Jesus himself. They often seem to be modern fabrications rather than historical realities, whether they are the 'Q community' which has become so popular today, or even the 'heretics' against which the second evangelist is supposed to be fighting. Because terms like 'community construction' are so vague, they therefore tend to say little more than the trivial definition of the *Sitz im Leben* of a tradition in terms of liturgy or mission preaching. In fact, the whole of the gospel tradition should really be called a 'community construction', because it was selected, translated, shaped, edited and finally written down by the 'community' – whatever this word may mean.

In reality, however, oral tradition was usually associated, not with anonymous communities but with well-known individual authoritative bearers of tradition. Such authorities already appear with Paul, when he speaks of Cephas, James, Barnabas, the 'apostles before me' (Gal. 1.17, cf. Rom. 16.7) or 'the Lord's brothers' (I Cor. 9.5). Thus the history of earliest Christianity, like that of the 'synoptic tradition', was not as anonymous and disparate as the representatives of radical form criticism suppose, or as people would want in these days when 'creative collectives' prove so popular. Clearly defined 'personalities' can be found at the beginning of earliest Christianity: John the Baptist, then in a unique way Jesus himself, and after that the authorities known to us. The transmission and formation of the oral tradition about Jesus certainly did not just by-pass the leading figures of the first community. Simon Peter, who is so often given pride of place, must have had a particularly prominent position in it. Of course we should not underestimate the particular theological work of forming and selecting from the tradition which was done by those who handed it on. But it is very difficult clearly to assign particular pieces of tradition in the texts to a community or a teacher. It is easiest in respect of the evangelists themselves, who belong to the second or third Christian generation. In the meantime it has long been recognized that they were not mere 'collectors' and 'redactors' of anonymous and amorphous traditions; like the bearers of the

tradition on whose shoulders they stand, they are themselves
theological personalities and probably also authorities and teachers
who in turn have obligations to an earlier tradition. For that very
reason, it is also improbable that there was no connection at all
between the authorities mentioned by our earliest witness, Paul,
like Cephas or John (Gal. 2.9), and the later evangelists. The history of earliest Christianity in the first sixty or seventy years down
to the time of the composition of the four gospels did not get lost
in an anonymous, unbounded and imaginary setting; it can still be
traced, and was influenced by the authority of particular persons
who were generally known at the time. This is as clear from I
Clement and the letters of Ignatius as it is from Acts and the letters
of Paul.

1.11 In this connection we may recall that the apologist Justin
describes the synoptic gospels – the only works of which he shows
knowledge – both in his *Apology* (66.3; 67.3) and above all in the
Dialogue with Trypho, some fifteen times, in an almost stereotyped
way, as 'reminiscences' (*apomnēmoneumata*), to which he regularly
adds the phrase 'of the apostles' (*Dial.* 100.4; 101.3; 102.5, etc.);
in one instance he speaks more exactly of the 'reminiscences composed by the apostles and those who followed them' (103.8). It may
be that in using this term, among other things the apologist *also*
wants to allude to the best known instance of the genre of
apomnēmoneumata, Xenophon's 'reminiscences' to Socrates. He
certainly knew them, because he quotes the fable of Heracles at the
crossroads from them in *Apol.* 2.11. However, we may suppose that
this stereotyped terminology is more than an apologetic artifice.
For Justin, his hearers and readers, the gospels really were
'biographical reminiscences' of Jesus written down by the apostles
or their pupils, and were comparable with the biographical reminiscences of antiquity, whose main subjects were the philosophers.
For example, Xenophon's *Memorabilia* are called by Aulus Gellius
dictorum atque factorum Socratis commentarii, i.e. 'reminiscences
of the words and deeds of Socrates' (*Noct. Att.* 14.3,5). This formula at the same time recalls the earlier report of the presbyter,
preserved by Papias, that Mark 'wrote down as Peter's interpreter

the *words and deeds* of the Lord as he *remembered* them (*emnēmo-neusen*), albeit not in the right order' (Eusebius, HE 3.39.15). In this connection Papias twice uses the word 'remember', and the second time even the composite form *apomnēmoneuein*, which Justin then took up again in his *Apology*: 'As they have taught who have written down as reminiscences (*apomnēmoneusantes*) everything concerning our redeemer Jesus Christ' (*Apol*. 33.5). Eusebius shows that this terminology is not limited to isolated occurrences; in PE 3.6.2 he calls the gospels the written *apomnēmo-neumata* of the disciples, while in an analogous way Clement of Alexandria can speak of *hypomnēmata* (Eusebius, HE 2.15.1; cf. 3.24.5). The Latin equivalent, *commentarii*, appears in Tertullian (*Ieun*. 10.3), who also describes the evangelists as *commentatores* (*Adv. Marc*. 4.2.4; *De resurrec*. 33.5; *De carne Christi* 22.1). Irenaeus also says several times that the evangelists hand down reminiscences (*Adv. haer*. 2.22.3; 4.2.3; 4.10.1: John; 5.21.2: Luke). One might also mention Luke again in this context. He twice speaks of the 'remembrance' of a 'saying of the Lord' (Acts 11.16; 20.35), a formula which recurs in I Clement (13.1; 46.7) and Polycarp (Phil. 2.3). Thus the theme of 'remembrance', which is fundamental to all historiography, can least of all be banished from the Jesus tradition.

It is not just a matter here of making the closest possible connections between the gospels and the ancient 'biographies of philosophers' in the style of *apomnēmoneumata*. The gospels are certainly 'reminiscences' of a particular kind. P. Wendland rightly protested against what was once the 'favourite habit of comparing the gospel tradition with Xenophon's *Memorabilia* and Arrian's accounts of the conversations of Epictetus' (*Die urchristlichen Literaturformen*, p. 266 n. 1). Between the two there is an educational barrier which was particularly high in antiquity. For Wendland, Mark has 'no individuality as a writer' (267); in other words, he had not been educated in the ancient schools, he writes barbaric Greek and has no proper rhetorical polish. But in Mark's work in particular, Wendland, following Herder, sees 'the living voice of a storyteller . . . the naive and fresh character of popular narration which has a sure touch in taking account of the means at its disposal and is well aware of their effects. To some degree this is an art, because it presupposes practice and tradition' (270). In other words, it is a natural talent for storytelling. This suggests that Mark himself had heard these stories or had himself told them on a number of occasions before he actually wrote his gospel. Presumably he himself had also had to pass on the tradition about Jesus, either as a Christian missionary or a helper in Peter's mission work. We should add that he was a story-teller who also knew how to arrange his material admirably, and could think and argue as a theologian. This is even more the case with Matthew and the more educated Luke. The ancient reader will probably have been well aware of the differences in style and education, say, between Mark and Xenophon; but he will also have noticed what the gospels had in common with the literature of biographical 'reminiscences' – and unlike the majority of German New Testament scholars today, he did not mind at all regarding the evangelists as authors of biographical reminiscences of Jesus which went back to the disciples of Jesus themselves. The question is whether we are right if we deny the gospels this biographical character altogether.

1.12 In what appears to some degree as a counter-movement to form criticism, in most recent times, above all in America, attempts have been made to see the so-called aretalogical romance as the closest parallel to the historiography of the New Testament. This form of romance was a special type of romantic biography with markedly religious and miraculous traits. The works which representatives of this approach have had in mind are the pre-Christian romance of Moses by the Egyptian Jew Artapanus; the *Life of Moses* written by Philo; the Platonic-type *Life of Apollonius* by Philostratus, which was published after AD 217; or even the still later lives of Pythagoras, by Porphyry and above all by Iamblichus. Whereas the early work by Artapanus is a partially grotesque-sounding Jewish-Hellenistic Haggadah relating to Moses, which has also left its mark on Josephus, the other works are extremely rhetorical compositions, and the two writings mentioned last, the lives of Apollonius of Tyana and Pythagoras, already presuppose a knowledge of the gospels. For example, among other works

Porphyry composed a sage and thorough criticism of the gospels. Indeed there are isolated and sometimes interesting parallels to the gospels, though a comparison shows even more the considerable, and even fundamental, differences. They consist not least in the fact that the gospels contain reports of a historical figure the remembrance of whom was still vivid, despite all the distortions in it, within the Christian community some thirty to sixty years after his death. By contrast, for example, the work of Philostratus was only written about 120 years after the hero's death at the wish of the empress Julia Domna, the widow of Septimius Severus.

With its rhetorical and romantic decoration it so concealed the figure of Apollonius, the Neo-Pythagorean and miracle worker who lived in the second half of the first century AD, that we can now see hardly anything of his historical personality. Despite all the parallels in points of detail, other autobiographical testimony to the 'aretalogical romance', for example the religious confessions in the *hieroi logoi* of the orator Aristides, the Imuthes-Asclepius aretalogy which is so illuminating for the history of mission (*Oxyrhynchus Papyri* 1381), or Book 11 of the *Metamorphoses* of Apuleius, are relatively far removed from New Testament 'history-writing.' The New Testament does not relate the religious experience of an individual with a deity in the first person singular, but the history of God with people whom he has chosen and sent, behind whom the individual pious man with his religious sensibilities and extraordinary experiences retreats into the background in an amazing way. What connects these texts with the writings of the New Testament – and distinguishes them from our modern understanding of the world – is their receptiveness towards miracle and direct divine revelation, though of course the earliest Christian texts are to a much greater degree constrained by the bounds of theological reflection. This is evident not only from the gospels and Luke's Acts of the Apostles, but even more from the letters of Paul, where to some extent we also could attribute an 'aretalogical' character to some autobiographical passages (e.g. II Cor. 11 and 12).

1.13 Thus the model for the collection and the literary presentation of the 'biographical' Jesus tradition is not to be sought either in the 'aretalogical romance' or in the autobiographical 'aretalogical confession', for which in any case we have hardly any clear pre-Christian examples, but rather in the accounts of history to be found in the Old Testament and Judaism, which to a large degree are composed of 'biographical' sections. As early as Genesis we find the 'biographies of the patriarchs', which at least in the case of Jacob depict the decisive events between his birth and his death in relative detail. There follows, from Exodus to Deuteronomy, the 'life of Moses', which is narrated in even greater detail; at the same time it includes the divine 'doctrine' entrusted to Moses. Then comes the history of the conquest of the promised land by Joshua, i.e. an account which is restricted to the activity of a man of God over a particular period of time. The narrative about David and his kingdom is hardly less detailed; it even introduces individual poetic compositions by the royal poet, inspired by the spirit of God (II Sam. 23.2). The Elijah–Elisha stories consist chiefly of accounts of miracles and narratives about disciples, and display numerous parallels to the gospel tradition. By contrast, Nehemiah's account of his actions is autobiographical in character. One common feature of most of these biographical complexes of Old Testament and Jewish tradition is that they are composed of individual narratives which contain particular striking scenes or anecdotes. They were primarily handed down in collections of oral tradition and even now show relatively few signs of intrinsic connections.

In his Apology *contra Apionem*, towards the end of the first century AD, that is, at about the time when the gospels and Acts were written, Josephus shows us that the educated Greek-speaking Jew understood the narrative writings of the Jewish canon as historical works *sui generis*, which differed fundamentally from the works of pagan historians by virtue of their divine authorization and inspiration and were therefore especially reliable. 'Not everyone was allowed to write', but only 'the prophets' (1.37). So they wrote in a reliable way the sacred history which extends from creation to the time of Artaxerxes I, who was identified with the Ahasuerus of the book of Esther and regarded as the contemporary of Ezra, the last prophet. By contrast, the later writings did not enjoy such a high reputation, because by that time 'the precise

succession of the prophets' had been interrupted (1.41). Conscious
though they were of the different character of their message, the
New Testament historians wanted to take up the tradition which
already existed. Whereas Josephus refers to the written testimony
of the prophets, Luke refers to the tradition (*kathōs paredosan*) of
those who 'from the beginning were eye-witnesses and preachers
of the word'. In describing himself in 13.52 as 'a scribe trained for
the kingdom of heaven', Matthew is referring to a new self-awareness of a special kind, which is governed by the subject-matter that
he is narrating. The same is true of the Gospel of Mark, who com-
poses his work as the *evangelium Jesu Christi*, and of the Fourth
Evangelist, who according to 19.35 and 21.24 grounds the authority
of his work in the testimony, indeed the authorship, of the beloved
disciple. In other words, the New Testament historical works are
not edifying romances for pious entertainment, but were written as
authoritative 'messianic narratives' which call for faith (John 20.31).

1.14 What distinguishes the content of the gospel accounts from
the 'biographical' historical narratives of the Old Testament is the
fact that they do not set out to relate in succession the activity of a
number of often very different 'men of God' who were active a long
time beforehand, but quite deliberately concentrate on the one
messianic-eschatological figure of Jesus of Nazareth, who lived
only a few years earlier. As Messiah and Son of God he discloses
eschatological salvation to all men, and his history is therefore itself
a saving message, a *euangelion*. Consequently, in the gospels everyone apart from Jesus, whether these are his disciples or his
opponents, must play a more or less static role. They have no
independent significance. The new element in the gospels is to be
found less in their external literary form than in the absolute, final,
unsurpassable, eschatological claim to revelation which they contain. However, without doubt it was this relationship with the
earlier 'holy' history of the Old Testament and Judaism and its
'biographical' narratives, coupled with the claim to fulfil and even
surpass the history of God with his people which was related
there, which from the beginning gave the earliest Christian tradition about Jesus its particular character. With a certain inner

necessity, this claim led to a particular form of historical writing as an account of the saving event.

Step by step, the oral tradition came to require an authoritative fixation and concentration in written form. This is true above all for the period after the death of the first generation, from the seventh decade AD onwards.

On the other hand, we find hardly anything comparable with the earliest Christian form of historiography in the literature of the other Hellenistic and Roman cults. True, the healing miracles of the gods were written down and collected in the sanctuaries of, say, Asclepius or Sarapis, and various writers, including the famous Demetrius of Phaleron, adviser to Ptolemy I in the founding of the cult of Sarapis, are said to have recorded in a number of books miraculous healings and instructions communicated by this god in dreams (Artemidorus, *Oneirocriticon* 2.44). However, miraculous features of this kind are still relatively far removed from the historical accounts of earliest Christianity. Probably the closest parallel, the recently discovered biography of Mani, a founder of gnostic religion from the third century AD, is in fact directly dependent on the earliest Christian tradition, that of Paul and the gospels.

By contrast, the Jewish rabbinic tradition, with a wealth of biographical anecdotes about significant teachers at its disposal which could easily have been developed into 'biographies', deliberately refrained from making a systematic collection of them. It put this material completely at the service either of the juridical and casuistic interpretation of the Torah in the Mishnah and Talmud, or of the interpretation of scripture in the Midrash. There the biographical anecdote is largely just an illustration and example of the special case of the Halachah, and has thus almost completely lost its particular historical significance. Thus the rabbis included the whole of their historical tradition in the interpretation of the Torah and subordinated that tradition to it. After the destruction of the sanctuary and the loss of Judaea, the events of the present were no longer worth writing down, since this present lay completely under the rule of the 'godless power', i.e. that of Rome. In effect the consciousness of a history of salvation which had produced Old Testament and Jewish historiography, passed over to earliest Christianity. We might ask whether this development under the rabbis was not, among other things, a reaction to the rise of the gospels. Even the lives of individual teachers, including the really great ones, like Hillel, Akiba, or Yehuda han-nasi, were completely subordinated to the doctrine of the true fulfilment of the commandments, i.e. the Torah.

One could, of course, speak of a self-contradiction in the phenomenon of the new 'earliest Christian history-writing'. What was the point of narrating the 'eschatological saving event', which was bringing an end to history, in terms of an ongoing history? Overbeck brought up this point, in connection above all with his criticism of Acts. The question is whether the activity and fate of Jesus and his disciples' experience of the Spirit did not bring about an elemental upheaval which compelled the earliest Christian communities to proclaim these events as a saving message in narrative form and to narrate them in the form of a proclamation. Precisely this will have transformed the awareness of the 'end of history' into a new 'kerygmatic' form of historiography (see pp. 47ff. below).

2

Acts as a Historical Source

2.1 In what follows, our particular interest will be not so much in the gospels as in Luke's Acts of the Apostles and the course taken by the message about Jesus *after* his ministry, his death and the events of the resurrection which gave rise to the Christian community. This is the subject-matter of Luke's second volume. The first feature about it which strikes us, is the almost objectionable eclecticism in the selection of material. However, in this respect it is not so very different from the gospels and the other historical works of antiquity. Individual events of particular significance regularly stand in the forefront of the ongoing narrative, and these are often linked together by brief – but in some circumstances historically valuable – summaries. We have the ascension and Pentecost, successes and the first persecution in Jerusalem, the martyrdom of Stephen, the calling of Paul the persecutor, the first conversion of a Gentile, the miraculous rescue of Peter, the first missionary journey of Paul and Barnabas, and the 'apostolic council'. All in all, the chronological arrangement is substantially better than that in the gospels, though it too has errors and inaccuracies. That need not surprise us: for Luke, the public activity of Jesus occupied a period of hardly more than a year, whereas the events depicted in Acts were spread over a period of about thirty years. It was easier and more necessary here to establish a chronological order. At the same time, there is also a striking concentration on individual authoritative personalities, the first two of which also play a part in the gospels. There are Peter and John, Stephen and Philip, Barnabas and Paul, and finally James the brother of the Lord. Peter remains the predominant personality of the first part; from 13.9 his place is taken by Paul, whom Luke up to that point has called Saul. From this point on, the description of Paul's divinely-guided career and his individual actions forces all other early Christian authorities into the background with an almost objectionable exclusiveness. Peter leaves the scene in ch. 15, and James and his elders disappear after their contentious encounter with Paul in 21.18–26. The last six chapters are entirely devoted to the apostle in his imprisonment: the Christian community comes into view only on the sidelines, as in Sidon (27.3), in Puteoli (28.14) and then in Rome (28.15). According to Luke, the communities in Palestine do not seem to have taken note of Paul's imprisonment. We are given consistent information about only a few main cities and communities: Jerusalem, Caesarea, Damascus, Antioch, Philippi, Thessalonica, Corinth, Ephesus, and finally Paul's goal, Rome, the capital of the world. Other figures and places, the fate of the majority of the 'twelve apostles', the beginnings of the church in Alexandria or Rome, are deliberately ignored. Even the reports about individual places and communities, which for the most part are thin, are not given for their own sakes; they are almost always passed on in connection with particular prominent figures, and primarily Paul. So we cannot even claim without further ado, as is the habit of so many scholars today, that Luke only knew what he reported about the early period of Christianity. He certainly knew a good deal more than he put down; when he is silent about something, there are usually special reasons for it. Only by this strict limitation of his material can he 'put his heroes in the right perspective'.

2.2   The title by which we know Acts, *praxeis tōn apostolōn* ('Acts of the Apostles'), does not do justice to its content and is therefore probably secondary; the genre of the work is that of a very special kind of 'historical monograph', a special history which describes the missionary development of a young religious movement in connection with two prominent personalities, Peter and Paul. I have already referred to this genre of 'historical monographs' (see p. 14 above); unfortunately we now have only fragments of the numerous works of this kind which once existed. In addition to the histories of cities, provinces and peoples already mentioned, there were accounts of philosophical schools like the works of Aristoxenus, the pupil of Aristotle, on Pythagoras and the Pythagoreans, and the book of Idomeneus the Epicurean on the Socratics. One example from the time of Luke is the *Aegyptiaca* of the Egyptian priest and Stoic Châiremon, who became tutor to the young Nero; he gave an idealistic picture of the Egyptian priesthood as the true Stoics. Examples relevant to Judaism which might be mentioned are the writings of predominantly Gentile authors 'about the Jews' (*peri Ioudaiōn*); in the case of most of them, all that we have are the names of authors and a few fragments. One can infer their often antisemitic character from the excerpts made by Josephus in *Contra Apionem*, from the *Apion* of Apollonius Molon or the fifth book of Tacitus' *Histories*. These Gentile polemical works were countered by Jewish apologies with the same title. The Tobiad romance preserved by Josephus in Book 12 of his *Antiquities* contains a family story as the theme of a monograph; I Maccabees, which essentially narrates only the rise of the priestly family of the Hasmonaeans, is oriented on Old Testament historiography. The work of Jason of Cyrene which has been condensed in II Maccabees, or the contemporary monographs of Philo on the persecution of the Jews in Alexandria and the delegation to the emperor Caligula, form a bridge from Jewish to Hellenistic historiography. The fact that Acts nevertheless is essentially different from all these 'analogies' lies first in the theological concerns of the author – the earliest Christian faith created an eschatological (and at the same time religious and missionary) awareness which was a revolutionary new development in antiquity –; and secondly in the fact that Acts cannot be separated from the Third Gospel: both books must be understood as a historical and theological unity.

2.3 Fortunately the historical works of antiquity, which have often been handed down only in fragments (see pp. 6f. above), are not the only sources at our disposal. They are supplemented by the original testimony of contemporaries in poetry or prose, by countless inscriptions and papyri, i.e. private letters, contracts or business documents, though these are essentially confined to Egypt. In the Hellenistic Roman period we are therefore best informed about everyday life there. The contemporary allusions of these original documents make a decisive contribution to criticism of historical writers proper; indeed often these reports are our only help towards putting them in a historical context. Aristophanes' comedies and Thucydides' history of the Peloponnesian war shed light on each other, and our detailed knowledge of the outcome of the Roman Civil War, the period of Pompey and Caesar, comes mostly from the many-sided work of Cicero, the personality of antiquity about whom we are best informed, above all through his own writings. The reign of Augustus is illuminated not only by Nicolaus of Damascus, Tacitus, Suetonius or Dio Cassius, but also by poets like Horace, Ovid and Virgil, and the letters of Pliny the Younger are a principal source for the time of Domitian, Nerva, and above all Trajan. The authentic letters of Paul play a similar role in connection with Acts, though the *auctor ad Theophilum* himself had no knowledge of them. In reality, it is only because of them that we can attempt a historical-critical assessment of Acts, while they in turn can only be understood in their particular historical and chronological context as a result of Luke's account. The historical reliability of Acts must be measured critically against Paul's original testimony. So on the one hand we can say that the letters of Paul and Acts explain one another. However, as primary sources, the letters of course are more important in this respect. On the other hand, without the account written by Luke, incomplete, fragmentary and misleading though it may be, we would not only find it almost impossible to put Paul and his work in a chronological and geographical setting; we would still be largely in the dark about the development of Paul's great mission around the Aegean and the events that led up to it, and about his concern to go to Rome and to Spain (Rom. 15.22–29). We only realize the significance of Luke's Acts as a historical source if we make a consistent attempt to eliminate the information it contains from our knowledge of earliest Christianity. For all his tendentious distortions, Luke's contribution to the historical understanding of Paul is essentially greater than many scholars want to suppose today. Paul's origins in Tarsus, his link with Jerusalem, the significance of Antioch and of Barnabas for the early Paul, the sequence of

Paul's letters, the length of his stay in missionary centres and the chronology of his activity – all these and much else would be completely or largely unknown to us without Acts.

A further source which explains Acts at many points and helps us to understand it better is the *Antiquities* of Josephus, which were written at almost the same time. As a result of this work we can, for example, establish a chronology for the reign of Herod Agrippa I (AD 41–10 March 44; cf. Acts 12 with *Antt.* 19.274–363); Josephus and Luke give two related but independent accounts of his death, though that in Luke has the colouring of popular legend (12.19–32, cf. *Antt.* 19.346–9). It is Josephus who enables us to understand references to the prophetic messianic rebels, Judas of Galilee and Theudas, whose historical sequence is reversed by Luke, and to the 'Egyptian who led four thousand *sicarii* into the wilderness' (21.38, cf. *Antt.* 20.169–72). The characterization of the procurators Felix and Festus, and of king Agrippa II, is confirmed and supplemented by Josephus. The expulsion of the Jews from Rome by Claudius (Acts 18.2) is endorsed by the famous note in Suetonius, where it is associated with Christian activities (see below, p. 108). Even individual inscriptions make valuable contributions. Thus the Theodotus inscription from Jerusalem puts the role of the Hellenists in Acts 6 in the right perspective (see below, pp. 71ff.), and the famous Gallio inscription from Delphi enables us not only to date Paul's stay in Corinth, but also to develop a chronology of Paul and earliest Christianity based on its dating. Thus at many points Acts is connected with other contemporary historical sources.

3

The Earliest Christian Histories as Sources for a History of Earliest Christianity and the Unity of Kerygma and Historical Narrative

3.1 After what has been said so far, we must go on to stress that in comparison with other areas and epochs of ancient history, and with due regard to the general fortuitousness and fragmentariness of the evidence that has come down to us (which has already been indicated above), our source material for the first decades of earliest Christianity, from John the Baptist to the persecution under Nero or the outbreak of the Jewish War, is not as bad as all that. Thus radical criticism, which in the end leaves us with nothing but a clean slate, on the whole bears witness only to its incapacity for real historical thinking, especially as it is often followed not so much by an honest 'we do not know' as by wild reconstructions. There is a kind of criticism which no longer deserves to be called critical, because it completely lacks self-criticism. For that reason we must understand the theologians' favourite – and much-disputed – adjective 'historical-critical' in the light of its subject-matter. To reject it would simply be a kind of false pretentiousness, because this goes against a real critical attitude. We could in fact extend the basis of our sources for earliest Christianity even further; for in addition to those already mentioned, the gospels, Acts, and the authentic and secondary letters of Paul, we also have a wealth of other, mostly pseudepigraphic, writings from the time between AD 70 and 110, from which we can draw conclusions about the 'time of the founders of Christianity'. In addition, there are reports in Papias, Hegesippus and Eusebius and notes in Josephus, Suetonius, Pliny the Younger and the rabbinic tradition.

Our knowledge of the Jewish and Hellenistic environment, enlarged by the discoveries at Qumran, the Gnostic texts from Nag Hammadi, rabbinic reports and numerous inscriptions and papyri, also helps towards historical reconstruction. It is obvious that we need to make a critical examination of the content of each report, and to distinguish between legend and history. However, this applies to all ancient history writing, as the formation of legends already began in the lifetime of great men. But even what are strictly speaking 'unhistorical legends' or 'ideal scenes' can be of historical value, because they tend to indicate the essential characteristics of a person or event and the general impression that they made, and because they express the earliest influence exerted by such a person or event. In our day it is impossible to decide with any certainty whether the vivid anecdotes about Demonax in Lucian really took place in the detailed form in which they are narrated, yet as a whole they give an impressive picture of this Cynic philosopher of whom Lucian had so high an opinion; furthermore, it does not occur to anyone to doubt his 'historicity', though we know him only from Lucian.

3.2 Measured by the 'riches' of early Christian sources, our knowledge of other phenomena from the history of ancient culture and religion is rather scanty. This is true, say, of Pythagoras and the early Pythagorean movement in Italy, the historical Simon Magus, the real Apollonius of Tyana and his spiritual grandson, Alexander of Abonuteichos, the founder of mysteries, the foundation of the cult of Sarapis or the Hellenization of the cult of Isis, the Essene movement or the methods of the Jewish mission. We owe our thorough knowledge of the origins of Christianity above all to the fact that Luke and similarly the authors of the other two synoptic gospels, and indeed to some extent even the author of the Fourth Gospel, were not simply preachers of an abstract message, but at the same time quite deliberate 'history writers' – one might also say storytellers – who proclaimed the new message of the coming of Jesus the Messiah through their historical accounts. Of course, they had little or no literary ambitions, and – Luke apart – no real training in literature or rhetoric; however, they did have a theological interest which was at the same time a historical one. In their accounts of the activity and suffering of Jesus of Nazareth they were concerned above all to relate the story of God's eschatological revelation of himself, his coming to men, and in so doing to complete the historical narrative of the Old Testament, which they all take up in some way, by describing the fulfilment of the promise. Luke then took this narration further with the story of the sending of the disciples, the coming of the Spirit and the mission which the Spirit directed, culminating in the work of Paul. In so doing he developed first beginnings which can be seen both in the gospel tradition and in the earlier letters of Paul. The earliest Christian history writers narrated this account of the eschatological consummation as a unique event which, though now past, determined both present and future, and embraced both time and eternity. It concerned all men and concluded the history of the old covenant once and for all, at the same time reconciling lost mankind with God. It was a historical report which, though a narrative, at the same time required faith in the action of God expressed in it. The time of the old covenant and the fulfilment of its promises in the present, determined by the activity and suffering of Jesus and dominated by his Spirit, did not need to correspond exclusively in a positive fashion. Indeed, in all probability, Jesus himself already described their relationship in an antithetical way: 'The law and the prophets were until John; since then the good news of the kingdom of God is preached, and every one enters it violently' (Luke 16.16). Jesus' critical remark about the new patch on the old garment and the new wine in old wineskins (Mark 2.21f.) already points to this antithesis, which is fully developed in Paul's remarks about the new covenant and the old (II Cor. 3.6,14), and which the Prologue to John's Gospel then paraphrases with the sentence: 'For the law was given through Moses; grace and truth came through Jesus Christ' (1.17). In his own way, Luke expresses this gulf in Acts by means of Stephen's speech in Acts 7, and then in the statement put in the mouth of Peter which refers to the law as a 'yoke which neither we nor our fathers could bear' (15.10), an interpretation of the Torah which was in sharp contradiction to Jewish tradition.

3.3 New Testament scholars were therefore ill advised when they allowed themselves to be persuaded that history and kerygma were exclusive alternatives. The consequence was the suggestion that the earliest Christian authors as a rule did not mean to narrate history proper, but simply to preach. By way of example, I might refer to some sentences from a much-quoted work on the Second Gospel: '*Euangelion* (in Mark 1.1) is set over the entire work as a kind of "title". It is a gospel. From the outset that means that his work is to be read as proclamation, and as such is an address and not a "report about Jesus". From this aspect, it is almost accidental that something in the way of a report also appears. In any case, it is only raw material. Sequence, chronological order – all this is certainly in the material or is at least intended there, but it is proclaimed in the present and for the present' (W. Marxsen, *Mark the Evangelist*, 1969, 131). Here the intention of Mark the evangelist is presented in a completely distorted way through the spectacles of a crude pre-understanding. No wonder that on the basis of such a caricature the evangelist Luke could be seen as an exception and be accused of treachery to the true gospel by presenting a theology of salvation history. In reality, the writers in the New Testament make their proclamation by narrating the action of God within a quite specific period of history, at a particular place and through real men, as a historical report. It is not a matter of chance that in his letters Paul sometimes refers by way of allusion to the narration of stories about Jesus. These allusions presuppose that the readers know more (I Cor. 11.23ff., 15.3ff.; Rom. 1.3; 15.8; Phil. 2.8; Gal. 4.4 etc.). We must assume that in his mission preaching – which fades right into the background in his letters – Paul also of course told stores about Jesus, and primarily the passion story, the account of the crucifixion of Jesus. We should not overlook the fact that we have no more than hints as to what Paul's mission preaching may have been: he had no occasion to repeat it at any length in his letters. These isolated references are therefore all the more important. In the ancient world it was impossible to proclaim as Son of God and redeemer of the world a man who had died on the cross, i.e. had suffered the shameful death of a common criminal, without giving a clear account of his activity, his suffering and his death. Those to whom the earliest Christian missionaries preached were no less curious than we are today. Certainly, they too will have wanted more information about the man Jesus. In other words, it was only possible to describe the exalted Jesus by telling of the earthly Jesus, his work and his death. The one who had been exalted to the right hand of God was no mere lay figure for the community. He was known from the narration of his ambassadors. Apocalyptic elaboration of the heavenly nature of the one exalted to the right hand of God, which is very much in the background in the books of the New Testament, was replaced by accounts of his saving work and cruel death in Galilee and Jerusalem, or at least, as in Acts (and even in Revelation), by a reference to the present effect of his Spirit and his Word and to the suffering of his community.

That favourite catchword, the 're-presentation' of the saving event in the earliest Christian preaching, should not be misused in this connection. By the very careful use of the aorist tense in talking about the death and resurrection of Jesus, Paul's terminology shows that he was not talking about just any repeatable or even timeless event, but about something *unique* (*ephapax*, Rom. 6.10). Strictly speaking, this event cannot really be 'represented' by preaching; rather, the audience which is addressed is taken back into the past event and made 'contemporaneous' with it. 'Do you not know that all of us who have been baptized into Christ Jesus were baptized into his death?' (Rom. 6.3). There cannot therefore be any proclamation of the gospel which is not at the same time a narration of past history. Even the shortest christological confession of earliest Christianity, 'Christ died for us', contains in the subject and predicate, 'Christ died', the germ of a historical, narrative element. By means of its past form, the Greek aorist *apethanen*, the verb 'died' expresses a finished, unique event from the past, and in my view the subject, Christ, is an indication that Jesus was condemned and killed as Messiah, *christos* in Greek, as the inscription on the cross (Mark 15.26) shows. It goes without saying that what was reported did not merely satisfy historical curiosity (which should not be despised), but also had unique significance for the present. Of course the earliest Christian historians were not archivists or archaeologists, who were interested in the past for its own sake. On the whole, ancient historians were not like this; they took up their pens to instruct their contemporaries about the present and the future (Thucydides 1.22). Furthermore, a large part of history-writing in antiquity was concerned with contemporary history. As a rule people wrote for the present and from the standpoint of a particular present. There was not yet a strict historical consciousness of the difference between the present and the past – at least in the modern sense. For the authors of the gospels, the saving event had taken place with Jesus of Nazareth in an immediate and still living past. If one likes to put it that way, they wrote 'eschatological contemporary history'. This distinguished them from the sacred primal history of the Pentateuch, where the living chain of those who handed on the tradition had long been broken, and people were forced back on the written word. True, the rabbis wanted to overcome this limitation by the doctrine of an ongoing oral tradition from Moses and Sinai, but in essentials they themselves were aware that it was a fiction. The special feature of the historiography of earliest Christianity was that what was reported here as an event of the most recent past had unique saving significance for all hearers, and that a happening which lay only a short distance back in the past at the same time contained God's offer of salvation for all men, which could be accepted in faith and trust and rejected in unbelief. The much disputed term 'salvation history' should be understood in terms of this particular 'offer of salvation' which is grounded in God's history with Jesus of Nazareth, and not derived from the false conception that in this respect talk must be limited to 'saving history'. From the human side, not least there was also the need to talk of disaster, for example in the misunderstandings of the disciples and their fear of suffering, in the treachery of Judas and Peter's denial, and indeed throughout the narrative of Jesus' passion. The unity between the proclamation of the gospel and the narration of history which is typical of earliest Christianity is evident from a redactional comment which Mark the evangelist puts on the lips of Jesus. In Mark 14.9, Jesus comments on the unknown woman who anointed him in Bethany: 'Truly, I say to you, wherever the gospel is preached in the whole world, what she has done will be told in memory of her.' Here Mark takes it for granted that the action of this woman will also be reported in all the churches in connection with the preaching of the good news, and that consequently proclamation (*keryssein*) and historiography (*lalein*) are inseparably connected. The fixing of the 'history of Jesus' in writing in the first description of his messianic activity and death – we might very well say: in the first 'Jesus-biography' – already derives from a fixed and widespread narrative tradition, on which the evangelist could build in a quite natural way. This is true above all of the passion narrative: I Cor. 11.23ff. indicates that Paul must already have known an extensive account with specific information.

For an ancient audience, the crucifixion of Jesus was such a fearful scandal that among the more learned public it had to be disguised in docetic fashion, because it was a grimly specific event which could not be reduced to a 'mathematical point' without content unless it were to be falsified. Such a reduction leads to abstraction, and abstraction volatilizes the underlying reality. Were the cross of Jesus to have become a mere symbol, to be manipulated at will, as happened in Gnosticism, then the scandal of the cross would have been removed. For that reason the passion story *had to be told* in detail by the earliest Christian missionaries – including Paul. If Paul could speak in very specific historical terms of 'the night on which the Lord Jesus was betrayed' (I Cor. 11.23), he must certainly have been able to say substantially more about this night and the betrayal of Jesus, and presupposed this knowledge among his Corinthian audience. His audience, too, must have known more about this 'betrayal of Jesus' and his suffering to the point of death, indeed 'death on the cross' (Phil. 2.8), than the mere fact of Jesus' death.

3.4 It is also striking that Paul too prepares a good deal of material for an 'Acts of the Apostles'. In I Cor. 15.2–11; I Cor. 9.1ff.; 1.12f.; 3.4ff., 21f.; Rom. 15.14ff. and above all Gal. 1 and 2, he presents individual sections which one could almost make into an ongoing narrative. Here he takes it for granted that the communities already have a good deal of knowledge about the persons and

events whom he mentions. Often he contents himself with allusions, because his readers were very much better informed than we
are today. What happened in the community of Jesus after the
resurrection was not without significance for belief in Paul's
Gentile Christian communities. One reason for this was that for
Paul himself, his apostolic activity was a direct and necessary consequence of the history of Jesus which formed the basis of salvation. It was this that filled up the interval between resurrection and
parousia, though we must always keep in mind Paul's relationship
with the other apostles. If Jesus, as the crucified one, was at the
same time the risen and exalted Lord, he had to send out his
messengers so that they could proclaim him as the salvation of
mankind (Rom. 10.12–18). That was why God had made Paul and
the other apostles 'messengers in Christ's place' (II Cor. 5.20); the
Risen One was himself at work in his apostolic messengers.

3.5   For precisely that reason, according to the earliest Christians
the saving event was 'history', which comprised not only the death
and resurrection of Jesus as the specific event lying at the heart of
salvation, but also his mission and his activity and the authentica-
tion of the apostles by the risen Jesus. For the apostles and
evangelists, for Paul as for Luke, this history as such was not *just* a
fabric of human effort or hybrid self-fulfilment, in short a 'product
of sin' (G. Klein, *ZNW* 62, 1971, 42). At the same time, in and
despite all human action it was God's act, the realization of the
divine will for salvation in the face of all human self-assertion.
However, in assessing this event, the basic presupposition is that
both the devastating judgment on 'history' as an attempt at human
self-realization and even more the recognition of the history of
Jesus and the apostles as the work of God are insights of faith.
They cannot be read out of the steady flow of events in positivistic
fashion, but presuppose that the audience is affected by the words
of Jesus and of his messengers. What we have here is not the
phantom of an isolated 'salvation history', to be delineated by
historical means, but an understanding in faith of the history of
Jesus in earliest Christianity itself as the event in which God acted
for the salvation of all men. This understanding of faith is at work

in the process of compelling men to retell the story of Jesus to the praise of God. Consequently modern historical, philological analysis of the historical sources of earliest Christianity, in search of facts, can never lead to the judgment that God himself was present in the history of Jesus and his first messengers; this judgment is derived from obedient attention to their message, which necessarily involves a historical account, a narrative. Paul himself emerges as the great example of the power of this message, both in his letters (I Cor. 15.10; Gal. 1.15ff.) and in Luke's account (Acts 9.15). The Risen One who encountered him was not a Gnostic hypostasis, but none other than the one man Jesus of Nazareth, who came from the Jewish people and whose physical brother James Paul had known (I Cor. 9.5; Gal. 1.19). In the last night before his death, Jesus had instituted the Lord's Supper and then had been crucified, after which God had exalted him into his presence. This Jesus thus embodied a whole history of his own, and as the exalted one at the same time caused the new message to be spread wider afield. That is, this Jesus was at the same time both the effective cause of the new eschatological community and its missionary proclamation. If Jesus was the basis of salvation, then Paul, as his 'thirteenth witness' (C. Burchard), was the incomparable instrument for the communication of this salvation. That is why Luke describes him as a unique example of a witness to Jesus; for that reason, too, Paul can also become the central apostle in the canon of the New Testament.

3.6 Now of course the form of historical narrative differs very widely among individual New Testament authors. A decisive role was played here both by the degree of their Greek or Jewish education and their theological thinking, their origin and the school to which they belonged. Luke has the greatest degree of formal rhetorical education; Matthew's background is the Jewish-Christian academy indebted to the Pharisaic tradition, whereas in John we find an almost esoteric community with a marked Jewish-Christian stamp, which in many respects is indebted to Palestinian Jewish mysticism. Here Mark is relatively the closest to the original events; in his work we can still find the effect of the strong missionary impulse which is also to be seen in Paul: his attention is still deliberately directed towards Galilee as the homeland of Jesus and the most important location of his activity, and to Jerusalem only as the place of his rejection and his passion. While the author has no literary education, he is a capable theologian and indeed a gifted narrator. He is probably identical with John Mark (Acts 12.12; 13.5; 15.37), who was later associated with Peter (I Peter 5.13) (see p. 92). He was certainly not an unknown Gentile Christian, as many scholars are fond of claiming today.

Thus the origin, education, style and manner of work of the individual authors are closely connected, and also govern the way in which they treat the traditions available to them.

It follows automatically from all this that the earliest Christian historical accounts never set out to be a rational means of proof for the truth and reality of the saving event which has its origin in God, capable of giving security by their demonstration and making faith superfluous. Rather, as narrative they are always at the same time testimony, which issues an invitation to understanding in faith. Of course one could also read such narrative in a negative sense, as is shown by the examples of the anti-Christian polemicists, Celsus or Porphyry, say in their evaluation of the passion story. However, a mere acknowledgment – in either a derogatory or even a neutral sense – would fail to do justice to the real aim of the narrator indicated in John 20.31: 'That you may believe . . .' All the history writers in the New Testament are agreed in this aim; even the 'recognition' of the reliability of the Jesus tradition in Luke 1.4 amounts to an acknowledgment which involves, rather than excludes, faith.

4

The Historical-critical Method

The thought that historical-critical knowledge is purely 'immanent' and 'value-free' is a modern 'achievement'. In ancient times people still hardly found it necessary shamefully to deny their 'pre-understanding' or 'heuristic interest'. Belief in the possibility of supernatural, divine interventions in the course of history and in miraculous events was the rule, and very few people rejected it altogether. The historical views of Herodotus, the first great Greek historian (fifth century BC), are based on his conviction of the absolute sway of inexorable destiny which no mortal man can escape, in which the gods cause misfortune to follow excessive good fortune and well-deserved punishment to follow hybris. Granted, in the most significant Hellenistic historian, Polybius (second century BC), Tyche the goddess of fate is usually simply a cipher for the changing and often arbitrary course of events, which in the last resort favours the most virtuous, i.e. the Romans; but in striking instances he too can claim the intervention of divine retribution. By contrast, according to the Stoic Posidonius, who lived a little later, continuing the history of Polybius and more than any other writer in antiquity introducing universal knowledge and philosophical construction into his historiography, history should never be taken to be under the domination of blind chance; rather, it bears witness to the meaningful sway of the divine 'Logos' or 'providence'. Diodorus Siculus, who saw real historians as 'ministers of divine providence' (11.3), is probably dependent on Posidonius. Dio Cassius, at the end of the second century AD and the beginning of the third, firmly believed in the historical significance of all kinds of divine guidance; in his first work he argued that the emperor Septimius Severus enjoyed divine favour, and he allowed himself to be guided by dreams in his own writing. As a high Roman official he knew and hated the Christians, which was reason enough never to mention them in his great historical work: he treated them as though they simply did not exist, then as now a favourite means of political polemic.

Thus by far the majority of ancient historians agree that history is not the work of men alone; at the same time it is a sphere of activity for superhuman forces: Tyche, the goddess of fate; or Heimarmene, an irrational divine will; or even the divine 'providence' of the Stoics. Only the Epicureans believed in the absolute sway of chance and arbitrariness, which man confronted with his free will. No wonder that ancient historical thinking found its consummation in a Christian work which at the same time represents the only great treatise on the philosophy of history to be found in the ancient world, namely Augustine's *City of God*. Its focal point, too, is not man and his controlling power; rather, there is a conflict between the *civitas terrena diaboli*, the earthly rule of the devil, and the *civitas Dei*, the rule of God. A consideration of history shows that whether as an individual or as a collective, man is not the 'measure of all things', but stands under the power of trans-subjective 'forces'.

In contrast to these very varied views of history among Greek and Hellenistic-Roman historians, the distinguishing feature of history-writing in the Old Testament and Judaism was the certain faith that the God who chose Israel was the sole Lord of history and guided it in judgment and in grace. There is a Hellenistic Jewish illustration of this: we have fragments of a dramatist called Ezekiel, which deal with the exodus from Egypt completely in the style of Aeschylus and Euripides, with the one difference that – in contrast to Greek tragedy – destiny plays no role in this drama; the whole event is subject to God's saving will. Despite all the differences, the New Testament narrators are closest to this Old Testament and Jewish picture of history. Once again we may single out Luke, as being the most significant historian of the New Testament. A comparison of his work with that of Josephus or the books of Maccabees, and here above all with II Maccabees, which goes back to Jason of Cyrene, shows his particular proximity to Jewish

Hellenistic historiography. Luke is evidently influenced by a firm tradition with a religious view of history which essentially derives from the Septuagint. His imitation of the style of the Septuagint shows that he wants quite deliberately to be in this tradition. Among Hellenistic historians it has a parallel in the imitation of Herodotus with his Ionic dialect, or of Thucydides, which is mocked so much by Lucian (15f.).

4.2 Our understanding of history is certainly quite substantially different from the views of history current in antiquity. Nevertheless, it would be a distortion were we to denounce the work of modern historians as a sterile, positivistic 'historical-critical method' which pinned down and collected the supposed 'brute facts', i.e. the real events, like so many butterflies. This is a vapid caricature which is probably perpetuated only by theologians. There is no real historiography, without interest and evaluation, without penetrating questions concerned with deeper connections, causes and effects, without reflection on chance and destiny, human greatness and human failure, guilt and fate. There is no historical research without 'pre-understanding' or heuristic interests. On the other hand this must be controlled and kept in check by our responsibility to what the sources say and the historian's integrity and love of truth. This concern for objectiveness need not, however, carry with it the neutrality of the uncommitted. As a Christian, one has to go one stage further and assert that the meaning and unity of history – contrary to all appearances – can be thought of only on the basis of belief in God's revelation which bears witness to the unity of creation and redemption. Just as we cannot produce proofs of God with historical methods and from a consideration of history, so it follows that the application of historical-critical methods cannot call for the recognition of an 'atheistic' view of history in which the question of the activity of God becomes illegitimate. The same thing is true of the categories of determination and freedom. Every time he asks about the deeper basis of historical events, the scholar quickly come up against impossible barriers, against the question 'Why?', which he can no longer answer adequately. Thus again and again the study of history demonstrates the deep dilemmas, indeed the intractability of our humanity; the mere consideration of past events cannot offer an answer to the questions which emerge here. Therein lies its significance and its limitation. It is all too understandable that even in antiquity the great historians seldom believed in progress, and were more inclined to pessimism. Tacitus is an impressive example of this.

By contrast, one of the unmistakable characteristics of the message of earliest Christianity and the history narrated in it is the way in which it uses the past to remind the onlooker, who at the same time is always also a hearer, of the fundamental question about the truth and falsehood of his existence. In so doing it makes it impossible for the hearer and onlooker to adopt an attitude of detachment, which is otherwise the case in study of the distant past. Rather, the hearer and onlooker is caught up into that former event in and with Jesus – one might even say 'into the presence of Jesus'. In this encounter with him and his history, which has such a unique significance for faith, because through it God shows himself to us as a loving Father, we are also assured of the meaning and the unity of history, for this love of the Father made manifest in Jesus unites us with all men, those past and those to come, and bears witness that we are all God's beloved creatures. Thus history can take on quite specific meaning and unity in the Lord's Prayer. In place of pessimism and belief in progress we have here a trusting appeal to the creator of the world and the Lord of history as 'our Father', a form of address which at the same time includes thanks and praise for his goodness. By calling him 'our Father', we hallow his name.

4.3 If we want to turn to that 'former event with and in Jesus', we must always also ask what really happened then, what the events really were which are reported to us by the earliest Christian historians. But today, in accordance with our awareness of the truth, such consideration presupposes historical and philological research into the New Testament sources, since without them a real scientific understanding of the New Testament has become impossible for us touay. Two things get in the way of such consideration. On the one hand a defamation in principle of the so-called 'historical-critical method', with its underlying anxiety about historical truth, and on the other hand a misuse of this method which mistakes its possibilities and limitations and changes it into a kind of dogmatic method, postulating with reference to it that 'what may not be cannot be'. The expression 'historical method' would be enough in itself; the term 'historical-critical' occurs above all in theological terminology and has an apologetic connotation. It is a matter of course, which really ought not to be stressed any further, that any scientific historical work must always also be critical. Without a critical analysis of the sources there can be no historical discipline, no investigation of past events. Here the 'historical-critical method' simply represents a necessary collection of the 'tools' for opening up past events; that is, it is not a single, clearly defined procedure, but rather a mixture of sometimes very different methods of working. Like almost all intellectual methods, it is constantly subject to the fluctuating intellectual trends which unfortunately are not always identical with real scientific progress. Therefore the adjective 'critical' must always also include self-criticism. If scholastic fixation is to be guarded against, criticism must always represent an open multiplicity of methods. This also rules out the absolute use of one particular method in exegesis. Similarly, we must be very careful indeed about calling 'events' of the past which can be reconstructed with its help straightforward, obvious 'plain facts'; as a rule, they in turn prove to have many possible significances. Each individual event can be seen by different witnesses at the same time from quite different aspects, which often seem to us to be contradictory. By contrast, to talk of a plain fact shows a tendency to simplify and devalue past reality. Often enough the use of the phrase in a derogatory fashion is often simply an attempt to justify an evasion of history itself. It would therefore be a good thing to remove this kind of language from theological terminology as being too abrupt and misleading. The real 'facts' of the past, what happened at one time, are accessible to us only in a very limited way. This is particularly true of events from the ancient world, because here the sources on which we base our investigations are so very limited and fortuitous (see pp. 3ff. above). Indeed we can only recreate a sketchy outline of the real world of the past with the inevitably inadequate means of our analysis and reconstruction. This is true both with Jesus, who taught peasants and fishermen on the shores of Lake Gennesaret, and with Paul, the greatest missionary and theologian of early Christianity, who founded the first as it were sectarian mission communities in the capital cities of the Roman provinces. In our business we all too often come up against the limits of 'historical-critical' work. Furthermore, when it is wrongly applied, this work does not revive past events, but dissolves them in the clouds of vague hypothesis. Sometimes it would be more appropriate here to talk of an unhistorical-uncritical method. Awareness of his own limitations and the constant lack of source material should therefore make the historian modest, and always open to correction in his attempts at reconstruction. However, he should not become a sceptic, since the texts with which he is dealing as a theologian and a New Testament scholar resist destructive scepticism as much as they resist unbridled fantasy. He has to approach them in a responsible fashion, in the awareness that the evidence about Jesus and earliest Christianity which has been entrusted to him conveys a power which has shaken mankind to the core and which continues to be influential today in creating faith and bringing about community.

4.4 The events of vanished ages come most to life where they can be depicted in vivid fashion; one might almost say, when they can be lived out all over again. Therefore the art of the historian consists in the degree to which he can make a vivid impression on the reader, bringing the dead past to life. It is not a matter of the dry accumulation of detail which puts one archive after another, much less a destructive radical analysis in which everything turns into a figment of the imagination. It was already the aim of such great biblical narrators as Mark and Luke to guide the hearer or reader into such genuine shared experience. They comprehended the nature of past events better than mere detailed records could have made possible. Luke, with his 'dramatic episodic style' (Haenchen), stood in a broad tradition of Hellenistic historiography which sought to bring historical reality vividly before the eyes of the reader by concentrating on particular paradigmatic events. The modern historian certainly cannot simply imitate this style, but he should also attempt in his account to make the ancient sources and their historical background clear and thus comprehensible. Here we come up against possibilities and tasks which leave far behind what one might suppose to be the primary goal of the academic historian, the knowledge of historical 'facts'. He cannot simply 'make the texts speak' in a single act of violence, but must first of all make them speak to himself; he must become attuned to them, and then carefully, step by step, with the help of the historical and philological methods at his disposal, attempt to hear individual tones and at the same time the whole work more clearly. Only where the historian and exegete is himself the best hearer will he also be able to help others to hear and understand better.

4.5 In all this, the most appropriate attitude for the scholar when dealing with the historical narratives of the New Testament is one which does not disregard *a priori* the testimony and the claim presented in these texts, but is prepared to 'listen' openly to what they have to say. Such an approach takes seriously the content of the texts – however strange they may seem to us – and attempts to understand them in terms of their intrinsic concerns. This also involves accepting, rather than denying, their claim to be kerygmatic historical reports. For example, when we enquire about the purposes of a New Testament author, we can never ignore the fact that such an author, who has a position within the Christian community and is at its service, does not seek primarily to display his theological individuality and originality, much less his rhetorical skill and historical learning. Keeping his own personality in the background, he works with existing traditions about the saving event which, while lying in the past, utterly governs the present of the community. Redaction-critical and structuralist approaches, so popular today, fail to do justice to this situation when in principle they ignore the question of the traditions standing behind the text and their historical basis, as being inessential and uninteresting. A text is never a completely isolated entity. We should therefore also guard against the temptation of a text fetishism. Precisely by isolating a 'text in itself' and giving it an absolute status, one ignores the historical reality which underlies it. Every text occurs in a particular 'con-text' and as such serves to give an indication; it has the character of witness. The earliest Christian narrators sought to describe God's acts in a particular realm of the past in such a way that they became the testimony of faith for the present; in so doing they neither present unalterable documentation nor do they dissolve the event which forms a basis for faith so that it becomes completely unimaginable. In their historical narratives we also encounter a sense of obligation to the traditions which give the community its foundation; one might even say that we come up against past truth and reality which as such is nevertheless at the same time completely present, along with a creative freedom which was a fruit of the spirit and which could venture to tell the old story in a new way so that the audience could take part in it. Only those who go into this character of the New Testament narrative material, so striking in comparison with other texts from antiquity, will also discover the manifold and tense relationship between the simple narrative as an apparent 'account of facts' and the complex reality which precedes it in time, underlies it, and in the last resort was the cause of the composition of these texts. Because of this dialectic between the account which is also testimony and the saving event to which it bears witness and which, because past, is inaccessible to a direct approach, our modern attempts at reconstruction – which have to be carried on for the sake of the truth – will always be no more than patchwork. We can only arrive at sketches and shadows of what once happened, and must therefore always be ready to correct our hypotheses. But even these 'sketches' and 'shadows' speak a language which is impressive and clear enough. If we dispense with them, we will have no understanding whatsoever of what took place at that time. However, no authentic faith can evade understanding and slightingly despise historical knowledge.

4.6 The historical method which is appropriate here requires extreme care, guarded intensity, responsibility and reverence towards the truth. Even Lucian, so ironical and critical, often stressed this reverence, which goes hand in hand with inner freedom (38,41,61). There should no longer be any room in contemporary Christian theology for an anxious apologetic which suppresses historical truth. On the other hand, the New Testament texts are too good for us to devalue them so that they become the objects of an unrestrained and ambitious competition. In this context, it must be obvious that over its history of almost two hundred years, so-called 'radical criticism' has led to uncritical speculations just as much as has apologetic and fundamentalist anxiety. The history of the radical criticism of Acts itself gives us many warning examples. The hypotheses of the hyper-critics coincide with the often so painful 'salvage attempts' by the learned Theodore Zahn in mistaking the true historical value of Acts and creating instead new apostolic romances which at one time go beyond Luke and at another completely pass him by.

Unfashionable Reflections on Luke as a Theological Historian

5.1 The argument introduced by H. Conzelmann (*The Theology of St Luke* (1954), ET 1960) and often repeated since then, that Luke divides history up into three periods, was certainly attractive, but nevertheless misleading. The *auctor ad Theophilum* did not set out to depict the history of Jesus as 'the middle of time', nor to present subsequent events in Acts as the 'period of the church'. In reality, the whole double work covers the one history of Jesus Christ, which also includes the interval between resurrection and parousia as the time of his proclamation in the 'last days' (Acts 2.17), and which Luke clearly distinguishes from the epoch of the old covenant as the time of the messianic fulfilment of the prophetic promises. The division of the work into two parts necessarily followed from the distinction between the activity of the earthly Jesus and his work as exalted Lord, who acts through the spirit in the preaching of his messengers. This necessary distinction between the earthly existence of Jesus and his activity as exalted Lord is already hinted at in the two levels of the early christological confessions and hymns (Rom. 1.3f.; Phil. 2.6–11; I Tim. 3.16). Of course Luke deliberately narrows down his account of the messengers of Christ stage by stage so that it culminates in his paradigmatic witness, Paul. The charge that he adopts an anti-eschatological attitude also rests on an error. Luke only attacks a misguided enthusiastic expectation of the parousia in the imminent future and the apocalyptic calculations associated with it, which lead the community astray (see Luke 17.20). In fact he means his work to introduce the reader to the time of perseverance in suffering and missionary proclamation which precedes the parousia. He finds exemplary embodiments of both these things in Paul. Luke's relatively positive attitude towards the Roman state is not only governed by the fact that as a forerunner of the apologists he wants to achieve public toleration and recognition by the Roman authorities of the new religion as it represents the true Judaism and thus deserves to share its special status – Haenchen's interpretation completely mistakes Luke's attitude – rather, he is well aware that the church will come up against further and increasingly more severe persecutions. In reality, like I Peter in a comparable situation, he wants to stress that the charges laid against the Christians are raised unjustly. A further point of view which influenced Luke was his experience that there were also thoughtful and upright officials who acted with tolerance towards the Christians. Perhaps we might describe one basic theme of Luke's two works, which are dedicated to a representative of the upper classes and addressed not least to readers from the educated middle classes with sympathy for Christianity, in terms of the invitation given in I Peter 3.15: 'Always be prepared to make a defence to any one who calls you to account for the hope that is in you.' Christians are not an anarchical, amoral, hole-in-a-corner sect, which shrinks back from public gaze (Acts 26.26). The reason for their activity and the bond which held them together is therefore not the 'hate against the human race' (*odium humani generis, Ann.* 15.44), of which Tacitus accuses them. Luke's historiography has precious little to do with cheap apologetic; the *apologia* called for here is governed by the responsibility of a faith which scorns the safe esoteric conventicle and which is not afraid of public discussion despite the threat of persecution, while at the same time knowing that God himself will have the last word through his Christ, the coming judge (10.42; 17.31).

5.2 Luke is no less trustworthy than other historians of antiquity. People have done him a great injustice in comparing him too closely with the edifying, largely fictitious, romance-like writings in the style of the later acts of apostles, which freely invent facts as they like and when they need them. There is a great gulf between him and the later romances about the apostles (see p. 12 above).

Going by ancient standards, the relative reliability of his account can be tested in the gospels by a synoptic comparison with Matthew and Mark. We have no reason to assume that he acted completely differently in Acts from the way in which he composed his first work, and that he made up his narrative largely out of his head. Of course, in some circumstances he rigorously omits everything that does not fit in with his narrative purposes; he abbreviates some events so much that they become almost incomprehensible, and hints at others quite briefly (see pp. 63f. below). At the same time he elaborates what he wants to stress, and makes use of multiple repetition as a means of writing. He can also combine separate historical traditions to serve his ends, and separate matters that belong together if as a result he can achieve a meaningful sequence of events. All this can also be found in the secular historians of Greek and Roman antiquity. On the other hand, one can hardly accuse him of simply having invented events, created scenes out of nothing and depicted them on a broad canvas, deliberately falsifying his traditions in an unrestrained way for the sake of cheap effect. He is quite certainly not simply concerned with pious edification at the expense of truth. He is not just an 'edifying writer', but a historian and theologian who needs to be taken seriously. His account always remains within the limits of what was considered reliable by the standards of antiquity. That means that the author's assurance in Luke 1.3 is more than mere convention; it contains a real theological and historical programme, though this cannot be measured by the standards of a modern critical historian. True, the speeches interspersed through Acts always also serve to develop Luke's own theological ideas, but as a rule he does this by the use of older traditions, and often attempts to give an appropriate characterization of individual speakers. Once again, this is the procedure which Lucian requires of the true historian: the words of the speaker should match his person and his concern (58). Thucydides (1.22) already stressed that 'it was difficult to recall with strict accuracy the words actually spoken', and so he presented them 'in the language in which, as it seemed to me, the several speakers would express the sentiments most befitting the occasion'. The style-critical method of separating redaction and tradition, which tends to be overdone, can be used only with the greatest caution in the case of Luke, since like all ancient historians who used existing material he did not simply copy out his original sources, where these were not authoritative sayings of Jesus, but reshaped them according to his own style. In essentials, he already treats sayings of Jesus in the same way as scriptural quotations (cf. Acts 20.35). His subtle feeling for style can be shown, for example, in the way in which in the first part of Acts, where the scene of events is predominantly in Jerusalem and Palestine, he works much more with 'semitisms' drawn from the Septuagint than in the second part of the work, where he describes Paul's mission to the Gentiles in Asia Minor and Greece and his imprisonment and journey to Rome. Nevertheless, all in all his style remains remarkably uniform throughout. On the basis of this far-reaching originality and unity of style one could claim that the whole of Acts has been shaped 'editorially', and attempt to provide stylistic justification for the caricature of Luke as an edifying romantic writer. In reality, however, this would be a disastrous mistake. In analysis, style-critical arguments must always be supplemented by historical and theological arguments. This is the only way of arriving at a considered judgment.

5.3 In any account of Luke's theology it should also be noted that the deliberate turning towards the past, which is more marked in Luke than in any other of the New Testament writers, has also influenced his theology. He resorts to time past, the period of the event which gave Christianity its foundation. He searched for old traditions; made enquiries of those who handed on the tradition and used source material. The 'historical sense' evidenced in all this also influenced his theological thinking. We cannot therefore assert that he simply projected his theological present uncritically on to the past; on the contrary, we should note how much his theology was shaped by archaic conceptions – if one can use 'archaic' in connection with a period of time of between fifty and sixty years – on which he stumbled in the course of his search for ancient tradition. He wanted to take his bearings on what for him was the authoritative primal age of faith, because more than his

Christian contemporaries he was capable of thinking historically. This is true of his simple exaltation christology, with no conceptions of pre-existence and mediation at creation; his predilection for the title 'servant of God' and his striking restraint over 'Son of God'; the definition of the eucharist as 'breaking of bread'; his enthusiastic conception of the spirit; the typically Lucan theology of the poor; and so on. Thus he is the first theological representative of an approach concerned to go back *ad fontes*, i.e. back to the primitive Christian sources (cf. Luke 1.1). We must regard it as a legitimate undertaking that in about AD 80 or 90, at a time of oppression by Domitian and the beginning of the Gnostic threat – which of course is hardly visible in his work and should not be overestimated as a theme – he should deliberately return to the beginnings. Faced with the danger of splits in the church and apocalyptic fanaticism, in his two-volume work Luke reminds that church of the earthly Jesus and the exalted Christ, who proclaimed himself through his messengers and his witnesses and guides the community through word and spirit. It is part of his paraenetic concern that the account in Acts often only hints at conflicts and thus plays them down. There were presumably more than enough disputes in the church of his time; Luke saw it as his task to overcome them with a view to the one Lord of the church and the coming judge, and by an orientation on the origins in which he had been at work. By stressing above all the struggle over the validity of the Jewish law in his account of conflicts within the church, Luke is in essentials simply stressing his relative reliability; for at the time when he wrote his work, precisely this question had long been decided in favour of an unlimited mission which took no account of the law; furthermore, Palestinian Jewish Christianity had lost its leading role in the church, at the latest after the martyrdom of James in AD 62. By depicting the Jewish Christians, including Paul, as essentially faithful to the law, Luke – against the historical situation of his time – is trying to say that the Christians are the true Israel and that the break with Judaism (i.e. with the community organized in the synagogue congregations of the Diaspora) was not caused by Christians, but by Jews (Acts 28.26ff.). The Christians had not left the synagogues of their own accord, but had been driven out of them by force. In fact we can hardly doubt that the milieu of the synagogue had been an important place for missionary teaching and discussion, both for earliest Christianity and indeed for Jesus himself. It was an area which will have been abandoned reluctantly and only under external compulsion. This is still the case even with Paul, who quite deliberately began his mission to the Gentiles with the 'god-fearers' in the synagogue. The report in Acts 16.3, that Paul had his later travelling companion Timothy, the son of a Jewish mother and a Gentile father, circumcised, is not a Lukan falsification. Timothy was a Jew because he had a Jewish mother. By refusing circumcision Paul would have supported apostasy and would no longer have been allowed to appear in any synagogue. That is precisely what he wanted to avoid. It was the majority in the Jewish synagogue congregations – understandably outraged – who expelled the earliest Christian apocalyptic trouble-makers. Luke also indicates that there were exceptions, in his account of the Jews in Beroea who willingly accepted Paul's message (17.10–12). Of course this break was long over by Luke's time; i.e. in this point too he does not introduce the present circumstances of his church into past history, but takes up a real problem from the past, though – as was his practice – doing so in somewhat schematized form. Certainly Paul's attitude to the law is unduly simplified, and indeed distorted, by Luke's emphatic references to his being a Pharisee (23.6) and his preaching in the synagogue. On the other hand, Paul himself stressed that he was a Pharisee and loved Israel (Phil. 3.5f.; Rom. 9.1f.; 10.1). We can hardly doubt that the Jews were responsible both for the expulsion from the synagogue of the Hellenists, who were critical of the law, and for the final breach between the Judaism which was renewed after the destruction of the Temple and the Palestinian Jewish Christians. We must also add that of all the non-Jewish writers of antiquity, Luke has by far the best knowledge of Judaism, its liturgy in the Temple and in the synagogues, its customs and its parties, and on the whole he reports them in an accurate and indeed positive way. There is not a trace in his work of the ancient antisemitism which was similarly not unknown to him (cf. Acts 16.10f.). In his time the Christians were evidently still themselves the victims of Gentile hostility to the Jews.

5.4 The favourite slogan and label 'early catholicism' is less helpful for understanding Luke; it cannot really make any contribution to a historical and theological understanding of earliest Christianity. On the contrary, it fits all too well with today's widespread desire for handy clichés. As far as Luke is concerned, both his enthusiastic conception of the spirit and his understanding of the ministry of the church, which at least outside Jerusalem still did not have any hierarchical structure, fail to match the label. Nor can one term 'early catholic' either his archaic doctrine of the sacrament, for which any 'sacramental magic' is still alien, or his no less archaic christology. The *auctor ad Theophilum* is oriented more on the past period of Christian origins than on the arrival of the second century. Here Matthew seems to be the more ecclesiastical and therefore more 'modern' theologian. It was his gospel which was to exercise the greater influence from the second century on, as he determined the future of the church's ethos; John, on the other hand, showed the way forward for christology. Unfortunately the early church paid too little attention to the way that in the Gospel of Luke Jesus' message of God's boundless love for sinners rings out most clearly, say, in the parables of the prodigal son and the Pharisee and the publican; even today this can sometimes be forgotten because of the blinkers which go with a radical criticism of Luke. Only Marcion found Luke's approach particularly attractive, and that was no great commendation for his work; perhaps that is the reason why it is not mentioned in the notes from Papias which have come down to us.

5.5 For the period which will be of particular interest to us, from the persecution of Stephen to the 'apostolic council' (see pp. 111ff. below), Luke makes use of two strands of source material in particular, though we can no longer make a consecutive reconstruction of them. These are: (*a*) the so-called Antiochene or Hellenist source, which in my view contained the stories of Stephen and Philip and the reports about Barnabas and Paul's early days;

(*b*) a collection of stories about Peter. We may assume that Luke did not take over everything that these sources contained, but made a careful selection from them to serve the purpose of his narrative. This purpose was to show the course taken by the gospel from the Jewish-Christian community in Jerusalem, to which he rightly accords central significance, step by step to Paul's world-wide mission to the Gentiles.

5.6 The author of the two-volume work is probably Luke the physician (Col. 4.14; cf. Philemon 24). He may have joined Paul on the so-called second missionary journey (Acts 16.10ff.) and later have accompanied him from Troas to Jerusalem (20.5 on), and finally from Caesarea to Rome (27.1 on). That is to say, the remarks in the first person plural refer to the author himself. They do not go back to an earlier independent source, nor are they a mere literary convention, giving the impression that the author was an eye witness. From the beginning, this is the only way in which readers – and first of all Theophilus, to whom the two-volume work was dedicated and who must have known the author personally – could have understood the 'we' passages. 'We' therefore appears in travel accounts because Luke simply wanted to indicate that he was there. However, his personal experiences are uninteresting. Paul remains the sole focal point. The differences between the picture of Paul in Acts and Paul's original letters, which are certainly considerable, may be explained by the interval of about thirty years between the events in which Luke shared and the composition of his work, and further by the fact that Luke presumably did not know Paul's letters. He may have known that Paul sometimes sent letters to his churches, but these were no longer available to him at the time when he wrote, between 80 and 90. When he finally became Paul's companion, all these letters – with the exception of Philemon and perhaps Philippians – had already been written. They were composed at the height of Paul's mission, during the so-called second and third missionary journeys, and Luke only joined Paul for any length of time on the journey to Jerusalem. At a later stage he evidently had no more opportunity of getting information about the apostle through his own works. Finally, although he was a companion of Paul and had great respect for this unique missionary Luke did not completely understand and assimilate Paul's theology. Those who reflect on the theological changes to be seen among once 'narrow Barthians' or 'strict Lutherans' over the past thirty years, or note how far imagination and reality have become confused in the legends about the church struggle over a period of only forty years, will be more careful in judging Luke than his strictest critics in recent decades. After all, he was a child of his time, who was still quite unfamiliar with the 'historical-critical method', did not have the possibility of easy access to information in well-filled libraries and archives, and was even less acquainted with the strict methods of New Testament seminars. It is without doubt a serious failing that Luke does not take up the Pauline theology of the cross and that justification by faith alone without the works of the law takes very much a back place with him (but cf. Acts 13.38f. for Paul and 15.11 for Peter). Still, which of Paul's pupils remained completely faithful to his master's heritage? Taking into account the so-called 'Deutero-Pauline' letters, can we not also include Luke among the 'disciples of Paul'? Those who cannot forgive him his questionable 'Paulinism' and his other 'freedoms' should at least consider how many people are proud of being the disciples of a great theological teacher and heap praise upon him, though in the meantime they have moved miles away from him. In how many cases might we not think it a blessing that the dead teacher is no longer in a position to note the errors and confusions of his pupils? Only those who are really completely without sin here can go on throwing stones at Luke because of his un-Pauline 'Paulinism'.

We only do justice to the significance of Luke as the first theological 'historian' of Christianity if we take his work seriously as a source, i.e. if we attempt to examine it critically, reconstructing the story which he tells by adding and comparing other sources. The radical 'redaction-critical' approach so popular today, which sees Luke above all as a freely inventive theologian, mistakes his real purpose, namely that as a Christian 'historian' he sets out to report the events of the past that provided the foundation for the faith and its extension. He does not set out primarily to present his own 'theology'.

In the second part of this book I shall attempt to provide, in paradigmatic form, a reconstruction of the period between the persecution of the 'Hellenists' and the 'apostolic council', i.e. of the decisive span of about twenty-five years. In this it will become clear what we also owe to Luke in terms of historical knowledge and understanding, because while we cannot use his work as the basis for a continuous 'history of primitive Christianity', we can attempt a sketch of developments from the first community in Jerusalem to the world-wide mission of Paul.

II

The Decisive Epoch of the
History of Earliest Christianity:
The Development of a World-
wide Mission

6

The Hellenists and their Expulsion from Jerusalem

6.1 Scholars since F. C. Baur have rightly supposed a historical nucleus in Luke's account of the tensions between the Christian 'Hebrews' and 'Hellenists' in Jerusalem (Acts 6.1ff.) and have suggested that it indicates a new and decisive stage in the development of the earliest community. One striking phenomenon here, which they often ignore, is the fact that the message of the crucified and risen Messiah Jesus of Nazareth also found its way particularly to Greek-speaking Jews a few years, and perhaps only months, after the resurrection event which formed the foundation of the community. These Jews came from a wide variety of places in the Diaspora and had settled in Jerusalem. This astonishing influence on outsiders, transcending the boundaries of language and culture, distinguishes earliest Christianity from all other Palestinian Jewish movements, the Sadducees and Pharisees, the Essenes and the Baptist movement, the activity of which was largely confined to Palestine before the destruction of the Temple. With the exception of Philip and Nicanor, the list of the 'seven' in Acts 6.5 does not contain any of the typical Jewish names which are attested for, say, Egypt or Palestine. Simply from the exclusively Greek names, one might suppose that the 'seven' came from abroad; the last of them, the proselyte Nicolaus, is said to have come from Antioch. According to Acts 11.20, the Jewish Christians driven out of Jerusalem, who first used Antioch as a base from which to embark deliberately on a mission to the Gentiles which took no account of the Jewish law, came from Cyrenaica and Cyprus, areas which from the time of the Ptolemies on had a large and completely Hellenized Jewish Diaspora. Perhaps one might recall at this point that according to

Mark 15.21 it was a Simon from the North African city of Cyrene who had carried the cross for Jesus, and that his sons, one with the Greek name Alexander and the other with the Roman name Rufus, presumably became members of the Christian community. Similarly, Acts 13.1 mentions Lucius of Cyrene and Barnabas from Cyprus among the prophets and teachers in the Syrian capital. Manaen (Menahem), the third person mentioned there, who is described as *syntrophos* of Herod the Tetrarch, had been a childhood companion or a close friend of Herod Antipas; that is, he probably came from the upper classes in Jerusalem or Galilee, who tended to have a Greek education. This was a sign that the new message also reached members of the upper classes. The development had presumably already taken place during the lifetime of Jesus (Luke 8.3). Some people have tried to see Lucius of Cyrene as representing a hidden reference to Luke himself, pointing out that the first person plural appears for the first time in the Western text of Acts 11.28. However, this hypothesis is very improbable.

6.2 The question is why it was that Greek-speaking Jews in particular were so attracted by the new eschatological message of salvation and in turn presented it with such zeal that they were persecuted and driven out of Jerusalem. In my view, the only reasonable explanation of this is that the proclamation of Jesus itself had features which were particularly fascinating for Diaspora Jews. From the beginning, the message of Jesus had affinities with the universalist Greek-speaking world and perhaps even with some themes in Greek thought. We can see in it not only close connections with Jewish wisdom, but sometimes also echoes of Greek gnomic wisdom and above all of Cynic thought. We find in it that universality which E. Käsemann has described by the phrase 'the call of freedom'. We can best understand that the aggressive preaching of the 'Hellenists' in the Greek-speaking synagogues of Jerusalem could lead to lynch law for their leader Stephen and to the expulsion of the group on the presupposition that the 'Hellenists' presented arguments the foundation of which is to be sought in the message of Jesus himself. They called for the eschatological abolition of Temple worship and the revision of the law of Moses in the light of the true will of God. Granted, their criticism of the Torah did not yet have that considered theological radicalism which we find with Paul, but it did set the eschatological authority of the revelation of the crucified Messiah Jesus above the authority of Moses and therefore the commandment to love above the ritual law (Acts 6.8–14). That means that the 'Hellenists' put forward the offensive claim that the significance of Jesus as the Messiah of Israel essentially superseded that of Moses in the history of salvation: the gospel of Jesus took the place of the Jewish gospel of exodus and Sinai as God's concluding, incomparable eschatological revelation. They understood their authority to make this criticism as a gift of the spirit, which they saw as a sign of the dawning of the eschatological age. The Aramaic-speaking Jewish Christians had a more restrained – one might almost say more conservative – attitude towards the Law. They remained more deeply rooted in the religious tradition of Palestine, which from the time of the Maccabees inevitably regarded any attack on Torah and Temple as sacrilege. Of course we should not suppose that in the earliest period even they were so strict about keeping the law as the Jerusalem community under the leadership of James seems to have been at a later stage (Gal. 2.1ff., 11ff.; Acts 21.18ff.), for they too were still under the direct influence of the preaching of Jesus.

6.3 The persecution which broke out as a result of the 'Hellenists'' criticism of law and cult probably consisted primarily in disciplinary measures directed by the synagogue against this group. Their opponents were the members of the Greek-speaking synagogues in Jerusalem (Acts 6.9), from which the Jewish-Christian Hellenists had themselves emerged (cf. Acts 9.29). However, we cannot exclude the possibility that the supreme Jewish judicial authority in Jerusalem, the Sanhedrin, dominated by the Sadduceean priestly nobility, was occupied with the new heresy, since the high priests and Sadducees had not only handed Jesus over to Pilate, but from the beginning had used violence against the leaders of the first community in Jerusalem (Acts 4 and 5). These disciplinary measures had not gone beyond the traditional floggings.

The Jewish authorities did not in fact have the right to inflict capital punishment, which was restricted to the Roman prefects (cf. Josephus, *BJ* 2.117; 6.302f.; *Antt.* 20.202). Luke's report that Paul, the Pharisee and pupil of the scribes, had acted as a judge on behalf of the synagogue and along with others had passed sentences of death (Acts 22.4; 26.10; cf. 9.1), is an exaggerated piece of elaboration, especially as elsewhere (22.19; cf. 26.11) Luke only has Paul inflicting synagogue punishments. However, we should no longer doubt that Paul was very much involved in the break-up of the 'Hellenist' community in Jerusalem. The use of the verb *porthein* in Gal. 1.13, 23 (cf. Acts 9.21) is an indication of this. The 'community of God' which Paul 'destroyed' was that of the 'Hellenists' in Jerusalem. We do not know of the destruction of any other community. Soon after Easter – presumably for linguistic reasons – the 'Hellenists' had formed a separate community for worship, led by the 'seven' of Acts 6.5. However, this liturgical independence seems very quickly to have led to tensions between them and the larger Aramaic-speaking 'mother community' (Acts 6.1ff.) which affected their organization and their social circumstances; theological differences, too, may have played a part here. Still, this small, Greek-speaking Messianic apocalyptic sect in Jerusalem did not remain active for very long. Suppression and persecution forced the Hellenists to emigrate and at the same time to extend their mission outside the holy city and Judaea.

6.4 The larger Aramaic-speaking part of earliest Christianity seems hardly to have been affected by these proceedings; according to Acts 8.1 the 'apostles' all remained in Jerusalem and were not driven out. This is certainly Luke's own way of putting things, but there must be some historical background to it. Nowhere else is there mention of a return of those who had been driven out and scattered, so presumably only the Greek-speaking Jewish Christians who had gathered around Stephen and the circle of the 'seven' were affected. They will not have found it too difficult to leave the city and Jewish Palestine; since they had returned from the Diaspora, their roots in Jerusalem will not have been as deep as those of the native Aramaic-speaking Jewish Christians. They probably saw the murder of Stephen as a sign of judgment on Jerusalem, the city where Jesus himself had been killed (Luke 13.34 = Matt. 23.37; cf. Heb. 13.12; Rev. 11.8). On sending out his disciples, Jesus had already said that they were to expect persecution and expulsion (Matt. 10.23a). Therefore the violent actions of their opponents will have confirmed the 'Hellenists' in their ways rather than disheartened them; it did not diminish their activity. The pogrom or the forced exile from Judaea could only strengthen them in their criticism of the Temple and the ritual law, and at the same time it served to reorientate their missionary efforts. Whereas in Jerusalem they had turned to their Greek-speaking fellowcountrymen in the Diaspora synagogues there, now – outside this heartland of Judaea – new groups came into view which we might term the outposts of Judaism. To turn towards despised and second-rate marginal groups was also fully in accord with Jesus' preaching. Chief among them were the Samaritans, who were regarded as heretics; in addition there were the Gentile 'godfearers', who were only loosely associated with the Jewish synagogue communities and had not yet undergone circumcision or proselyte baptism: the boundaries between them, mere 'sympathizers' with Jewish customs, and the real Gentiles were blurred. To give an example: in *Antt.* 20.195 Josephus could call even Poppaea, Nero's wife, a 'godfearer' (*theosebēs*). She may have cherished certain sympathies for Jewish religion; she was not a monotheist, as she obviously took part in pagan cults. Thus the 'Hellenists', driven out of Jewish Palestine, were gradually forced to go beyond the circle of full Jews and also to turn to Gentiles who were interested in Judaism; in other words, they paved the way towards a mission to the Gentiles, which in the end had to mean disregarding the law.

6.5 We can only follow the geographical expansion of the young Christian movement in one or two places. It is quite possible that small Jewish-Christian communities had already developed out of Galilee in the adjacent cities on the Phoenician coast, in Damascus or in Transjordania, especially as Jesus himself had already been at work outside the borders of Galilee. However, we do not have any reliable reports of this. Still less do we have any reason to suppose that the real impulse towards the mission among the Gentiles came from these first small communities outside Palestine. It is striking here that Paul and Luke agree that Galilee played no part in the further development of earliest Christianity. Paul mentions only Jerusalem and the communities in Judaea and does not mention Galilee at all; in Luke, Galilee appears only once on the periphery, in a redactional note (Acts 9.31). In other words, out-of-the-way, 'backwoods' Galilee quickly lost its significance for the further history of earliest Christianity and could not regain it even after the destruction of Jerusalem in AD 70. The sole reason why it emphatically occupies the centre of Mark's Gospel is that it was known as the place of Jesus' activity, and that it could be contrasted with disobedient Jerusalem. Certainly there is no reflection here of a later new significance of the Galilean communities for the church as a whole. Nor can this be established in any way in the other early Christian sources. All conjectures about the role of the Galilean communities in the rise of the Gospel of Mark lead to groundless speculations. Even in the first century AD, Jewish Galilee was in no way more strongly 'Hellenized' than Jerusalem and Judaea; rather, because of the frontier situation there, xenophobia and Jewish nationalism were more highly developed there than say in the Jewish capital, Jerusalem, with its international stamp and its world-wide connections.

6.6   The communities outside Judaea – where they existed at all – received their real missionary impulse from the arrival of the 'Hellenists', who extended their missionary efforts beyond the Jewish synagogues. We find occasional hints in Luke about the existence of such communities in the Phoenician cities (Acts 11.19; 15.3). Their characteristics can be inferred from their positive attitude towards Paul. According to the account in Acts 21.3–7, in the first person plural, Paul and his companions were given free hospitality on the journey to Jerusalem by the communities in Tyre and Ptolemais-Acco; according to Acts 27.3, the same thing happened in Sidon on the journey to Rome. This hospitality is clearly different from the restrained reception Paul had in Jerusalem (21.15ff.), where only a minority gave Paul a warm welcome. We may see this as an indication that these Phoenician communities were more in sympathy with the Pauline mission than the people of Jerusalem. This becomes quite clear from Paul's reception in the house of Philip in Caesarea (Acts 21.8ff.). This former member of the 'seven' also seems to have approved of Paul's work and aims. Damascus was evidently another community in which the exiled 'Hellenists' carried on their activity. This is the only explanation why Paul the Pharisee should have been sent to this important trading city – probably more by his Greek-speaking synagogue friends in Jerusalem than by the Sanhedrin – to guard against new disturbances from the messianic sect in the synagogue there (Acts 9.20), which according to Josephus was large and influential (*BJ* 2,559). Here, too, Luke has dramatically exaggerated the legal competence of the delegate from Jerusalem in speaking of a commission from the supreme Jewish authority, the high priest, to bring any Christians there bound to the Jewish capital (9.2; cf. 22.5). On the other hand, it made a good deal of sense for the Jewish 'Hellenists' in Jerusalem to send to Damascus someone who was experienced in dealing with Christians, so that he could initiate the same kind of disciplinary measures against the refractory apostates as in Jerusalem. Luke may also be right in saying that the initiative for this mission came from Paul himself (9.2). What happened to Paul after his conversion – the fact that quite apart from his time in Arabia he remained in Damascus for two years, was probably baptized there and accepted into the community, and finally that according to the evidence of the communities in Judaea he eventually 'proclaimed the faith', i.e. taught and did mission work there, having been formerly a persecutor (Gal. 1.15ff., 23; Acts 9.19ff.; cf. II Cor. 11.32f.) – all this is conceivable only if the community there accepted his gospel, which from the beginning probably did not involve acceptance of the law. So this community, too, seems to have been dominated by the Jewish-Christian 'Hellenists'.

6.7 Luke gives us the best example of the activity of the 'Hellenists' in the two stories about Philip, which he presumably selected from a larger number of similar narratives. In the list of the 'seven' in Acts 6.5, Philip is mentioned in second place after Stephen, and in Acts 21.8 he is given the title 'the evangelist'. He must evidently have played a significant part in the 'Hellenist' group. One striking feature of the mission legends selected by Luke is that they stand in sharp contrast to the instruction in Matt. 10.5 which comes from strict Jewish-Christian circles and is ascribed to Jesus: 'Go nowhere among the Gentiles, and enter no town of the Samaritans' (Matt. 10.5). According to Acts 8.5, however, Philip immediately goes 'into a city of Samaria' and according to 8.26 the angel sends him on the 'way to the Gentiles'.

6.7.1 Another striking feature is the various forms of ecstatic 'guidance of the spirit', of the kind that emerge as early as the account of Stephen, above all in the second narrative (Acts 8.26, 29,39ff.). This feature is supplemented by the account of the four daughters of Philip endowed with prophetic gifts (21.9). Quite independently of Luke, we hear about these prophetic women later from Papias, in the letter of Bishop Polycrates of Ephesus to Victor of Rome and from the Roman Presbyter Gaius. Philip is said later to have moved with them to Hierapolis in Phrygia (Eusebius, *HE* 3,31,39). Two of the daughters are said to have remained single and one got married in Ephesus. Papias says he has heard miracle stories associated with them. In this stress on the spirit and the gift of prophecy even among women, we may suppose that we have an archaic, enthusiastic feature typical of the 'Hellenists'. According to Luke, Philip founded the mission in Samaria and we have no reason to doubt his report. Thus the second man among the 'seven' after Stephen took a missionary initiative which can best be understood as a consequence of his christological thinking. For at this very point he could take up the positive attitude of Jesus towards the Samaritans (Luke 9.52ff; 10.30ff.; 17.16; John 4); presumably he also saw in them, contrary to Matt. 10.5f., a typical example of the 'lost sheep of the house of Israel'. Unlike the Jewish Christians who observed the law strictly, he felt that the risen Jesus had sent him to these 'heretics' in particular. However, it was perhaps Luke who for the first time connected his mission with the visit of Peter and John to Samaria in Acts 8.14ff. O. Cullmann may be right in suggesting that John 4.38f. indicates two stages in the Samaritan mission, a first through Philip or the 'Hellenists', and a second, later one through Peter and the Jerusalem church. Points of contact for the mission preaching to the Samaritans may have been that they too rejected Temple worship in Jerusalem, and even more the Pharisaic traditions associated with the Torah, and that they did not expect a political royal Messiah, but a prophetic redeemer figure along the lines of Deut. 18.15–18.

6.7.2 The story of the conversion of the Ethiopian 'finance minister' depicts the conversion of a 'godfearer'; the eunuch could not become a complete proselyte because of his physical defect (Deut. 23.2). Legal barriers of this kind no longer existed for the Hellenists. By transferring his missionary activity to the realm of the cities of Gaza, Azotus-Ashdod and Caesarea, and taking up residence in Caesarea, Philip concentrated on the predominantly Gentile Hellenistic areas of the coastal plain, where the contrast between Jews and Greek-speaking Palestinians was particularly marked. Jesus' example may also still have been influential here: at a certain point he left the Jewish Galilee and stayed in the Hellenistic Phoenician territories of Tyre, Sidon and Caesarea Philippi (Mark 7.24,31; 8.27). There may also have been some eschatological motivation. Philip's mission to the Gentiles 'cities of the Philistines' in the completely Hellenized coastal area could also be regarded as an attempt to change the old prophecy of judgment in Zeph. 2.4 into a blessing.

6.7.3 It is very probable that Philip and other 'Hellenists' in this area gradually and step by step went over to a mission to the Gentiles which did not involve the law: in the first instance, this 'freedom from the law' will have been a matter of ignoring the requirement for circumcision and the demands of the ritual law. This gave rise to the question of the relationship between these new Jewish-Christian Hellenistic communities and the communities in Judaea, which spoke Aramaic. Possibly the separation of

'Hebrews' and 'Hellenists' in terms of organization and worship, which was already to be found in Jerusalem (Acts 6.1ff.), continued here. But we must also reckon with the possibility that to begin with, the early Jewish-Christian community in Jerusalem tolerated without taking offence the move towards the mission to the Samaritans, the 'godfearers', the relatively uncommitted 'sympathizers' and finally also to individual Gentiles outside Jewish territory. There too, during the early period, the inner freedom which derived from the preaching of Jesus may have been much stronger than it was at a later stage. Furthermore, to begin with, even the 'Hellenists' do not seem to have envisaged a large-scale mission to the Gentiles. Further stimulus was needed before that could take place. Therefore what is reported in Acts 8 is of decisive significance for Luke himself, because here the commission presented by the risen Jesus in Acts 1.8 is being fulfilled. As a result of the expulsion of the 'Hellenists' from Jerusalem, the gospel was passed on to Samaria and finally, in the figure of the Ethiopian on his way home, reached 'the ends of the earth' (cf. Zeph. 3.10; Ps. 68.32; Luke 11.31). In ancient geography, Ethiopia was the extreme boundary of the habitable world in the hot south.

7

The Calling of Paul

7.1 Final freedom from the limitations of the law and the full development of the mission to the Gentiles are inseparably bound up with the person of the former Pharisee Saul-Paul. He was presumably born in Tarsus in Cilicia, i.e. in the Greek-speaking Diaspora, but was the son of a Pharisee and Palestinian Jew, who at the same time had Roman citizenship (Acts 22.3; 23.6; 26.5; Phil. 3.5f.). The report preserved by Jerome, that as a very young man Paul came to Tarsus with his parents from Gischala in northern Galilee as a prisoner of war, is hardly historical in its present form, since it is difficult to reconcile with the information that the apostle had Roman citizenship by birth. Were Jerome's story true, Paul would not have been a full citizen, but only a freedman. We do not know where Jerome got this remarkable information from. It could go back to a second-century author, say Hegesippus. According to what Luke tells us, Paul was not educated in the Diaspora, but in Jerusalem, and there is no reason to doubt that he was in the school ('sat at the feet') of Gamaliel I, the son (or grandson) of the great Hillel (Acts 22.3). Even later, the Hillel family always had a particular interest in the Diaspora, the Jewish mission, and Greek language and culture. Hillel himself had come from Babylon to Jerusalem as a Diaspora Jew. Talmudic tradition says of Gamaliel's grandson, who bore the same name and founded the patriarchy, that in his house five hundred children learned the Torah and five hundred learned Greek wisdom (*Sota* 49b; BQ 83a), that is, command of the Greek language and Greek rhetoric and training and rabbinic thinking were not absolute opposites. Not only traditional Jewish wisdom schools and schools of the Torah, but also Greek schools, were to be found in Jerusalem from the third century BC onwards. In what goes for critical scholarship, where there is a tendency to doubt that the young Pharisee Paul was educated in Jerusalem and carried on his persecution there, unfortunately far too little attention has been paid to the significance of Paul's own remark that he was a Pharisee and as such was 'blameless in the law' (Phil. 3.6), or that he exceeded by far the majority of his contemporaries in *iudaismos*, i.e. in study of the law (Gal. 1.14). We know nothing of any form of organized Diaspora Judaism or of Pharisaic schools outside Jerusalem before AD 70. Evidently it was only possible for a Pharisaic pupil seeking to be a scribe to make a real study of the law in the holy city itself; this was not only the cultic but also the intellectual centre of that part of Judaism which observed the law. Even today the rabbinic schools of the law, the so-called *yeshiboth*, are again primarily concentrated on Jerusalem. Zion and the Torah belonged and still belong very closely together. Furthermore, unless we accept that Paul the Pharisee had his scribal training in Jerusalem, it remains quite inexplicable how this supposedly completely Hellenized Jew from Tarsus in Cilicia could have found his way to Damascus (cf. Gal. 1.17; II Cor. 11.32). Jerusalem, the religious centre for Jews who observed the law strictly, must have been much more important to him (cf. Rom. 15.19). Only in the period after the Bar-Kochba rebellion do we hear of the founding of Pharisaic schools outside the Holy Land, in Rome and above all in Babylonia. By contrast, the rabbis were very sceptical about the Jewish and Hellenistic education given in Alexandria.

7.2   Thus intellectually Paul moves between two worlds: he lived in two different language-areas and cultures. This is already evident from his double Hebrew-Latin name, Saul-Paul. Belonging to two cultures was what he had in common with the 'Hellenists' who were driven out of Jerusalem. In Jerusalem, his own spiritual home will have been the Greek-speaking synagogues in the holy city, of which there were evidently a large number (Acts 6.9). Against this background it is very easy to see how he, the 'zealot for the law' (Gal. 1.14; Phil. 3.6; Acts 22.3), could have participated actively in the persecution of Stephen and some time later have been sent to Damascus, to combat the disturbances caused by the Christians who had been driven out of Jerusalem. If we put the so-called 'apostolic council' in the year AD 48 or 49, that would make his calling AD 32 or 34. In other words, we should not separate his vision of Christ, which he himself regards as the last 'appearance' of the Risen Lord (I Cor. 15.8), too far from the event of the resurrection which brought the Christian community into being. The earliest developments in the post-Easter community must have been very stormy ones. In his encounter with Jesus, exalted to God, whom he had earlier rejected with extreme hate as a seducer of the people and a deceiver (cf. *bSanh* 43a) who had met with divine judgment, Saul-Paul experienced a decisive turning point in his life. Even as a persecutor, he must have become acquainted with the basic features of the tradition about Jesus and the theology of the church in controversies and legal hearings; i.e., as a Pharisee he will have known 'Christ after the flesh' (II Cor. 5.16). This much misused phrase of Paul's refers to his own Pharisaic past as a persecutor of Christians and a hater of Christ, and not to the so-called historical Jesus. It has lost its significance for the apostle. Now he no longer knows Christ in this way. When he stresses in Phil. 3.6 that he 'persecuted the community *zealously*', he is clearly referring to the use of violence in the cause of the law; he was zealous to keep the Torah intact. Contemporary Judaism was familiar with Phinehas as a model for such zeal: according to Num. 25 this man killed with his own hands a Jewish apostate and the Gentile woman who led him astray, and because of this was given the promise of a special priestly covenant with God. Psalm 106.30 says that Phinehas did atonement by his zealous act and that this 'was accounted to him for righteousness'. It is very probable that before his conversion Paul the Pharisaic scholar thought precisely in these terms. The Damascus event brought a radical break for him, an unexpected and total change of life. The one who hitherto had been a persecutor, who had joined in the destruction of this group and in so doing had appealed to the Torah which was being endangered by the Hellenists, now recognized as a result of his encounter with the risen Christ that the way to salvation indicated by the Torah and God's crucified Messiah must inevitably stand in fundamental opposition. In other words, he thought through to the end the criticism of the law put forward by Jesus and the Hellenists, and drew all its theological consequences. The result of his recognition that Christ represents the end of the law to all believers in being the way to salvation (Rom. 10.4), and that faith is 'reckoned' by God 'as righteousness' (Gen. 15.6; Rom. 4.3; Gal. 3.6), in other words that God justifies the ungodly (Rom. 4.5; cf. 5.6), was an unqualified affirmation of the mission to the Gentiles. Christ had called him, and from now on sent him as his messenger to the 'peoples' (Gal. 1.16). Here Paul understood himself as one of the 'justified godless'. His understanding of himself as a sinner who has received God's mercy is still reflected in the Deutero-Pauline I Timothy: '. . . that Christ Jesus came into the world to save sinners, of whom I am the foremost' (1.15).

7.3   Although Paul says nothing to this effect in Gal. 1, the Greek-speaking Jewish-Christian community in Damascus, which he had been sent to suppress, gave him a warm welcome and introduced him into their community of faith. The Jewish Christian Ananias, mentioned by Luke in Acts 9.10ff., probably played a decisive part in this, perhaps as an intermediary between the Christians there and Paul, who was still unknown to them. Of course we can no longer say whether this introduction to the community took place before or after Paul's stay in 'Arabia', over which we are very much in the dark. Galatians 1.15ff. is written so much in an attempt to reduce to a minimum any connection between Paul and other communities and authorities, that we must reckon with the possibility that Paul himself passes over essential events in silence; thus we also know nothing about his close connection with the community in Antioch, extending over many years, as representatives of which he and Barnabas went to the 'apostolic council'. We are also completely uninformed about the duration and the purpose of his time in Arabia. It may have only lasted a few months. Perhaps Paul made his first attempts at mission in Arabia; but there is no way of telling. Whereas Paul himself says that he visited Jerusalem only after three years (Gal. 1.18), Luke leaves the duration of his stay in Damascus uncertain; he speaks in indefinite terms of 'many days'

(Acts 9.23). Paul seems to have spent the longest part of these two or three years, even according to his own account, in or around Damascus. Eventually he drew down on himself the wrath of the Nabataean sheikh responsible for the security of the caravan routes, who was in turn responsible to king Aretas (AD 9–39), and because his life was threatened, fled by night from the city with the help of members of the Christian community. As the gates were guarded, friends lowered him down in a basket through a hole in the city wall. It is not improbable that the influential and politically powerful Jews of Damascus had a hand in this affair, rightly disappointed at the transformation of Paul the Pharisee into a Christian missionary; at all events, one should not play off II Cor. 11.32f. and Acts 9.23ff. in this connection. Presumably they simply depict the same development from different perspectives. Paul probably visited Jerusalem after this escape in order to get to know Peter, as he himself says (Gal. 1.18). He may have waited so long before visiting the mother community in the Jewish capital because of some difficulties of communication with Jerusalem. This would not be at all surprising after what had happened, both in the 'Hellenist' communities and even more with Paul himself, who was presumably the first representative of a mission to the Gentiles which in principle did not take the law into account. At the same time, Paul will have been anxious about the threat from his former friends in the Greek-speaking synagogues in Jerusalem.

7.4 On the other hand, the fact that Peter/Cephas received the visitor from Damascus and gave him hospitality for two whole weeks shows that such a divide was not insuperable. What was discussed during this not inconsiderable space of time will always remain a mystery. The two most significant figures in earliest Christian history will have exchanged views on what interested them; I myself feel that for Paul this will have included the Petrine tradition about Jesus, which, as is shown by the role of Peter in all the gospels, was the dominant one in the Greek-speaking communities of the Roman empire (*inter alia*, see p. 92). At the same time, they will have got to know each other better.

When Paul speaks about Cephas in his later letters, he always presupposes that Peter is well known not only to him but also to the communities. Peter also appears in all the gospels as the most important figure among the disciples, and is therefore in principle at the head of the various lists of disciples. After Peter, Paul goes on to mention James the brother of the Lord. Paul also made his acquaintance at the same time, though his main conversations were with Peter. According to both Galatians and Luke, Peter and James were also Paul's most important contacts in Jerusalem on later occasions, and in other places as well, as is shown both by I Corinthians and the clash in Antioch (2.11ff.). Here too there is some agreement between Paul's own evidence and the account of the later 'apostolic council' in Acts. Of course, at one point Luke's report in Acts 9.26ff. is misleading, where it speaks in general terms of 'the apostles': Paul did not make the aquaintance of any of the other apostles. However, it should be noted that even Luke does not claim that Paul received authorization from the Twelve. There can be no question of his playing a subordinate rule: 9.28 can even be taken to imply that he stood on the same footing. The possibility that the former persecutor was introduced by Barnabas, his later companion on missions to Peter and James (cf. Acts 9.27) and not to the (twelve) apostles, need not have been Luke's invention. It is quite understandable that Paul may have used a middle man in making contact with the authorities in Jerusalem, since we may assume that there were considerable differences at the time between the principles of his mission and those of the majority of the Jerusalem community. Of course the supposed fear of the former persecutor, mentioned by Luke in Acts 9.26, is incredible; according to Gal. 1.23 the community had been informed a long time before that their former opponent had become a Christian missionary. However, it is a tendency of Luke to tone down tensions brought about through intrinsic theological factors by attributing them to external causes. The restraint towards and indeed 'fear' of Paul could have been caused by the unusual new theological insights of the former Pharisee and opponent of Christianity. On the other hand, it is not improbable that after being separated for two or three years from his former friends in the Diaspora synagogues of Jerusalem, Paul attempted to begin a discussion with them, as in Acts 9.29; furthermore, he may have made them so angry that after two weeks he had to interrupt his stay and make off with great speed. If Paul had left the city in fear of his life, that would explain why subsequently he avoided it for so long. He had no reason to go into background details in Galatians, where he had to play down his contact with Jerusalem as far as possible and therefore limited himself to brief allusions. There is one further indication that Paul tried to carry on his mission in Jerusalem. According to Rom. 1.16; 11.14; and I Cor. 9.20 he felt obliged to present his message not only to the Gentiles but always also to the Jews, and in Rom. 15.19 we find a remark to which too little attention has been paid, namely that he has preached the gospel of Christ 'from Jerusalem and the surrounding area' (or less probably: 'and in a wide circle') to Illyricum. This information must have some support in historical reality; we can hardly assume that the apostle is not telling the truth here. In other words, at this point Paul seems to be referring to missionary proclamation in Jerusalem itself, however brief that may have been. The *en kyklo* could refer to his activity in Damascus, 'Arabia' and possibly Caesarea (Acts 9.30), and to the journey from Damascus to Jerusalem. Of course none of these considerations can give us complete certainty. The problem is not made simpler by the fact that Luke has Paul telling an excited crowd in Jerusalem about a vision of Christ which he had in the Temple (Acts 22.17–21), and which came to him after his conversion outside Damascus. In this vision it is the exalted Lord himself who commands Paul to leave the city without delay, as his testimony will not be accepted there: the Lord will send him instead 'to the people who are far off'. Perhaps Luke here is following a tradition which is connected with Paul's own testimony in Rom. 15.19, according to which the Pauline mission started in Jerusalem itself. Of course the content of the vision coincides completely with Luke's pattern of a mission to the Jews, rejection by the Jews, mission to the Gentiles, which runs like a scarlet thread right through his work (cf. 13.46; 18.6; 28.25ff., etc.).

7.5 It is very possible, indeed probable, that in the early days Paul did not feel so clearly as at a later time, before and even more after the 'apostolic council', that he had been singled out and given a very special position as the missionary to the non-Jews. In the first years after his calling he may *also* have made attempts (which we may suppose on the whole to have come to nothing) to win his Jewish contemporaries over to his gospel, regardless of the fact that in principle he preached salvation apart from the law. This did not exclude the possibility that for love of his own people (Rom. 9.1ff.; 10.1; 11.14), he lived 'for those under the law as one under the Law' (I Cor. 9.20), in order to win them over (cf. Acts 16.3; 21.26), or at least so as not to limit the possibilities of his missionary activity. Jewish Christians continued to play an essential role among those who helped with his mission and the communities which he founded. Although he could still bring individuals to faith (Rom. 11.14), at this point – quite understandably – he usually came up against bitter rejection. Thus not least we may suppose that Paul's own disappointments in the mission to his fellow Jews underlie his talk in Rom. 10.21; 11.7ff. of disobedience and the hardening of Israel. However, in contrast to the majority of Jews, the 'godfearers' who were to be found in the vicinity of the synagogue – as also later, at the time of the great 'missionary journeys' – will have been an attentive audience for his preaching. Strictly speaking (that is, according to the law), 'godfearers' were still Gentiles as far as the Jews were concerned. Josephus shows that 'godfearing' women were particularly numerous in Damascus: the Jewish mission had also already had a powerful effect in Antioch (BJ 2.560; 7.45). According to BJ 2.463, on the outbreak of the Jewish war, every city in southern Syria had 'sympathizers with the Jews who came under suspicion': as they 'appeared doubtful to both sides', there was no concern to exterminate them out of hand – as happened in the case of the Jewish minorities – but 'as a mixed group they were feared as though they were real strangers'. We might well ask whether in his mention of this special group Josephus was not referring to the Christians, who were still regarded as a Jewish sect even in the first century AD. In this setting on the periphery of the synagogue congregations

Paul and also the 'Hellenists' will at first have been somewhat restrained, but in due course – at least in Antioch – they will have devoted all their energies to missionary work. They will also have spoken to non-Jews, and will not have required them to be circumcised or to observe the ritual law and the regulations over food, as these had become insignificant for ultimate salvation. They could expect a sympathetic hearing in particular among those groups on the periphery of the synagogue congregations who were interested in the ethical monotheism of Judaism. This was so for a number of reasons. First, the Jewish eschatological pattern of argument presented by the Christian missionaries permeated with prophetic and apocalyptic elements, will still have been clearly understood to a large degree by Gentile sympathizers with Judaism. On the other hand, the Christian message will have been almost incomprehensible to a genuine worshipper of Sarapis or Dionysus or a follower of the 'Syrian goddess'. By way of preparation, it was still necessary to argue for some form of ethical monotheism before preaching to real pagans (cf. I Thess. 1.9f.; Acts 14.15ff.; 17.22ff.); in other words, as far as they were concerned, the original eschatological kerygma of the Jewish Christians had to be supplemented by elements from Jewish-Hellenistic mission preaching. Among the 'godfearers' who visited the synagogues, as opposed to real Gentiles, belief in the authority of the prophetic writings of the old covenant, to which Christians referred, could already be taken for granted. However, they were relatively uninterested in the ritual law and Temple worship, which were so important for Palestinian Judaism. Because they had not been circumcised and did not observe the law in its entirety, in the eyes of Jews who were obedient to the law these 'godfearers' always remained second-class citizens. Proselytes were buried in the Jewish cemeteries in Jerusalem and Rome and elsewhere in the Diaspora, but not 'godfearers'. From an official point of view, despite their visits to synagogue worship and their partial observance of the law, the 'godfearers' continued to be regarded as Gentiles, unless they went over to Judaism completely through circumcision and ritual baptism. The satirist Juvenal describes how in Rome at the end of the first century the fathers of full proselytes contented themselves with the observance of the sabbath and abstinence from pork, without circumcision and complete conversion to Judaism. It was only the sons who went completely astray, seduced by the bad example of their fathers and going beyond it:

> And see no difference between eating swine's flesh, from which their father abstained, and that of man; and in time they take to circumcision. Having been wont to flout the laws of Rome, they learn and practise and revere the Jewish law, and all that Moses committed to his secret tome, forbidding to point out the way to any not worshipping the same rites, and conducting none but the circumcised to the desired fountain. For all which the father was to blame, who gave up every seventh day to idleness, keeping it apart from all the concerns of life.
>
> (14.98ff., translation by G. G. Ramsay, Loeb Classical Library)

For the missions carried on by the 'Hellenists' and Paul, the distinction which was evident here even to the pagan satirist, in which only the second generation went over to Judaism completely, was a thing of the past, since circumcision and the observance of the whole of the Torah, its 613 commandments and prohibitions, which hitherto had been a hindrance, had now lost their essential significance. The way to true, eternal life (cf. John 14.6) was no longer the fulfilment of the law, but obedient trust in God's eschatological saving work, revealed through his Messiah. There was no longer scope for a distinction between mere 'godfearers' and full proselytes among the Gentile Christians, who had themselves baptized and went to Christian worship. The new message of salvation could appear to outsiders as a universal, 'unrestricted' Judaism, without the burden of the law, which educated pagans mocked as superstition (cf. Acts 15.10,28; Gal. 5.1).

Paul's move to his home town of Tarsus (Acts 9.30) could be an indication that to begin with – as perhaps already in 'Arabia' – he did his mission work as an individualist and an outsider; it is questionable whether at this early period (*c.* AD 34–36) there was already a Christian community worth mentioning in Tarsus in Cilicia. How far he was successful there we do not know. It is striking that he never makes explicit mention at a later stage of communities in Cilicia and Syria (cf. simply Gal. 1.21; 2.11), and that only Luke tells us that he came from Tarsus (Acts 21.39; cf. 9.11). We get the impression that he came to regard this period of his activity as a closed book. After he was summoned to Antioch by Barnabas probably before the end of the thirties (Acts 11.25), we must suppose that in addition to his own towering theological thinking and missionary energy, he was also involved in shaping the kerygma of the Greek-speaking Jewish Christian community in Syria. Strictly speaking, we can only talk of a 'pre-Pauline' community in the strict sense for the two to four years before his conversion (*c.* AD 32–34), or at most until the end of the thirties. Thus the designation '*pre-*Pauline community', which appears so often in academic literature, is often misleading from a chronological point of view. It would be more accurate to speak of 'parallel communities' or even 'non-Pauline communities'.

8

Peter and the Mission to the Gentiles

8.1 In contrast to the picture of earliest Christianity outlined by F. C. Baur and still quite influential even today, Cephas-Peter was not the typical representative of a Jewish Christianity which practised a strict observance of the law, and therefore was not Paul's real opponent. He did not belong to the group of 'Judaists'; according to all that we know, he did not require Gentile Christians in principle to be circumcised and to observe the ritual law. On the contrary, he must have taken up a mediating position in the confrontation which was gradually shaping up. On the one side were the Christians from Palestine and particularly Jerusalem, who were practising increasingly strict observance of the Torah and formed a majority; on the other side were the communities outside the areas of Jewish settlement which had been founded by the 'Hellenists'. Indeed, at a slightly different time, he followed a similar course to the 'Hellenists'. This 'tolerance', and indeed 'liberalism', of the former Galilean fisherman probably derived from the fact that as a disciple he was particularly close to Jesus and at a later stage could not deny the memory of the freedom which he had seen embodied in the person of his master. It is very probable that Peter passed on to the Greek-speaking community a large part of the tradition about Jesus preserved by Mark. Papias' later note about the Gospel of Mark (Eusebius, HE 3.39.15), which goes back to earlier reports by the presbyter (see pp. 27f. above), has some historical value and is not simply to be dismissed as a spontaneously invented, apologetic fabrication. In the years between AD 130 and 140, and seventy years after the martyrdom of Peter, reliable traditions about this great figure of the earliest church had not yet been completely suppressed by pseudepigraphical, fictitious fabrications.

Moreover, Papias was concerned to explore the knowledge of trust-worthy, ancient bearers of the tradition. The apocryphal *Gospel of Peter*, the Pseudo-Clementine *Kerygmata Petrou* and the *Acts of Peter* presumably came into being only in the second half of the second century AD; the *Apocalypse of Peter* was perhaps composed at the same time and II Peter shortly before. It is striking that in this later literature about Peter, Mark and his Gospel no longer play any part; people perhaps claimed to have regained direct access to the authority of the apostle without going through a man of the second generation. Precisely because it is so extremely brief, the note in Papias has quite a different character. I Peter 5.13 also suggests that an earlier tradition underlies it.

To begin with, the sphere of Peter's activity was limited to Jeru-salem and Jewish Palestine. This is for example confirmed by the fact that according to the legends in Acts 9.32–43, and in complete contrast to Philip, he only visited the purely Jewish cities on the coastal plain round Lydda and Joppa and was summoned to the predominantly Gentile residence of the Roman prefect, Caesarea, against his will. In other words, he did not seek out the Gentile capital of Palestine of his own accord. The fact that in Joppa he stayed with a tanner who was despised because of his unclean trade (9.43) is another indication of Peter's broad-mindedness. It also says much for his 'liberalism' that in the earliest period – when he was still the leader of the Twelve in Jerusalem – he tolerated the relative 'independence' of the 'Hellenist' group by allowing them to have their own assembly for worship without expelling them from the church, and that at a later stage he was involved in mis-sion in Samaria. In my view, Acts 8.14–25 comes from a collection of stories about Peter: the account was worked over by Luke and connected with Philip's mission in such a way as to give the impression that this was being inspected by the authorities in Jerusalem. In the original report – as in the *Pseudo-Clementines* and the *Acts of Peter* – Simon Magus was presumably the exclusive opponent of Peter. It says much for the originality of the report that in Luke Peter encounters Simon in Samaria, whereas accord-ing to the apocryphal acts of the apostle the first meeting takes place in Jerusalem: after that Simon, vanquished by Peter, flees from Judaea to Rome (*Actus Vercellenses*, ch. 23; cf. Syr. *Didascalia* p. 120, 23). Here too Luke follows his practice of saying very much less than he knows. He certainly introduces only parts of the stories about Peter which are known to him. The story of Cornelius (Acts 10.1–11.18) shows that Peter supported the baptism of an individual 'godfearer' whose profession as a soldier prevented him from becoming a full Jew, along with his family, without requiring circumcision beforehand. The outpouring of the spirit as a 'divine verdict' before the baptism may have been original in this narrative. Even some circles in the Palestinian community rated the specific eschatological revelations and instructions of the Lord above the ritual commandments of the Torah, which for them had been superseded by the coming of the Messiah. In other words, now, under the sign of the dawning of the messianic age, the normative source of revelation was the Messiah and Son of God himself, exalted to the presence of God, and no longer the Torah which Moses had once received on Sinai. The authority of the one who had said, 'Something greater than Jonah is here . . . something greater than Solomon is here' (Matt. 12.41; Luke 11.32,31), inevitably had to surpass that of Moses and was in a position to correct it. This is precisely what is indicated by the antitheses in the Sermon on the Mount, which show the fundamental difference between the community on Sinai and the Messiah as the one who proclaims the true will of God: 'You have heard that it was said to them of old time . . . but I say to you' (Matt. 5.21f., cf. 27f., 31f., 33f., 38f., 43f.). The tension between Moses and his Torah on the one hand and the authority of the Messiah Jesus on the other was created for the Palestinian community by the preaching of Jesus, and to begin with still continued to create a critical ferment within it. Only gradually – not least from the pressure of the Jewish milieu and under the influence of James the brother of the Lord – was obedience to the law and a more decisive concern for the Torah developed here, although the attitude of the Palestinian Jewish Christians was not completely unanimous even on this point. As late as the beginning of the second century AD, Jewish Christians in Capernaum were criticized for having broken the sabbath and having bewitched the nephew of R. Joshua so that he rode an ass on one sabbath day (*KohR* 1,8 4). On the one hand rabbinic polemic charged the Jewish-Christian heretics with laxness towards the law, while on the other hand we have reports of learned discussions with individual Jewish Christians over questions of the Halakah.

Finally, the fact that Paul could stay with Peter in Jerusalem for fourteen days indicates that there was a fundamental readiness for understanding between these two apostles, who were so different in origins, education and character. If there were nevertheless tensions between them, these will hardly have stemmed from a conflicting attitude towards the Jewish law; here we have two different personalities, coming from completely different spheres of tradition, assured in their views and meeting face to face.

8.2   When in about AD 43 or 44 King Herod Agrippa I, a friend of the Sadducees, had James the son of Zebedee beheaded (Acts 12.2), arrested other members of the community (12.1), and compelled Peter temporarily to leave Jerusalem or, more probably, the area of Palestine under the king's control (Acts 12.17), the more conservative James, the Lord's brother, with his stricter attitude towards the law, took Peter's place in the earliest Jewish community. Although James had not been one of the disciples during the lifetime of Jesus, but had been critical of his brother (John 7.5; Mark 3.21,31ff.), from now on his influence grew steadily. His rise was helped by his blood relationship with Jesus, his exemplary observance of the Torah which earned him the title 'the Just', and certainly by the particular force of his character. It was probably not least his personal attraction and his fidelity to the law which made possible the continued existence of the Jerusalem community in what was becoming an increasingly difficult situation. He seems to have achieved a fruitful and peaceful relationship above all with Pharisaic circles, whereas the attitude of the Sadducean priestly nobility towards the Jewish Christians always remained a negative one. One reason for this may have been the fact that the family of Jesus himself had always been close to the atmosphere of Pharisaic piety. This would also explain why Jesus and the earliest community argued with the Pharisees and their scribes more than with any other Jewish groups and why the earliest Christian eschatology is at many points so akin to Pharisaic apocalyptic. Here Jewish scholarship, which is now fond (wrongly) of describing Jesus as a 'special kind of Pharisee', has rightly perceived the historical connection, even though it has drawn the wrong conclusions. When in AD 62, during the vacancy in the procuratorship caused by the death of Festus, the Sadduceean high priest Annas, the son of the Annas of the passion narrative, had James the Lord's brother and other Jewish Christians put to death because of some alleged breaches of the law, other groups who were faithful to the law – probably Pharisees – protested against such partisan justice. They made their protest both to King Agrippa II, the guardian of the Temple, and to the procurator Albinus who was on his way from Alexandria, and secured the immediate deposition of the high priest (Josephus, *Antt.* 20.200ff.). The markedly different attitudes of the Pharisees and the Sadducees towards earliest Christianity in Luke's account could well go back to Jerusalem tradition, and should in no way be regarded as a figment of Luke's apologetic. In all probability the question what to make of the messianic apocalyptic sect of Christians, who were nevertheless not concerned to cause political disturbances, was a matter of controversy between Sadducees and Pharisees. The authority which the Jesus of Matthew's Gospel accorded to 'the scribes and Pharisees' (Matt. 23.2) is also – at least partially – to be seen against this background. Luke's mention of Christian Pharisees in Acts 15.5 and James' reference in 21.20 to the numerous Jewish Christians who are 'zealous for the law' may well accord with historical reality. The increasing influence of James in the years after the persecution by Agrippa I can be recognized from the fact that in the 'apostolic council' of AD 48 he is mentioned first of the three 'pillars' *before* Peter and John the son of Zebedee (Gal. 2.9). We should not question the fact that this list reflects a hierarchy, in view of the numerous lists of disciples in the New Testament which follow the sequence of Peter, James the son of Zebedee and John (Mark 3.16f.; 5.37; 9.2; 13.3; 14.33; cf. also the list of the brothers of Jesus in 6.3, with James at their head). We can see how much even Peter himself had to fear from the Jewish Christians close to James and thus from their master in the instance of his clash with Paul in Antioch

(Gal. 2.11ff.). Here Peter's fundamentally 'liberal' attitude to the law is even more evident, since before the messengers from James arrived in Antioch, he had eaten with Gentile Christians virtually as a matter of course. In his outspoken polemic, Paul confirms that Peter lived 'in a Gentile and not in a Jewish way' (Gal. 2.14). In Paul's view, Peter threatened the truth of the gospel not through his strictness over the law, but through his vacillation or his opportunism. Possibly Peter could appeal to a vision as justification for his 'liberal' attitude, and Luke inserted this into the context of the Cornelius narrative (Acts 10.9ff.). It also emerges from Acts 11.2ff. that Peter had been attacked in Jerusalem for his 'lax' position over the Torah. We may therefore assume that he personally had never shared the strict standpoint of the Judaists; indeed we have to suppose that the evident decline of his influence in the mother community of Jerusalem was connected with his relative laxness towards the Torah. By contrast, James was well aware that in the long run the Jewish-Christian community could only continue to exist in the predominantly hostile setting of Jerusalem if it proved to be a model of obedience to the law. Only in this way could it be sure of the neutrality (cf. Acts 5.38f.) or the tolerance of the Pharisees in the face of the open hostility of the Sadduceean nobility. After the withdrawal of the 'Twelve', James, at the head of the elders, was able to take over complete control of the Jerusalem community. Given this situation in Jerusalem, the only possibility for Peter, who in Gal. 2.7 is depicted as the one who is really responsible for the mission to the Jews – which in Paul's opinion was not very successful (cf. Rom. 11) – was to move out into the Greek-speaking Diaspora, where we can see his activity in Antioch and Rome, and at least his influence in Corinth.

8.3   Just as Paul did not give up the mission among the Jews completely, so too we are not to assume that at a later period Peter limited his work to them only. The example of Cornelius shows that 'godfearers' entered his missionary perspective at a very early stage. After the evident failure of his preaching to his own people, Peter must have become increasingly interested in the mission to the Gentiles, especially as for both Jewish and Gentile Christians

he had a unique authority. Peter was the first witness of the resurrection, a close disciple of Jesus from the beginning and a first-
hand communicator of the tradition about Jesus. The best explanation of Paul's opponents in II Corinthians is that they were representatives of a mission sponsored by Peter which was in competition with Paul, especially as Peter-Cephas must already have
exercised considerable influence on the Corinthian community
(see I Corinthians), which must have caused difficulties for Paul
(I Cor. 1.12; 3.22; cf. 15.3). This is why the controversy between
the apostle and his opponents in II Cor. 10 and 11 is so laborious
and why the theological differences are so hard to understand. Paul
cannot and will not speak openly here. Close as Peter's standpoint
was to the 'Hellenists' over the law, he probably found it difficult to forget the severe humiliation to which Paul had subjected
him in Antioch, especially as the Jewish-Christian leaders of the
community there, along with Barnabas, had evidently thought that
Peter was in the right and had supported him (Gal. 2.13). From
now on the community in Antioch, and therefore probably the
communities in Syria, generally came under Peter's influence. In
my view this explains the special role played by Peter in the Gospel
of Matthew, which was written in Syria (14.28f.; 16.16ff.; 17.24;
18.21); this goes beyond the picture of Peter presented in the
Gospel of Mark, which was written in Rome, and is also in the
Petrine tradition. By contrast, in all the gospels James the brother
of the Lord fades into the background. In the long run the community in Judaea inevitably became isolated from the Gentile
Christian church. This break with the Syrian metropolis also
explains why Paul persistently keeps quiet about his long period of
activity in Antioch, apart from the one significant mention in
Gal. 2.11: 'But when Cephas came to Antioch . . .'

9

The Decisive Breakthrough in Antioch

9.1 This brief sketch of developments in connection with Peter has taken us well ahead of historical sequence. The second focal point alongside Jerusalem in the history of earliest Christianity was the community in Antioch, founded by the exiled 'Hellenists' and already mentioned on a number of occasions. Antioch was the third largest city in the ancient world after Rome and Alexandria and capital of the combined Roman province of Syria and Cilicia during the period in question. The Roman governor in Antioch was even responsible in some respects for the acts of the prefects in Judaea. In other words, there were direct political connections between Judaea and Antioch, in a way that did not exist between Alexandria and Egypt. Antioch was the first great city of the ancient world in which Christianity gained a footing. There are hardly any parallels in the sociology of religion to the astonishing fact that in the briefest period of time the Galilean Jesus movement, which to begin with was a purely rural phenomenon, became a predominantly urban community in Jerusalem and then took on a decidedly cosmopolitan flavour in Antioch. This social form was to be typical of the Pauline mission, as of the subsequent three centuries of church history. This energetic drive from remote Galilee, thought of as barbaric and uncivilized, to the Jewish capital and finally to the main cities of the Roman empire, is an expression of the vitality and missionary force of the new Jewish apocalyptic sect. Luke will be right in his note deriving from the Antiochene source (Acts 11.20), that the complete breakthrough to an open mission to the Gentiles first took place in the freedom and openness of the capital, and as a result of the stimulus provided by the Hellenists who had been driven out of Jerusalem and were

not completely at home there, so that from now on the observance
of the Torah was of virtually no significance at all. Now a mission
to non-Jews became an independent task and no longer happened
sporadically in particular isolated cases; it was not limited to the
'godfearers', but in a fairly systematic way was now directed towards all the Gentiles. Here, too, the crucial factor may have been
the direction of the Spirit, combined with a number of basic
theological considerations. The task of bringing together a people
of God composed of both Jews and Gentiles now took the place of
mission to the Jews, which hitherto had been assumed to have
priority.

9.2 We come up against a further development with Paul and
probably also with Barnabas, who deliberately shifted the focal
point of their missionary work entirely in the direction of non-
Jews. For Paul, according to Gal. I.15f., an inclination towards
a mission to the Gentiles already goes back to his call outside
Damascus; in the case of Barnabas this shift will only have taken
place after his arrival in Antioch and perhaps when he had come
under the influence of Paul. Paul also provided a theological and
apocalyptic basis for the priority of the mission to the Gentiles.
According to Romans 11, as far as he was concerned the 'full
number of the Gentiles' determined by God had to be achieved
before the coming of the Kyrios, so that 'the jealousy of Israel'
might be aroused through the belief of the nations and at the
expected parousia 'all Israel would be saved' (11.11,25f.). The fact
that Paul (and Barnabas) identify themselves so emphatically with
the mission to the Gentiles in Gal. 2.2ff., and that Paul negotiates
with the Jerusalem authorities over it in an exclusive fashion,
shows that the systematic and intensive move towards the Gentiles
and the priority for the Gentile mission which resulted from it had
not become a matter of course recognized by every community,
even outside Jewish Palestine. Furthermore it needed a special
theological justification, and who better to provide it than Paul, the
former Pharisaic scribe? We should probably see the sporadic
mission among the 'godfearers' and 'sympathizers' as a pre-
liminary stage, distinguishing it from the deliberate and systematic

Gentile mission which accorded priority in the history of salvation to preaching to non-Jews. This last stage was helped by the freedom accorded by the Syrian capital; it also presupposes a large degree of independence from the Jewish synagogue communities and a certain detachment from the tendency, long prevailing in existing Christian communities, to give priority to the mission to the Jews. Above all, of course, it presupposes detachment from the mother community in Jerusalem. Presumably, too, the political influence of the synagogue community was not as great in the metropolis of Antioch as it was in Damascus or Caesarea. There were fewer difficulties to be expected from this quarter. According to Acts 11.22f., on hearing of this revolutionary innovation, the Jerusalem community sent a delegate to Antioch, Joseph Barnabas. Barnabas was a Levite from Cyprus, but according to Acts 4.36f. he seems to have belonged to the earliest community in Jerusalem from the beginning. In Antioch, he followed the new pattern with enthusiasm: he summoned Paul to Antioch from Tarsus, went on missionary journeys with him, and about ten years later successfully represented with him the concerns of the Antiochenes in Jerusalem. This sending of Barnabas as an 'inspector' to the new development in Antioch comes much too close to Luke's particular bias for us to be able to accept it without further ado. On the other hand, there is no reason at all for following Haenchen and others in supposing that from the beginning Barnabas was one of the 'Hellenists' who had been driven out of Jerusalem and was one of the founders of the community in Antioch. Luke had no reason to falsify reality so crudely. In view of the later significance of Barnabas, one would have expected in that case that he would already have been mentioned in connection with the 'seven'. There is no reason to doubt that the Levite from Cyprus was originally one of the core community in Jerusalem directed by the 'Twelve' (Acts 4.36; 9.27), i.e. was one of the 'Hebrews'. There are a number of indications that these so-called 'Hebrews', i.e. the Aramaic-speaking, relatively more numerous section of the community in Jerusalem, did not form a 'monolithic block', particularly in the early period. A large proportion of them will have been openly sympathetic to developments outside Palestine, while at the same time mistrusting the heightened emphasis on obedience to the law in Palestinian Jewish Christianity. In addition to Barnabas, other representatives of such a position in the Christianity of Jerusalem, who also kept closely in touch with the freer Greek-speaking communities, will have been Barnabas' nephew or cousin, John Mark, later to be the author of the earliest gospel; Silas-Silvanus, the Jerusalem Christian who accompanied Paul on the second missionary journey; the prophet Agabus; and probably also the Cypriot Mnason, who according to Acts 21.16 gave Paul lodging on his last visit to Jerusalem. The designation 'Hebrews' in Acts 6.1 does not mean that none of the members of this group had a command of Greek, but simply that their mother tongue was Aramaic. We may assume that all the people mentioned were bilingual. For these reasons I would think it most likely that Barnabas deliberately made the transition from Jerusalem to Antioch – one might almost call it a 'retreat' – for theological and personal reasons. The common factors which united the Levite from Cyprus and the Pharisee from Tarsus were not only the shared conviction of the necessity of a mission to the Gentiles which did not require observance of the law, but also their bachelor status and the freedom it gave them from depending on the communities for their support. Paul earned his daily bread as a leather-worker; we do not know what Barnabas did for his living. Perhaps both had the opportunity of working together in their craft, as Paul did later with Prisca and Aquila in Corinth and Ephesus (Acts 18.2f.). It was here that the city-dwellers Paul and Barnabas differed from the Jerusalem apostles and the brothers of Jesus, who had been predominantly Galilean fishermen and peasants, and to whom large cities were originally alien. Craftsmen from the cities were more mobile and more independent than countryfolk from Galilee, who also had to care for their wives and children (I Cor. 9.4–6); because of this they were more dependent on support from the communities than Paul and Barnabas.

In bringing his acquaintance Paul, the former scribe, from Tarsus to Antioch, Barnabas will certainly have further strengthened the new activities of the community there in the sphere of the mission to the Gentiles, and will have stimulated theological thinking. Possibly Paul had already made contact with Antioch before-hand and influenced developments there. Of course we know virtually nothing for certain apart from the few pieces of information which Luke gives us. Paul's almost fourteen years of activity in the then double province of 'Syria and Cilicia' (Gal. 1.21; 2.1) form one of the great unknown areas in a history of Christianity. Virtually all that is certain is that it was there, in the milieu of the self-confident and active community in Antioch, that Paul's later programme for the missionary conquest of the then known world was gradually prepared and brought to maturity.

9.3   The fact that the members of the new messianic community in Antioch were given the peculiar Latin-type designation *Christianoi/Christiani* (Acts 11.26; cf. I Peter 4.16), presumably by the Roman authorities there, indicates that they had become an independent organization over against the Jewish synagogue community. To the outsider, the successful messianic sect could now appear as a group on its own, which had detached itself from Judaism. It was given its own name, the independent character of which made it fundamentally different from earlier designations like 'Galilean' or 'Nazorean' (Acts 24.5), which had referred to Jewish groups. Of course we have no more than a remote idea of the difficulties involved in this process of detachment and the conflict associated with it. We learn from the Byzantine chronographer Malalas, who incorporated earlier Roman sources, that during the reign of the emperor Caligula (AD 37–41) there were anti-Jewish disturbances in Antioch, as there were in Alexandria. Possibly these hastened on the independence of the new Jewish-apocalyptic movement.

9.4.1   There is a certain intrinsic parallelism between the development of the earliest Christian conception of mission and the development of christology. This parallel development, too, is hinted at in Luke's account. In Luke, as in Paul, the absolute *ho kyrios* or *ho kyrios Iesous* (*Christos*), 'the Lord' or 'the Lord Jesus Christ', is by far the most frequent christological title. This corresponds to the terminology of the Greek-speaking community outside Palestine. It is all the more striking that the absolute *ho kyrios* in the first five chapters of Acts is rarely related to Jesus, quite against the usage elsewhere (2.47; 5.14; cf. 1.21: *ho kyrios Iesous*; in 4.33 the reading is uncertain); by contrast, it is referred much more frequently to God (2.25; 3.20; 4.26; cf. *kyrios* on its own in 2.20f., 39; 3.22). In Acts 2.36, as in Rom. 1.3f., there are hints at an archaic adoptionist christology: through the resurrection God has made Jesus *kyrios* (Ps. 110.1) and *christos*, 'Lord' and 'Anointed'. Furthermore, only in these first chapters have we four instances of the very archaic designation of Jesus as 'servant of God' (3.13,26; 4.27,30). Another frequent usage is the designation of Jesus as Messiah, the titular *christos* (2.31,36; 3.18,20; 4.26; 5.42), which only emerges later in preaching directed towards the Jews (9.22; 17.3; 18.5,28; 26.23). Similarly, the single mention of the Son of man by the martyr Stephen (7.56) is another of the archaic relics in Luke's account of the early period. Even if all these christological allusions were to be 'redactional', this terminology is quite certainly not fortuitous; rather, the titles have been chosen deliberately. In other words, here too Luke works with the 'historical-theological' understanding which is his hallmark. In reality, however, it is extraordinarily difficult to distinguish between 'redaction' and 'tradition' in Acts: to deny in principle the presence of earlier traditions in the speeches composed by Luke makes them incomprehensible and is no more than an interpreter's whim.

9.4.2 The title 'Son of God' is completely missing in the first chapters. It appears – and not by chance – only once in connection with Paul's preaching (9.20); furthermore Luke makes the apostle quote the saying about the Son of God in Ps. 2.7 in his speech in Pisidian Antioch (13.33). It is equally deliberate that when Luke makes Peter address the family of Cornelius, i.e. on the first occasion when a number of Gentiles are converted, he puts in his mouth the saying that Jesus Christ is 'the Lord of all' (*houtos estin panton kyrios*), a formulation which must be interpreted in the light of Rom. 10.12: 'For there is no distinction between Jew and Greek; the same Lord is Lord of all and bestows his riches upon all who call upon him.' The universalist christology of the 'Hellenists', who now saw the risen and exalted Jesus as the Lord of all men, rather than as the exclusive Messiah of Israel, exercised pressure towards a universal mission without the limitations of the law. In commenting in Acts 11.20 that the Jewish-Christian 'Hellenists' from Cyprus and Cyrene had for the first time 'spoken to the Greeks also, preaching the Lord Jesus' (*euangelizomenoi ton kyrion Iesou*), Luke gives an apt rendering of their central christological formula. The acclamation *kyrios Iesous*, 'Jesus is the Lord' (I Cor. 12.3; Rom. 10.9; Phil. 2.11), became the fundamental confession of the Greek-speaking Gentile-Christian communities as we come across them in the letters of Paul. The use of the title *kyrios* cannot be explained as a borrowing from pagan cults, say from some alleged gods of the mysteries (there is no pre-Christian evidence that the mystery gods were called *kyrios*); rather, it is a consequence of christological thought. Even in the earliest community in Jerusalem, people had called upon the exalted Son of man with the words *maran'atha*, 'our Lord come' (I Cor. 16.22; cf. Rev. 22.20), and presumably the phrase 'my Lord' in Ps. 110.1, 'Yahweh (pronounced as *'adonai*) said to my Lord (*'adoni*), "Sit at my right hand" ', was already applied to the one who was risen and exalted to the right hand of God. In its Aramaic version, the beginning of Ps. 110.1 has a good play on words: *'amar marē l'emari...'* Contrary to earlier mistaken claims, there is evidence that *marē* was also used in Palestinian Judaism in the absolute form as a designation of God. This is demonstrated not only by the Job Targum from Cave 11Q of Qumran but also by the Aramaic fragments of Enoch from Cave 4. The next step was then taken in the early Greek-speaking community with the idea that God, the Father, i.e. the *kyrios* of Septuagint, transferred his name Kyrios to the risen and exalted Son. This transference of the name Kyrios is expressed, for example, in Phil. 2.9ff. by the formula 'and he gave him the name which is above every name'. Whereas in the early Palestinian community the title Messiah had already suppressed that of Son of Man, which could not be used in the kerygma because it was so puzzling, in Greek-speaking communities outside Palestine, *kyrios* very soon took the place of the titular *christos*, which was equally incomprehensible to non-Jews and was regularly confused with Chrestos, a popular name for slaves. Thus the earlier acclamation *christos Iesous*, which had been formed on analogy with *kyrios Iesous*, quickly became a proper name even among Jewish Christians. Paul still uses it in this way. The designation of Christians in Antioch as *Christianoi* shows that this process of christological transformation, at the end of which Christos was understood as a proper name rather than as a title, was already complete towards the end of the thirties.

9.4.3 Equally as a consequence of consistent christological thought, the conceptions of the pre-existence of Jesus, his mediation at creation and his sending into the world were then developed in the Greek-speaking community. Only by the introduction of the category of pre-existence could the uniqueness, the absoluteness and the finality of the eschatological revelation of God in his Messiah Jesus of Nazareth be maintained and proclaimed over against the heavenly hierarchy of angels and pre-existent Wisdom or Torah. The development of christological thinking, the departure from the authority of the law of Moses and the progress towards the Gentile mission therefore went hand in hand. Paul already takes for granted the christological conceptions mentioned here. The fact that at a later period Luke is more restrained towards them and does not make use of statements about pre-existence and mediation at creation is presumably connected with the archaic – one might almost say 'historically accurate' – character of his christology.

9.5 In practice, the fundamental and unqualified move towards a mission to the Gentiles made by the 'Hellenists' in Antioch and probably even before them by the outsider Paul gave this mission priority over the mission to the Jews. Communities now began to form in 'Syria and Cilicia', which at that time had been combined into one Roman province. Here real Gentile Christians came to be more and more predominant, even if the Jewish Christians or the former 'godfearers' would long continue to maintain spiritual leadership. In effect, virtually all the theologically significant figures in the church of the first century AD come from Jewish Christianity or its milieu. Even Luke, who in my view is the only Gentile Christian among the evangelists, seems to have been a former 'godfearer'. This is the only explanation of his knowledge of the Septuagint, of the apocryphal and Hellenistic Jewish literature which went with it, and of the institutions of the synagogue, which would be unique for a non-Jew in antiquity. Of course, the transition to a planned mission to the Gentiles did not from the start include the idea of a mission to the whole world. To begin with, even the activity of the missionaries who did not require obedience to the law was limited to a relatively small geographical area: the double province of 'Syria and Cilicia' and perhaps Cyprus as well (Acts 11.19).

9.6 It is remarkable that we know nothing at all about Christianity in Egypt during the first century AD. Acts 18.24 mentions Apollos, the Jew from Alexandria; however, we have to ask where he made his first contact with the Christian message and whether he may not have come to Ephesus as a disciple of John the Baptist and only have been converted to Christianity there by Prisca and Aquila. Only the later version of Acts in Codex D reports that Apollos had already been instructed in the gospel in his native city of Alexandria (18.25). This note is hardly likely to have any historical value. Possibly Egypt, and above all Alexandria, with its great Diaspora, were originally a focal point of the Jewish-Christian mission. The proportion of Jewish inhabitants in Egypt and Cyrenaica was greater than that in all the other provinces of the Roman empire outside Syria. More Jews lived there than in their mother country, Palestine. As a result of the fearful Jewish rebellion and the subsequent extermination of Judaism in AD 116–17, the early Jewish-Christian communities in Egypt will have disappeared almost completely. A further reason for the absence of information could be the fact that the Roman authorities – as is clear, for example, from the letter of Claudius – regarded the departure of Jews from Judaea to Alexandria and Egypt with a certain degree of mistrust. On the other hand, it is by no means improbable that the community in Rome was founded by 'Hellenists' who had been driven out of Jerusalem, as there were very

close contacts between Jews in Jerusalem and those in the Roman
capital from the time of the conquest of Jerusalem by Pompey in
63 BC and the subsequent transportation of numerous prisoners of
war to Rome (Philo, *Leg. ad Gai.* 155f.). Perhaps Paul's reference
to Andronicus and Iunia(s), 'men of note among the apostles' –
probably in Jerusalem – and who were 'in Christ before me',
should be explained against this background (Rom. 16.7). As the
name Iunia(s) is found only as a woman's name, the early Christian
exegetes regarded them as a married couple. An obscure note preserved by Augustine (*Ep.* 102.8), which is said to go back to
Porphyry's work against the Christians, reports that the 'law of the
Jews' came from Syria to Rome during or shortly after the reign of
Caligula (March 37–January 41). As there is evidence that Jews
lived in Rome as early as the end of the second century BC, this
report may refer to the Jewish sect of the Christians, who first of
all attempted to carry on their missionary work within the Jewish
synagogues in Rome. The well-known note in Suetonius about the
frequent 'disturbances caused by Chrestus' among the Jews of
Rome (*Claudius* 25,4) may then be connected with the attempt of
the Jewish Christians there to go over to a Gentile mission apart
from the law even in Rome; in the end the disturbances led to an
expulsion of at least part of the Jews from Rome in AD 49, in which
presumably the Jewish Christians were particularly involved as
being the instigators (acts 18.2).

9.7 A first and essentially still cautious extension of the mission
beyond the boundaries of the province of 'Syria and Cilicia' took
place as a result of the so-called first missionary journey of Barnabas
and Paul, which took place even before the 'apostolic council'. The
first stopping place was Cyprus. Remarkably enough, Luke gives
no indication here of the communities on the island which had
presumably already come into existence: according to Acts 11.19,
'Hellenists' who had been expelled had also arrived there. Luke is
probably silent here because this island later became the particular
mission territory of Barnabas and John Mark (Acts 15.39), and he
was only interested in the development of the Pauline mission.
Here as elsewhere, Luke's account is abbreviated and describes

developments in a straight line. He only keeps in view the development which leads to Paul. He brushes almost everything else aside. We also hear nothing from Luke about the founding of communities in Egypt, Cyrenaica, northern and eastern Asia Minor, Armenia, East Syria, the Parthian kingdom or Italy. It is no coincidence that on this journey visits are limited to the parts of Asia Minor nearest to Cilicia: Pamphylia, Pisidia and Lycaonia; this shows how slow the geographical expansion of the mission proved to be. There is no reason to banish this journey to the realm of legend; we may assume that the great journeys in the Aegean were preceded by briefer forays into the areas adjacent to Cilicia and that it was the 'apostolic council' which first gave Paul freedom to embark on a world-wide missionary plan, still not evident from the first journey. What we have is a limited undertaking which starts from Antioch. In the Deutero-Pauline II Timothy (3.11), a tradition which is quite independent of Acts speaks of the suffering of the apostle in (Pisidian) Antioch, in Iconium and in Lystra. We find these three cities mentioned in precisely the same order in Acts 13 and 14, where Paul and Barnabas are expelled by force from every city. The stoning of Paul in Lystra is confirmed by his own mention of having once been stoned: II Cor. 11.23–33 (25). Luke did not know this shattering enumeration of the sufferings of the apostle: he would hardly have missed the opportunity for an effective account based on the 'thrice have I been shipwrecked, and I have spent a night and a day on the deep'. This reference to three shipwrecks suggests that Paul travelled considerably more than Luke indicates. Paul's mention of having suffered the synagogue punishment of thirty-nine strokes and his 'thrice have I been scourged', the punishment inflicted by the Roman authorities, also go far beyond what Luke tells us. We hear of a scourging only in Acts 16.22f. In other words, this brief journey to Cyprus and Asia Minor could serve as an example for a number of similar trips in Syria and Cilicia and in the areas of Asia Minor adjoining it to the west and north. Paul does not say clearly in Gal. 1.21–2.1 where he spent the fourteen years after his first visit to Jerusalem. All we hear from him is that from there he went 'into the region of Syria and Cilicia'; here was the focal point for his missionary activity. This by no means excludes individual ventures during this period which took him outside the area in question. So we have no reason to date the journey in Acts 13 and 14 after the 'apostolic council' and to put the council earlier, reversing Luke's order. That would make insuperable difficulties for the whole of early Christian chronology, which rests on the Gallio inscription, Luke 3.1 and Gal. 2.1. At the same time, it is clear that the transition to a consistent mission to the Gentiles did not necessarily amount to a 'world mission'. To begin with, the mission to the Gentiles could be carried on within the confines of a province. The programme of a mission to the whole 'world' put forward by Paul in Rom. 10.18 and 15.7ff., by Mark in 13.10, by Luke in Acts 1.8 and in the missionary command of Matthew 28.18f. was gradually developed from the 'Hellenist' mission in Antioch which was carried on apart from the law. Although such mission was indicated by certain universalist promises in the Psalms and Deutero-Isaiah (cf. Ps. 19.5 = Rom. 10.18; Ps. 117.1 = Rom. 15.11; Isa. 52.15 = Rom. 15.21), it only became possible as a result of the fundamental eschatological priority accorded to the Gentile mission over against the mission to the Jews which is so typical of Paul. Presumably Paul was the first to develop this conception of religious, ethnic and geographical universalism and to give it a theological basis; others – perhaps even including Peter himself (cf. Mark 13.10) – simply followed in his footsteps. After the negotiations in Jerusalem Paul sought to implement this super-human programme as 'apostle to the Gentiles' (Rom. 11.13) in his great journeys which took him from one Roman province to another. He planned to travel as far as Spain, that is, to the bounds of the then known world (Rom. 15.2; cf. Rom. 10.18 = Ps.19.5). The 'apostolic council' was a milestone on this route.

The so-called 'Apostolic Council' and its Consequences

10.1 Despite the partially contrary developments in Antioch and Jerusalem, connections between the two communities were never completely interrupted. True, there will have been good reasons for Paul to have kept away from Jerusalem for fourteen years; nevertheless, there is no reason to mistrust Luke's reports about visits from Jerusalem to Antioch. Thus according to Acts 11.27ff., prophets travelled from Jerusalem to the Syrian capital. Luke singles out Agabus for mention from them, because he is said to have prophesied a world famine. This is probably to be interpreted in apocalyptic terms, as a forecast of part of the messianic woes. In reality, of course, we know only of famines in limited areas during the reign of Claudius: according to the calculations made by J. Jeremias, one took place in Palestine in the years between AD 47 and 49. According to Luke's account, at that time Barnabas and Paul had brought a collection to Jerusalem at the request of the church in Antioch to support the distressed communities in Judaea. However, according to his own remarks in Gal. 2.1, Paul cannot have taken part in this journey; furthermore, it is hardly possible to refer the note in Acts 11.29 to his visit to the 'apostolic council' in Acts 15.2ff. We must also rule out the possibility that the 'council' began early in 43 or 44 for chronological reasons; we know nothing about a famine at this point either. The journey into the border regions of Asia Minor related in Acts 13 and 14 was not a consequence but a presupposition of the 'council'. Paul's fear in Gal. 2.2, 'lest I should run or have run in vain', in fact points to quite a considerable activity of mission preaching which already lies behind him. Nor are we to make a connection between the persecution of the earliest community by Herod Agrippa I and the resolutions of the so-called 'council'. Agrippa I presumably wanted to make himself popular among the leading groups in Jerusalem, i.e. in Sadduceean circles. From the crucifixion of Jesus down to the death of James the brother of the Lord in AD 62, the Sadduceean priestly nobility rather than the Pharisaic scribes will have been the real proponents of a harsh policy towards the new messianic sect in Jerusalem. The names of the three 'pillars' in Gal. 2.9 indicate that the 'apostolic council' took place after the death of James the son of Zebedee, since in the earlier gospel tradition in Mark and Matthew he is always put before his brother John, but after Peter: i.e., he was superior in rank to his brother John. It is only Luke who puts John the son of Zebedee before his brother James, which in my view is a sign that John continued his activity and was not killed along with his brother. Of course the disputed journey of Barnabas and Paul in Acts 11.29f.; 12.25 cannot entirely be a Lucan invention; for instance, it could refer to a journey which Barnabas undertook by himself. In that case Luke will have added the name of his later companion Paul, just as at an earlier stage he sometimes puts John alongside Peter (3.1,3f., 11; 4.13,19; 8.14). The Levite from Cyprus will have brought his young relation John Mark back to Antioch on the return journey (12.25); Mark then accompanied Barnabas and Paul on their journey to Cyprus, but after landing on the coast of Asia Minor in Pamphylia, he lost heart and returned to Jerusalem (13.13). In that case, in the report of this visit we would have one of those inaccuracies which appear often in Luke's account. Thus in Acts 12.2 Luke reports the execution of James (the son of Zebedee) by Herod Agrippa I and a little later, in 12.17, without any further explanation has Peter sending a message to James: he does not say that this is now quite a different James, namely the brother of Jesus. Clarity and exactitude – as in so many other ancient historians – were not *always* his strong point. But he was also quite certainly no imaginative romance writer; such inaccuracies could well go back to the sources which he incorporated.

10.2   In all probability, the contrary developments in conditions in the two communities led to the appearance in Antioch towards

AD 48 of quite different visitors from Jerusalem, who suddenly put in question the mission to the Gentiles which had already been under way there for some ten years. Their visit is connected with the opposed theological development in Jerusalem, where in the meantime a group had developed which called for radical obedience to the law; it bitterly repudiated the acceptance of 'godfearers' into the community without circumcision, a practice which had sometimes been followed by Peter, and made the observance of the law of Moses a fundamental condition of salvation. This course of events may be connected with increasing pressure from the Jewish milieu in Palestine and the constant danger of new persecutions (I Thess. 2.14f.), the increasing influence of James the brother of the Lord and the 'elders' (cf. Acts 11.30; 12.17), the decline of the influence of the former disciples of Jesus, the 'Twelve', and with it the decline of the direct tradition about Jesus in Palestine. We can see a similar development in the fact that parts of the Jesus tradition had been reshaped in Palestine in a legalistic form (Matt. 5.18; 10.5; Luke 16.17; Matt. 23.2f., 23c). To begin with, at any rate, the Jewish-Christian visitors from Jerusalem probably observed the missionary activity for a while, noted the equal rights of the Gentile Christians in Antioch, and then came forward with their strict legalistic demands which were concentrated above all on circumcision. They must have posed the severest of threats to the existence of the community, which had meanwhile become Gentile-Christian in character. In Gal. 2.4 Paul speaks abruptly of 'false brethren secretly brought in, who slipped in to spy out our freedom which we have in Christ Jesus, that they might bring us into bondage.' This reference, which in my view alludes to earlier developments in Antioch, shows that such freedom was not generally enjoyed even outside Palestine; it was practised consistently only by isolated communities; Antioch evidently played a leading role here. Certain groups within the Jerusalem community saw this as a dangerous tendency towards apostasy, about which they wanted their delegates to bring back information, so that they could adopt some counter-measures. The Antiochenes now launched a counter-attack, so as to reach clarity over this question which threatened the existence of the community. To this end they sent Paul and Barnabas, as the most capable and most experienced representatives of the mission to the Gentiles, on a visit to Jerusalem (Acts 15.2). According to Paul, the decisive impetus towards this was given by a special 'revelation' (Gal. 2.2), whether this came from the utterance of a prophet in the community (cf. Acts 13.1ff.) or a particular visionary experience on Paul's part. He expressly stresses this point in Gal. 2.2, for in writing to the Galatians he is concerned to bring out his complete independence of all human authorities. It was not the wish of a community but a divine command which caused him to undertake the difficult journey to Jerusalem. For this reason he is almost completely silent about the preliminaries to the 'council'. Luke gives us some valuable indications in this direction in Acts 15.1ff. According to 15.2, Barnabas and Paul travelled with a number of companions; Paul himself only mentions the Gentile-Christian Titus (Gal. 2.3), whose presence posed a certain challenge to the Judaists in Jerusalem. Barnabas, who was just as important for the negotiations in Jerusalem, and whose significance is probably unduly played down in Paul's account in Galatians, also had one or more companions. People in Antioch thought that the delegation to Jerusalem made sense because they were aware that the Judaistic agitators who had been at work in the community had so far had only some of the community in Jerusalem behind them; in other words, they hoped that it would still be possible to reach a positive agreement. Presumably Paul and Barnabas were also chosen as delegates because they could put forward the most convincing theological and scriptural arguments. The point at issue had to be discussed with theological arguments, and that meant with the help of a spirit-guided interpretation of the Old Testament, which on the whole remained holy scripture for earliest Christianity. According to Paul's judgment in Gal. 2.2, a complete break with the earliest community in Jerusalem could have made all previous missionary work towards non-Jews seem meaningless. For him, a division in the church was inconceivable. On the journey there they instructed the communities in 'Phoenicia and Samaria' founded by the Hellenists (Acts 15.3), which were more strongly exposed to the influence of the community in Jerusalem by virtue

of their geographical situation. Evidently they were by no means
ill-disposed to the concerns of the delegates from Antioch. In
Jerusalem the delegates were first introduced to the whole community (Gal. 2.2; cf. Acts 15.4), and then the real negotiations
were carried on with representative leaders of the community, i.e.
according to Paul's reliable report, with the three 'pillars'. In contrast, Luke talks of the 'apostles', who were indispensable for him.
Here, along with their spokesman Peter, they appear for the last
time in his work; the 'elders' already appear beside them. In Acts
15.22, Luke reports that the 'apostolic decree' proposed by James
had the approval of the apostles and elders, 'along with the whole
community'. It was resolved to send two messengers from Jerusalem to Antioch along with Paul and Barnabas, who were to
present the decree to the community there in the form of a written
document (15.22–29). Thus for the author of Acts the conflict was
resolved harmoniously and to the satisfaction of both communities.
According to Luke, real opposition to the Gentile mission is inconceivable; for him the earliest church, with the apostles at its
head, was completely guided by the spirit of God (cf. Acts 15.28).
This idealistic picture certainly does not correspond to reality,
which was much more varied and complicated; the situation has
probably also been simplified in Paul's biographical account in
Gal. 2.1–10. Nevertheless, the succession of apostles and elders
marks inner changes in the Jerusalem community which resulted
in James and the elders taking over the leadership, gradually sup-
pressing Peter and the older group of apostles. The fact that in
Luke the two most important speeches are attributed to Peter and
James corresponds with the stress on the three 'pillars' in Paul's
account. Whereas for Paul the Lord's brother occupies first place
among the 'pillars', Luke attributes to him the closing remark
which resolves the conflict, with the proposal of the so-called
'apostolic degree'. For Luke, too, James is the decisive authority
who ends the dispute with a compromise which required Gentiles
to refrain from eating meat offered to idols, tasting blood and flesh
which had not been slaughtered, and to refrain from sex outside
marriage. However, Paul knows nothing of legal concessions of
this kind; indeed he asserts that no obligations were laid on

Barnabas and himself (Gal. 2.6). Here we may trust him, rather than Luke's account (see below, p. 120).

10.3   In reality, the resolute and unyielding approach of Paul and Barnabas to the 'pillars' had met with success. These did not accede to the demand of the radicals that the Greek Titus should be circumcised, but recognized the right to a mission apart from the law through the two delegates and the community in Antioch. We can no longer discover in detail the reason for this astonishing success. The convincing arguments of Paul the scribe in explaining his gospel (Gal. 2.2) may have had something to do with it, as may have some considerations of church politics. The people in Jerusalem did not want either to destroy the mission communities in northern Syria which had been built up after years of work or to split the church, especially as the missionary practice of the Syrian communities had been tolerated for many years. Exceptions had even been made within Palestine in special cases, as the Cornelius episode shows; and there were also Gentile Christians in the Greek speaking coastal cities. The Jerusalem church probably saw this as a problem which had long been acute in the Jewish mission to the Diaspora, and which at the same time had been a matter of dispute. One could hardly be more 'legalistic' than those Jewish Diaspora communities which not only tolerated a wide circle of 'godfearers' around the core community of the synagogue, but even welcomed them, and which in matters of conflict advised prominent Gentile sympathizers that it would be better not to be circumcised – to avoid scandal and persecution (Josephus, *Antt.* 20.34–42). Furthermore, the representatives of the strict trend in Jerusalem were evidently still in the minority: Luke may be right in speaking of Pharisees who had joined the Christian movement and were now introducing their Pharisaic conception of the law into Jewish Christianity (Acts 15.5; cf. Matt. 23.2f., 23). Of course from now on they would be gaining more and more influence on the further development of the earliest Christian community in the holy city, thus sharpening the tensions with the predominantly Gentile-Christian mission communities. Luke himself gives a clear picture of the conflict-ridden situation in his account of Paul's last visit to the

earliest community in Jerusalem (Acts 21.17–26). It becomes particularly clear at this point that he knew more than he wanted to say.

The victory of Paul and Barnabas became obvious by the fact that
they incurred no kind of legal obligations. In reality, the 'apostolic
decree' which Luke attributes to James – probably not by chance –
goes back to a compromise achieved some time later without Paul,
which after the clash in Antioch (Gal. 2.11ff.) was intended to
restore the broken table-fellowship between Gentile Christians and
Jewish Christians who observed the law. Possibly James was able
to assert his position here. In contrast to Paul, Barnabas and the
Antiochene community seem to have accepted this compromise.
A resolution of this kind became particularly significant in areas
where the Jewish-Christian element was still relatively strong, say
in Syria or Phoenicia and in parts of Asia Minor. Paul, by contrast,
never acknowledged it or practised it. His letters do not contain
any clear references to the 'decree', though its effects can be traced
elsewhere until well into the second century. Probably the apostle
lays so much stress on his freedom from obligations in Gal. 2.6
because his opponents in Galatia had insinuated that he had taken
on such obligations. In this connection, as in his account of Paul's
conversion, Luke may have drawn on sources some of which con-
tradicted Paul's account and regarded the decree as part of the
'apostolic council', even if it was drawn up later. Here once again
one is tempted to think of the so-called 'Antiochene source'. One
may perhaps infer from Acts 21.25 that Luke knew that Paul himself had not recognized the 'apostolic decree': there James presents
it as something new and apparently unknown to him.

10.4 Of course the problem addressed in the 'apostolic decree'
emergèd in the form of the dispute between the 'weak' and the
'strong' even in the Pauline communities, and then again in Rome.
However, the apostle sought to resolve it less by authoritarian
instructions than by an appeal to the commandment to love and
the freedom of faith. Typical of his judgment in this connection is
the lapidary sentence which he puts at the end of the discussions
of this question in Rom. 14: 'Whatever does not proceed from
faith is sin' (v. 23). Not a single word points to the existence of the

'apostolic decree'; either he did not know it or, as seems to me more probable, he showed by his rejection that he ignored it.

According to Paul, the only real 'obligation' imposed by the Jerusalem community was that the two missionaries to the Gentiles should arrange a collection for the 'poor' in Judaea among their mission communities. As there was a severe famine in Palestine in AD 47–49, we can see why this collection should be particularly necessary. However, in my view, the 'poor' are not simply the materially poor; what we have here is a religious title which the earliest community adopted and which is preserved in the later designation of the Palestinian Jewish Christians as 'Ebionites'. The Essenes of Qumran had already called themselves 'the poor'. Whereas Paul understood the collection as a sign of gratitude for the gospel which had gone out from Jerusalem (Rom. 15.27), the Jerusalem authorities could have seen it as a parallel to the Jewish didrachma tax for the Temple (Matt. 17.24ff.), through which the Jews in the Diaspora sought to express their special connection with the sanctuary. In a form fixed by law, this tax was still relatively recent; it probably dates from Hasmonaean times. Exodus 30.11–16 (cf. 38.25f.) was appealed to as its justification. In Palestine it receded in the face of other offerings for sanctuary and priests, but became all the more important as a bond between Diaspora and Temple. Matthew 17.24ff. shows that it was a matter of dispute in the earliest community. People paid it, although they had been freed from it by the coming of the Messiah, in order not to give offence to their Jewish fellow-countrymen. In that case the leaders of the earliest community in Jerusalem would have introduced a new obligatory offering by analogy with the Temple tax, but in a freer form, so as to further acknowledgment of the legal pre-eminence of the original community in Jerusalem and Judaea and its place in the history of salvation. Less probable is the interpretation of the collection as an anticipation of the eschatological pilgrimage of the Gentiles to Zion in which, according to the prophetic promises, the nations of the world bring their gifts to the holy city. It is typical of Luke's way of working that in his account of the 'council' and the Pauline mission he gives the impression that he knows nothing at all about the collection, apart from the fact that when Paul speaks to defend himself before Felix (Acts 24.17) he seems very well informed about it. Luke does not always say everything that he knows, and when he does, he can mention facts which are important – to us – only in passing.

10.5 We can no longer discover the exact wording of the agreement, much less the way in which it was interpreted by the different parties involved. It is improbable that Paul is giving a literal quotation from a written document in Gal. 2.7. In reality the decree was not concerned primarily with a division of the mission to Jews and Gentiles between Peter and himself, but with an enquiry of the community in Antioch, which he – and Barnabas – represented in Jerusalem. In addition, we may suppose that the agreement reached there served as a precedent for other Syrian communities which also had missions to the Gentiles and were confronted with similar problems. The concluding formula in Gal. 2.9 seems to me to be decisive: 'that we should go to the Gentiles and they to the circumcised'. From this it emerges that the delegates from Antioch were entrusted with the responsibility for the mission to the Gentiles and the 'pillars' in Jerusalem with the responsibility for the mission to the Jews. Thus not only Paul and Barnabas as missionaries, but also the whole community in Antioch, took on a special significance alongside the mother community in Jerusalem and the authorities there. By contrast, the transference of the mission among Jews and Gentiles to Peter and Paul in Gal. 2.7f. is probably an *ad hoc* formulation of the agreement from Paul's perspective which makes clear further developments down to the writing of Galatians: in the years after the 'council', according to his own understanding Paul became *the* missionary to the Gentiles (I Cor. 15.10; Rom. 11.13), just as Peter, who had probably left Jerusalem for good, now appeared as the main representative of the mission to the Jews. James did not take any active part in mission. As leader of what was – in his view at any rate – the main community, he deliberately remained in the holy city until his martyrdom in AD 62.

10.6   The Jerusalem agreement also meant that Paul's gospel, and
with it his apostolate, was recognized to be legitimate by the
authorities in the earliest community. His account in Gal. 2.1–10
is not easy to understand because of its parentheses and anacolou-
tha; another difficulty it poses lies in the fact that here Paul puts
his person and work so very much in the centre of things, whereas he is completely silent about the obligations of the Antiochene
community and treats his companion Barnabas in a very nig-
gardly way. The constant shift between the first person singular
and the first person plural should be given particular attention
here. At this point Paul's distinctive – one might even say unique
– apostolic self-awareness becomes evident. He certainly did not
make any special arrangements with the Jerusalem community on
his own account. Nevertheless, in the tense situation of the letter
to the Galatians, he relates the whole of the agreement to himself.
We must not overlook this one-sidedness in his autobiographical
account; however, Luke's narrative, with its tendencies towards
harmonization, is even more questionable.

A further question is whether the Jerusalem authorities, above
all James, did not see the agreement in quite a different light from
that indicated by Paul in his letters. If it were strictly observed, it
would have produced a division of missionary work which in practice could not be implemented in either geographical or personal
terms. If it were taken seriously, would not this division have to
lead to a separation between Jewish and Gentile Christian communities in terms of organization, worship and discipline, a division which would be far more damaging than the earlier linguistic
difference between 'Hellenists' and 'Hebraists' in Jerusalem because it involved nationality and obedience to the law? Were it to
come about, all that these different Christians would have in common would be their future salvation; present *koinonia*, fellowship,
say, in the Lord's Supper, would be put in question. The separation of Jewish and Gentile Christians at the eucharist, to which
Peter, Barnabas and the other Jewish Christians acceded, terrified
by the visit of the delegates from James, probably indicates the
solution towards which James was striving. Only a clear separation
could have prevented Jewish Christians, like Peter himself, from

constantly breaking with the laws of purity in a predominantly Gentile-Christian setting and gradually assimilating themselves to their Gentile-Christian environment. Of course it was far too late for a division of the kind that James probably favoured to be put into effect; the relative failure of the mission to the Jews and the extension of the Gentile-Christian communities automatically took it *ad absurdum*. Even the compromise represented by the 'apostolic decree' was in the long run seen more as a sign of retreat than as success for the 'ritualists'. That is the case, although to begin with they too developed their missionary activities and sometimes achieved considerable success. One of these was in Syria, where for centuries there is evidence of strict Jewish-Christian communities even outside the Jewish areas of settlement. In Matthew's community, which in my view is to be looked for in the borderland between Syria and Palestine, and which affirmed the mission to the Gentiles unconditionally, the separation from Jewish worship was evidently not too far back in the past. Evidently it took place finally only after the destruction of the Temple. Further instances are the false teachers in Galatia and the Judaizing angel-worshippers in Colossae, who were bothered about the purity of food and drink, about 'festivals, new moon and sabbaths' (Col. 2.16). Even Ignatius himself had to combat Judaists in Magnesia and Philadelphia, and Cerinthus was accused not only of docetism but also of Judaism. Despite Paul, the Jewish-Christian element exercised more influence in Asia Minor than is generally supposed. One of the tragic developments in the history of Christianity is that the 'church of the Jews', which showed great powers of perseverance even after AD 70, was not tolerated and supported in the further history by the Church of the Gentiles, despite the warning given by Paul in Rom. 11.17ff.

10.7 F. C. Baur was quite right when, like the Reformation theologians before him – he put the question of the validity of the law and the problem of the Gentile mission at the centre of the history of earliest Christianity. However, 'thesis' and 'antithesis' were not in schematic confrontation, as he argued, nor was the synthesis which allegedly produced so-called 'early Catholicism' just a later result. Historical developments were much more varied and much more complicated than Baur supposed. The term 'early Catholicism', so often misused, is inappropriate and does not add anything to our understanding of earliest Christian history. We would do better to avoid it altogether, as it leads us astray into a cliché-ridden approach to earliest Christianity, coupled with distorted judgments. If we want to, we can find 'early-Catholic traits' even in Jesus and Paul: the phenomena thus denoted are almost entirely a legacy of Judaism. Real history cannot in principle be reflected in dogmatic clichés, not even in those which purport to be 'critical'. From the beginning, men ready to compromise, like Barnabas and Peter, tended towards that 'synthesis' which was necessary both historically and theologically for the unity of Jewish and Gentile Christians to be preserved in the church and for the world-wide mission to be affirmed. To start with, we do not have just the abrupt 'nomism' of the Jerusalem community, but the overwhelming impact of the criticism of the Torah contained in Jesus' preaching, which was principally effective among the 'Hellenists' and led to the beginnings of the Gentile mission. An increasing regression towards legalism only came about in Jerusalem as time went on, not least because of pressure from the Jewish environment. The ultimate theological consequences of the 'Hellenists' ' criticism of the law were drawn by Paul, their former persecutor, for whom God's eschatological revelation in Christ once and for all excluded the law as a way of salvation. Despite the inner tensions and considerable suspicions, at the 'apostolic council' the Jerusalem community, which was by no means at one on this issue, in principle gave the green light to a universal mission to the Gentiles which did not call for obedience to the law. However, in a strange reversal of the situation, a little later in Antioch there was that momentous clash between Paul and the advocates of the 'synthesis' (Gal. 2.11ff.) which led to Paul breaking off his ties with his earlier base in Antioch and with his companion Barnabas. He began his great missionary journeys quite independently, with the aim of winning the Roman world province by province to 'the obedience of faith'. For all his harmonizing, even Luke cannot completely conceal this abrupt breach.

According to his account in Acts 15.36ff., there was a 'bitter dispute' (*paroxysmos*) between Paul and Barnabas in Antioch: in fact Luke simply gives as the reason for it the question whether John Mark, Barnabas' relative, should be taken with them to help with the mission after he had failed so lamentably on the so-called first journey (13.13). It seems to me possible that Luke knew about the deeper reasons for the argument, but deliberately kept quiet about them. The ways of the two missionaries, who had worked successfully together for so long, parted for ever. However, after the great disappointment and apparent defeat in Antioch, there now began for Paul the most successful and theologically most fruitful period of his activity, which represented the decisive turning point in the further history of the church.

10.8 As a permanent result of the approximately seven years of missionary work in Asia Minor, Macedonia and Achaea which now followed, we have the authentic letters of Paul, which were written on these subsequent journeys. One or even two letters may come from his imprisonment in Caesarea or in Rome. The completely new situation is illuminated by the surprising choice of Silas-Silvanus from Jerusalem as his new partner. Once Paul – to some degree against his will – had been freed from his obligations towards Antioch and Barnabas, he now attempted, as an independent missionary, to build up a more positive relationship with Jerusalem, which he had avoided over the previous fourteen years. How far he met with permanent success is another question. Perhaps he counted on the support of the more liberal Jewish-Christian wing in the Jewish capital. However, developments there worked against him. Nevertheless, he tried to maintain the connection. In his letters it is no longer the Syrian capital, but only Jerusalem, which has a significant role. He mentions only Jerusalem, and not Damascus or Antioch, in the great survey of his missionary work in Rom. 15.19, where it forms the starting point of his proclamation. After finishing his work in the Greek-speaking provinces of the East, before setting off for Rome and Spain, fate met up with him, as he probably expected (Rom. 15.30ff.; cf. Acts 20.22ff.), in the holy city, which had an irresistible attraction for him. Signi-

ficantly enough, we do not hear in any way that he was supported
by the community in Jerusalem during his trial. Did the community feel itself to be compromised by his criticism of the law
(Acts 21.21)? He only began his planned journey to Rome two
years later, as a prisoner, to appear before the emperor's judgment
seat there.

10.9 It is a strange contradiction that the clash in Antioch
brought Paul into conflict with Peter, the one man in the community who as a close disciple of Jesus had probably always had a
somewhat 'free' view of the Torah, and had proved this in Antioch
also, through eating with Gentiles. Of the authorities in Jerusalem,
Peter was presumably the one who understood Paul's concerns
best. When James took over the leadership of the Christian community in the holy city, Peter was forced to do mission work outside Palestine in the Greek-speaking Diaspora, and we may assume
that in the long run he did not confine himself to the mission to the
Jews here, especially as his own 'liberal' approach must have been
something of a hindrance. In this way tensions developed between
his work and that of Paul, which are hinted at in the letters to the
Corinthians and probably also in certain apologetic remarks made
by Paul in Romans. Willy-nilly, Paul and Peter became competi-
tors in the mission field, although the question of the law hardly
stood between them any more. In I and II Corinthians, where it
seems to me that Paul often argues with representatives of Peter's
mission and their attack on his own apostolate, the law as a way
to salvation is no longer a matter for discussion. Perhaps the persecution in Rome under Nero then brought them together again.
I Clement 5.2–7 shows both Peter and Paul going to martyrdom
hand in hand: they are 'the greatest and most righteous pillars':
'Peter, who by reason of wicked jealousy, not only once or twice
but frequently endured suffering and thus, bearing his witness,
went to the glorious place which he merited. By reason of rivalry
and contention Paul showed how to win the prize for patient
endurance. Seven times he was in chains; he was exiled, stoned,
became a herald in the East and West . . . he taught the whole
world righteousness, and reaching the limits of the West he bore

his witness before rulers. And so, released from this world, he was taken up into the holy place and became the greatest example of patient endurance.' True, Peter is mentioned here first, but the author does not seem to want to say too much about him: for Clement the Gentile Christian, as for Luke, Paul is the real representative of the world-wide mission.

In the same kind of way as Clement of Rome, Luke puts Peter and Paul together at the centre of Acts and gradually makes Peter fade into the background and Paul come forward: as far as he is concerned, the legitimation of the mission to the Gentiles is virtually Peter's last work (Acts 15). This represents a clear choice in favour of the 'thirteenth witness' and proves that the author of the work dedicated to Theophilus, for all the theological problems which he presents to the Paulinism of modern theology, was a decided Paulinist himself, albeit of a very distinctive kind. The central section of Acts, from the controversy between 'Hellenists' and 'Hebrews' down to the council of Jerusalem, describes the way taken by the message about Jesus from the apostolic community to the mission work of Paul. In it, for Luke, the proclamation of the risen Lord begun by the twelve apostles is brought to consummation. In accordance with his ideal of an apostle, Luke may be somewhat restrained in bestowing the title on Paul (Acts 14.4,14), because he was not one of the 'Twelve' who had accompanied Jesus from the beginning and were witnesses of the resurrection (1.21f.). Still, however, for Luke Paul is the model missionary; indeed, when one takes into account his suffering for Christ's sake (9.16), he is a unique witness to Jesus. It is also quite consistent with Luke's point of view – seeing that he does not mention Paul's letters and probably did not even know of them – that the authentic letters of Paul should form the centrepiece of the so-called 'apostolic writings' in the New Testament canon. As missionary and teacher, Paul became the real *apostolos* for the church, and at the same time he is the only one whom we really know more closely. Presumably Luke, without knowing it, made a decisive contribution towards giving Paul's work this unique position in the early church. His 'moderate' Paulinism, which by virtue of its character is something of a problem for us, has helped to find a

place in the canon and a significance in the church for the real Paul
and his writings. Furthermore, the work of Luke which emerged
from this Paulinism remains a unique and valuable historical
source for the history of earliest Christianity. It helps us to a better
historical and theological understanding of the way in which the
former Pharisee and scribe became the model missionary for the
church, even where Luke tones down rifts and conflicts because of
his tendency to harmonize. Precisely in his unilinear description
of the course taken by the earliest Christian mission from the
Hellenists in the group around Stephen to Paul's thoroughgoing
mission to the Gentiles in the fifties, Luke shows himself to be the
first Christian 'historian'. The church down to the present day
owes more to his work than theologians are usually wont to allow.

III

Historical Methods and the Theological Interpretation of the New Testament

1 Criticism of 'the historical-critical method'

1.1 Talk about '*the* historical-critical method' is questionable.

1.1.1 In reality there is a variety of 'historical methods'.

1.1.2 This variety of methods corresponds with the multiplicity of historical research and its results.

1.1.3 Historical research must always remain open to the testing of new methods. In some circumstances the discovery of new phenomena calls for the application of new methods.

1.1.4 The applicability and appropriateness of historical methods becomes evident from their subject-matter; that is, it becomes evident during the process of research and not in abstract reflection on 'the historical-critical method' *per se*.

1.2 In the last resort, the reasons for the constant appeal to '*the* historical-critical method' in theological discussion over the past seventy years have been psychological and dogmatic.

1.2.1 The clearest expression of this can be found in Troeltsch's distinction between 'historical' and 'dogmatic method'.

1.2.2 One of the chief reasons is anxiety about the devaluation of 'dogmatic method', which is regarded as unscientific, whereas '*the* historical-critical method' is thought to be scientific.

1.2.3 There has not been enough critical reflection on the limits and consequences of this 'historical-critical method', which has been reduced to a 'dogmatic' positivism.

1.2.4 The fundamental axiom of '*the* historical critical method' is the postulate of 'one reality' which can be comprehended by men and is at their disposal; in history this presents itself as 'the similarity in principle of all historical events' (Troeltsch).

1.2.5 The 'omnipotence of analogy' as 'the key to criticism' (Troeltsch) is the sole arbiter in the establishment of facts and their causal connection.

1.2.6 Thus the present-day experience of reality – which in any case is a limited one – is made the decisive criterion for what can and what cannot have happened in the past.

1.2.7 In the sphere of 'biblical history' in particular, we keep coming up against the question of the possibility of 'unparalleled events'. With its dogmatic fixation, the 'historical-critical method' must rule out this possibility *a priori*.

2 The multiplicity and complexity of the horizons of historical knowledge and the consequences for 'historical' and 'theological understanding'

2.1 Past events present themselves to us in an overwhelming multiplicity.

2.1.1 Historical reconstruction and interpretation necessarily lead to a simplification of what were originally much more complex circumstances.

2.1.2 The danger of simplification can only be countered by a multiplicity of methods which are appropriate to the subject-matter.

2.1.3 In the realm of ancient history the fortuitousness and fragmentariness of surviving sources and the distance between the ancient consciousness and our own can very easily lead to a simplified representation of past reality.

2.2 The multiplicity of perspectives of historical onlookers produces very different horizons of knowledge.

2.2.1 Critical control of our own pre-understanding and heuristic interests can limit these, but cannot exclude them altogether.

2.2.2 In the history of culture and religion in particular, in some circumstances a positive pre-understanding and existential interest in the subject-matter presented by the sources are the presupposition of a true understanding.

2.2.3 Knowledge of historical facts does not in itself amount to understanding. Rather, the latter is primarily identical with grasping the intention of the author of a text.

2.2.4 On the other hand, the claim that we might be able to understand the intention of the author of a text better than he does himself (W. Dilthey) is often questionable.

2.3 The variety of historical horizons of knowledge leads to a variety of ways of communicating the insights gained from the sources.

2.3.1 Complete intersubjectivity is most easily possible in the sphere of establishing clearly defined facts.

2.3.2 Intersubjectivity is already limited in the sphere of understanding cultural history and the interpretation built upon it.

2.3.3 In the sphere of value judgments, or the positive or negative answer to the truth-claim of historical sources, persons or groups, intersubjectivity is often only a contingent possibility and as such is not under our control.

2.3.4 Putting it very crudely, in the case of statements about historical sources which contain a truth-claim affecting us ethically or religiously, i.e. 'existentially', one could speak of three possible 'stages of knowledge': knowing, understanding and assenting or dissenting. The possibility of controlling communication diminishes with each stage.

2.3.5 In historical-theological exegesis it is all-important that historical and systematic-theological attempts at understanding should go hand in hand in the sphere of 'understanding', so that the truth-claim of the text being interpreted is expressed in a way commensurate with the contemporary situation.

2.3.6 The acknowledgment of theological truth in a statement made by a text can be prepared for, but not produced, by the use of historical method. Conversely, an inappropriate application of historical methods can distort the truth-claim inherent in a text both for me and for others.

2.4 When it comes to the question of certainty, there is a difference between historical and theological judgments. Theological judgments give unique saving significance to particular events of the past.

2.4.1 Historical knowledge leads to the 'accidental truths of history' (Lessing), which as a rule can only lay to claim to a sharply graduated scale of degrees of probability. They cannot, therefore, ever have ultimate significance for me.

2.4.2 On the other hand, faith is grounded in the certain promise. Theological judgments must therefore take the form of assertions: *tolle assertiones et Christianismum tulisti* (Luther).

2.4.3 Thus theological judgment will assign some degree of certainty to the 'fact' of God's free communication of himself at a specific point in history, which historical research either cannot or will not achieve, for all its methods.

2.4.4 Historical research provided access for theology to its decisive content by means of biblical disciplines and church history. However, it cannot provide a basis for the truth-claim of theology. This basis lies in the certainty of the divine promise in Jesus Christ, behind which we cannot investigate, a promise which comes to us in the unity of the message of the Old and New Testaments and to which new witness is constantly borne in the history of the church.

3 The necessity of historical discovery of truth and its limitations

3.1 The content of history accessible to historical methods proves to be the 'collective consciousness' of mankind which is gained from the past.

3.1.1 The task of historical scholarship is the constant expansion and correction of the content of this 'consciousness'.

3.1.2 The falsification, suppression and rejection of historical information and insights can be compared with the act of 'supression': not only do they contradict the universal demand for objective truth, but they can even lead to disruptive self-deceit.

3.1.3 The constant expansion, control and correction of the historical 'consciousness' is in principle to be affirmed by theologians as a 'good work' of discovering truth.

3.2 Since the naive unity of 'history' and 'biblical historical narrative' was shattered in the Enlightenment, theology is bound to carry on research into extending, controlling and correcting the knowledge of its past for the sake of material truth.

3.2.1 This historical research within theology cannot either confirm or refute the claim of Christian faith to validity, but it does serve to extend and correct the historical 'understanding of the world as a whole in theology'.

3.2.2 The steadily growing challenge from historical research to theology compels theologians to reflect on what they are really doing and thus increases their self-awareness and their involvement in the subject-matter.

3.2.3 For example, Lessing's criticism that 'accidental truths of history can never become proofs of the necessary truths of reason' reminds the theologian that he is not primarily concerned with 'necessary truths of reason' but with God's free self-disclosure of himself in Jesus Christ.

3.3 Just as the human consciousness – which cannot be separated from man's 'self-understanding' – is faced with the meaning of our existence as individuals, so as part of mankind's 'universal consciousness' it is confronted with the meaning and unity of history.

3.3.1 The question of the meaning of our existence as individuals cannot be detached from the question of the meaning of human history as a whole. The answer to the first question also entails an answer to the second, and *vice versa*.

3.3.2 Of course we cannot give any answers here with the instruments of historical method. Answers can only be given by 'theological judgments'.

3.3.3 Such an answer should not be given either – in crude existentialist terms – by reducing its scope to individual existence, or – in crude Marxist terms – by elimianting it in the form of a utopia which affects only the masses.

3.3.4 For the individual as for mankind as a whole, the question of meaning is resolved in connection with God as Creator and Lord of history and with the kingdom of God as the consummation of creation and history.

3.3.5 There are christological reasons for a reference of this kind: i.e., as Creator and Lord of history and thus also of the future, God discloses himself to man through the revelation of his love in Christ Jesus as the 'one Word of God that we have to hear, that we have to trust and to obey in both life and death' (First thesis of Barmen).

4 The New Testament as a historical source and witness of faith and the appropriate application of historical methods

4.1 As a result of their authorization by the church, the writings collected together in the New Testament are the earliest surviving sources of the primal event which is the foundation of the Christian church, 'the documentation for the preaching on which the church is founded' (Martin Kähler).

4.1.1 At the same time they are testimonies of faith pointing the hearer to God's disclosure of himself for the salvation of all mankind, which took place in Jesus of Nazareth and was proclaimed in the apostolic preaching.

4.1.2 An appropriate historical and theological interpretation of the writings of the New Testament must express this twofold character which they have as the earliest historical sources and testimonies of faith.

4.1.3 Through their form as 'kerygmatic historical narratives' or as 'kerygmatic historiography', large portions of the New Testament texts or writings demonstrate that the message of salvation as a form of address is always at the same time also – at least in essence – the report of a saving event, and that it is based on a historical event which can also be investigated by historical methods.

4.2 'Theological exegesis', which thinks that it can 'interpret' the New Testament without the application of the relevant historical methods, is not only deaf to the question of truth but is also in danger of distorting what the texts say and falling victim to docetic speculation.

4.2.1 The application of historical methods in the exegesis of the New Testament is required, in particular, by the fact that the writings of the New Testament bear witness that God has spoken once and for all in a particular human being at a particular time.

4.2.2 Consequently we cannot talk theologically of God's disclosure of himself in Jesus and the apostolic testimony without at the same time grasping the form and content of this communication by means of historical research.

4.3 The New Testament writings do not require for their interpretation specifically 'theological method of interpretation' which is qualitatively different from all 'historical methods'.

4.3.1 This means that the New Testament should not either be isolated from other ancient sources, nor should it be totally reduced to their level. Like any text which requires a deeper understanding and contains a claim to the truth, it inevitably requires the application of appropriate 'methods of interpretation' which are in accord with it.

4.3.2 These include, first, investigating the earlier history of the way in which 'God has spoken' (Heb. 1.1) in the Old Testament and in Judaism, as this has taken concrete form in the language and character of the writings of the New Testament. We need also to consider their influence and the tradition through which they have been interpreted.

4.3.3 Not only does the interpreter need to pay careful attention to the subject-matter of the material which he is interpreting; in addition he needs to be open in such a way as to be able really to 'perceive' the message which he encounters in the New Testament, to fall in with it and to respond to its 'claim'.

4.3.4 Thus the truth of the New Testament message does not need any additional methodological 'guarantees'. The faith of the church and the efficacy of Holy Scripture are expressed in this freedom.

4.4 To accept and agree to its truth-claim is not a work to be accomplished but an unmerited gift. It continually leads the interpreter back to the venture of daring to interpret the text. Only through constantly being 'conquered' by the message of the New Testament does the exegete really become a 'theological interpreter': *Illuminatio est actus gratiae, quo Spiritus per ministerium verbi docet et sincero magis magisque informat* (Hollaz).

4.4.1 The experience of constant acquaintance with the texts of the New Testament thus opens our eyes to the contours of its 'christological centre'. It can be paraphrased by phrases like *solus Christus, sola gratia, justificatio impii* or *theologia crucis*. This is an expression of the gift of the unmerited communication of meaning through encounter with the crucified and risen Jesus Christ as the Word of God which is addressed to us.

4.4.2 The church's tradition of interpretation gives the theological exegete some basic helps towards understanding and at the same time forms the basis for his criticism. It will certainly enrich interpretation, but at the same time it must consistently submit itself to critical examination by the message of the New Testament.

4.4.3 The pre-understanding of faith which emerges here is not a certain possession but, like all theology, is constantly under attack. It will certainly enrich interpretation, but on the other hand it must keep submitting to critical questioning from the message of the New Testament itself.

4.4.4 In all this we can never escape the appropriate application of historical methods. We cannot avoid the question of historical truth and are always in danger of engaging in speculative constructions which take us a long way from the text. It is exegesis which begins from a prior understanding based on faith that will make use of the historical methods at its disposal with particular care and accuracy.

CHRONOLOGICAL TABLE

Tiberius AD 14–37

Aretas IV, King of Nabataea,
9 BC–AD 39
Caiaphas, Jewish high priest,
AD 18–37
Pontius Pilate, Prefect of Judaea,
AD 26–36/37

Cailgula, March AD 37–January
AD 41
Claudius, AD 41–54
Herod Agrippa I, king over all
Palestine, AD 41–44

Famine in Palestine, c AD 47–49

Expulsion of the Jews from Rome
(Edict of Claudius), AD 49

Gallio, proconsul of Achaea, May
AD 51–April AD 52

Nero, AD 54–68

Felix, procurator of Judaea,
AD 52–58(?)

Festus, procurator of Judaea,
AD 58(?)–62
Albinus, procurator of Judaea,
AD 62–64
Nero's persecution of Christians
in Rome, AD 64
Outbreak of the Jewish War,
AD 66

Appearance of John the Baptixt,
AD 27/28
The death of Jesus, Passover
AD 30
Persecution of the 'Hellenists';
execution of Stephen, c AD 31/33
Converson of Paul, c AD 32/34

Paul's first visit to Jerusalem,
AD 34/36
Beginning of the Gentile Mission
in Antioch, c AD 34/38

Martyrdom of James son of
Zebedee; Peter leaves Jerusalem,
c AD 43/44

'Apostolic Council' (James at the
head of the earliest church);
clash between Peter and Paul in
Antioch, c AD 48
Paul in Corinth, c winter
AD 49–50 – summer AD 51
Paul in Ephesus, c AD 52/53 – 55/56
Paul's second stay in Corinth
(Romans), c winter AD 55/56 or
56/57
Arrest of Paul in Jerusalem,
Pentecost AD 56/57
Imprisonment in Caesarea,
c AD 56/58 or 57/59
Journey to Rome, winter AD 58–59
or 59–60
Martyrdom of James the brother
of the Lord, AD 62
Martyrdom of Peter (and Paul?),
AD 64
Flight of the Jerusalem church to
Pella, AD 66

BIBLIOGRAPHY

PART ONE

Chapters 1 and 2 (specialist studies of *Acts* are listed under Chapter 5)

H. Bengtson, *Einführung in die alte Geschichte*, Munich ⁶1969

T. Boman, *Die Jesus-überlieferung im Lichte der neueren Volkskunde*, Göttingen 1967

A. Dihle, *Studien zur griechischen Biographie*, Göttingen 1956

D. Esser, *Formgeschichtliche Studien zur hellenistischen und zur frühchristlichen Literatur unter besonderer Berücksichtigung der* Vita Apollonii *des Philostrat und der Evangelien*, Bonn dissertation 1969

P. Fiebig, *Altjüdische Gleichnisse und die Gleichnisse Jesu*, Tübingen 1904

——, *Jüdische Wundergeschichten des neutestamentlichen Zeitalters unter besonderer Berücksichtigung ihres Verhältnisses zum Neuen Testament bearbeitet*, Tübingen 1911

——, *Der Erzählungsstil der Evangelien im Lichte des rabbinischen Erzählungsstils untersucht . . .*, Leipzig 1925

——, *Die Gleichnisreden Jesu im Lichte der rabbinischen Gleichnisse des neutestamentlichen Zeitalters*, Tübingen 1921

M. Grant, *Ancient Historians*, London 1970

E. Güttgemanns, *Offene Fragen zur Formgeschichte des Evangeliums*, Munich 1970

Histoire et historiens dans l'antiquité, Sept exposés et discussions par K. Latte & J. de Romilly . . ., Vandoeuvres-Genève 2–8 Août 1956 (Entretiens sur l'antiquité classique 4)

F. Klingner, 'Römische Geschichtsschreibung', in id., *Römische Geisteswelt*, Munich ⁵1965, 66–89

F. Leo, *Die griechisch-römische Biographie nach ihrer literarische Form*, Leipzig 1901

Lucian, *How to Write History*, Loeb Classical Library 6, London 1959

A. Momigliano, *The Development of Greek Biography*, Cambridge, Mass. 1971

G. Perl, 'Der Anfang der römischen Geschichtsschreibung', *Forschungen und Fortschritte* 38, 1964, 185–9; 213–8

P. Schäfer, 'Zur Geschichtsauffassung des rabbinischen Judentums', *Journal for the Study of Judaism* 6, 1975, 177–88

K. L. Schmidt, 'Die Stellung der Evangelien in der allgemeinen Literaturgeschichte', in *Eucharisterion, Hermann Gunkel zum 60. Geburtstag, dem 23. Mai 1922 dargebracht* . . . II, Göttingen 1923, 50–134

E. Schwartz, 'Geschichtsschreibung und Geschichte bei den Hellenen', *Die Antike* 4, 1928, 14–30

G. N. Stanton, *Jesus of Nazareth in New Testament Preaching*, London 1974, 117ff.

D. R. Stuart, *Epochs of Greek and Roman Biography*, Berkeley 1928

G. Theissen, *Urchristliche Wundergeschichten*, Gütersloh 1974

P. Vielhauer, *Geschichte der urchristlichen Literatur*, Berlin–New York 1975

C. W. Votaw, 'The Gospels and Contemporary Biographies', *The American Journal of Theology* 19, 1915, 45–73; 217–49

F. W. Walbank, 'History and Tragedy', *Historia* 9, 1960, 216–34

U. von Wilamowitz-Moellendorff, 'Hellenische Geschichtsschreibung', in id., *Reden und Vorträge* II, Berlin ⁴1926, 216–46

Chapter 3

M. Hengel, 'Kerygma oder Geschichte', *Theologische Quartalschrift* 151, 1971, 323–36

——, *Crucifixion*, London and Philadelphia 1977

H. Ristow & K. Matthiae (eds), *Der historische Jesus und der kerygmatische Christus*, Berlin 1960

J. M. Robinson, 'Kerygma and History in the New Testament', in H. Koester and J. M. Robinson, *Trajectories through Early Christianity*, Philadelphia 1971, 20–70

J. Roloff, *Das Kerygma und der irdische Jesus*, Göttingen 1970

G. N. Stanton, *Jesus of Nazareth in New Testament Preaching*, London 1974

Chapter 4

W. G. Doty, *Contemporary New Testament Interpretation*, Englewood Cliffs 1972

E. Krentz, *The Historical-Critical Method*, Philadelphia 1975

H.-I. Marrou, *The Meaning of History*, Baltimore 1966

H. Strasburger, *Die Wesensbestimmung der Geschichte durch die antike Geschichtsschreibung*, Wiesbaden 1966

P. Stuhlmacher, *Schriftauslegung auf dem Wege zur biblischen Theologie*, Göttingen 1975

Chapter 5

C. K. Barrett, *Luke the Historian in Recent Study*, London 1961

The Beginnings of Christianity, Part I, *The Acts of the Apostles*, ed. F. J. Foakes-Jackson & K. Lake, Vol. II: *Prolegomena;* III: *Criticism*, London 1922

O. Betz, 'The Kerygma of Luke', *Interpretation* 22, 1968, 132–46

E. M. Blaiklock, 'The Acts of the Apostles as a Document of First Century History', in W. W. Gasque & R. P. Martin (eds), *Apostolic History and the Gospel, Biblical and Historical Essays, presented to F. F. Bruce on his 60th Birthday*, Exeter 1970, 41–54

C. Burchard, *Der dreizehnte Zeuge*, Göttingen 1970

H. J. Cadbury, *The Making of Luke-Acts*, London ²1958

H. Conzelmann, *The Theology of St Luke*, London 1960

M. Dibelius, *Studies in the Acts of the Apostles*, London 1956

J. Dupont, *Les Sources du Livre des Actes*, Bruges 1960

W. Gasque, *A History of the Criticism of the Acts of the Apostles*, Tübingen 1975

E. Grässer, 'Die Apostelgeschichte in der Forschung der Gegenwart', *Theologische Rundschau*, Neue Folge 26, 1960, 93–167

——, 'Actaforschung seit 1960', *Theologische Rundschau*, Neue Folge 41, 1976, 141–94, 259–90

E. Haenchen, 'Die Apostelgeschichte als Quelle für die christliche Frühgeschichte', in *Die Bibel und wir, Gesammelte Aufsätze* II, Tübingen 1968, 312–37

J. Jeremias, 'Untersuchungen zum Quellenproblem der Apostelgeschichte', in *Abba*, Göttingen 1966, 238–55

G. Klein, 'Lukas 1, 1–4 als theologisches Problem', in *Rekonstruktion und Interpretation, Gesammelte Aufsätze zum Neuen Testament*, Munich 1969, 237–61

K. Löning, *Die Saulustradition in der Apostelgeschichte*, Münster 1973

I. H. Marshall, *Luke: Historian and Theologian*, Exeter 1970

J. C. O'Neill, *The Theology of Acts in its Historical Setting*, London ²1970

E. Plümacher, 'Lukas als griechischer Historiker', *Paulys Realencyclopädie der classischen Altertumswissenschaft*, Neue Bearbeitung, Supplementband XIV, 1974, 235–64

——, *Lukas als hellenistischer Schriftsteller*, Göttingen 1972

H. Steichele, *Vergleich der Apostelgeschichte mit der antiken Geschichtsschreibung*, Munich dissertation 1971

V. Stolle, *Der Zeuge als Angeklagter*, Stuttgart-Berlin 1973

E. Trocmé, *Le 'livre des Actes' et l'histoire*, Paris 1957

P. Vielhauer, 'Zum "Paulinismus" der Apostelgeschichte', in id., *Aufsätze zum Neuen Testament*, Munich 1965, 9–27

A. Wikenhauser, *Die Apostelgeschichte und ihr Geschichtswert*, Münster 1921

PART TWO

Accounts of the History of Earliest Christianity

F. F. Bruce, *New Testament History*, London [2]1971
H. Conzelmann, *History of Primitive Christianity*, London 1973
F. V. Filson, *A New Testament History*, Philadelphia and London 1965
L. Goppelt, *Apostolic and Post-Apostolic Times*, London 1970
——, *Christentum und Judentum im ersten und zweiten Jahrhundert*, Gütersloh 1954
H. Lietzmann, *A History of the Early Church* Vol. I, London 1935
A. Schlatter, *Die Geschichte der ersten Christenheit*, Gütersloh 1926

Books on the Earliest Christian Mission

H. Frohnes & U. W. Knorr (eds), *Kirchengeschichte als Missionsgeschichte*, I, Munich 1974
F. Hahn, *Mission in the New Testament*, SBT 47, London 1965
A. von Harnack, *The Expansion of Christianity in the First Three Centuries*, two vols, London 1904-5
M. Hengel, 'Die Ursprünge der christlichen Mission', *New Testament Studies* 18, 1971/72, 15-38
H. Kasting, *Die Anfänge der urchristlichen Mission*, Munich 1969
S. G. Wilson, *The Gentiles and the Gentile Mission in Luke-Acts*, Cambridge 1973

Books on Paul

G. Bornkamm, *Paul*, London and New York 1971
G. Eichholz, *Die Theologie des Paulus im Umriss*, Neukirchen-Vluyn 1972
R. N. Longenecker, *Paul, Apostle of Liberty*, New York 1964
A. D. Nock, *St Paul*, London 1938
H. Ridderbos, *Paul*, Grand Rapids, 1975 and London 1977
B. Rigaux, *Saint Paul et ses lettres*, Paris-Bruges 1960
A. Suhl, *Paulus und seine Briefe*, Gütersloh 1975

Commentaries on Acts

O. Bauernfeind, *Die Apostelgeschichte*, Theologischer Handkommentar zum Neuen Testament 6, Leipzig 1939
F. F. Bruce, *Commentary on the Book of the Acts*, The New London Commentary on the New Testament, London [3]1962
H. Conzelmann, *Die Apostelgeschichte*, Handbuch zum Neuen Testament 7, Tübingen [2]1972
E. Haenchen, *The Acts of the Apostles*, Oxford and Philadelphia 1971
K. Lake & H. J. Cadbury, *The Beginning of Christianity*, Part I, *The Acts*

of the Apostles, ed. F. J. Foakes Jackson & K. Lake, Vol. IV, *English Translation and Commentary*, London 1933
——, (ed.), ibid. Vol. V, *Additional Notes to the Commentary*, London 1933
G. Stählin, *Die Apostelgeschichte*, Das Neue Testament Deutsch 5, Göttingen 1962

Chapter 6

B. W. Bacon, *The Gospel of the Hellenists*, New York 1933
L. W. Barnard, 'Saint Stephen and Early Alexandrian Christianity', *New Testament Studies* 7, 1960/61, 31–45
F. C. Baur, *Paulus, der Apostel Jesu Christi* I, Leipzig ²1866, 45ff., 49ff.
J. Bihler, *Die Stephanusgeschichte im Zusammenhang der Apostelgeschichte*, Munich 1963
H. J. Cadbury, 'The Hellenists', in *The Beginnings of Christianity*, Part I, Vol. V, London 1933, 59–74
P. Cousins, 'Stephen and Paul', *The Evangelical Quarterly* 33, 1961, 157–62
O. Cullmann, 'Secte de Qumran, Hellénistes des Actes et Quatrième Évangile', in *Les manuscrits de la Mer Morte, Colloque de Strasbourg 25–27 mai 1955*, Paris 1957, 61–74
E. Dinkler, 'Philippus und der ANER AITHIOPS (Apg 8.26–40)', in *Jesus und Paulus, Festschrift für Werner Georg Kümmel zum 70. Geburtstag*, Göttingen 1975, 85–95
E. Ferguson, 'The Hellenists in the Book of Acts', *Restoration Quarterly* 12, 1969, 159–80
W. Foerster, 'Stephanus und die Urgemeinde', in *Dienst unter dem Wort, Eine Festgabe für Professor D. Dr. Helmuth Schreiner zum 60. Geburtstag am 2. Marz 1953*, Gütersloh 1953, 9–30
P. Gaechter, 'Die Sieben (Apg 6.1–6)', in id., *Petrus und seine Zeit*, Innsbruck 1958, 105–54
P. Geoltrain, 'Esséniens et Hellénistes', *Theologische Zeitschrift* 15, 1959, 241–54
W. Grundmann, 'Das Problem des hellenistischen Christentums innerhalb der Jerusalemer Urgemeinde', *Zeitschrift für die neutestamentliche Wissenschaft* 38, 1939, 45–73
M. Hengel, 'Zwischen Jesus und Paulus, Die "Hellenisten", die "Sieben" und Stephanus', *Zeitschrift für Theologie und Kirche* 72, 1975, 151–206
I. H. Marshall, 'Palestinian and Hellenistic Christianity: Some Critical Comments', *New Testament Studies* 19, 1972/73, 271–87
B. Reicke, *Glaube und Leben der Urgemeinde*, Zürich 1957, 115ff.
M. H. Scharlemann, *Stephen: A Singular Saint*, Rome 1968
R. Scroggs, 'The Earliest Hellenistic Christianity', in *Religions in*

Antiquity, Essays in Memory of Erwin Ramsdell Goodenough, Leiden 1968, 176–206

M. Simon, *St Stephen and the Hellenists in the Primitive Church*, London 1958

A. Strobel, 'Armenpfleger "um des Friedens willen" (Zum Verständnis von Act 6.1–6)', *Zeitschrift für die neutestamentliche Wissenschaft* 63, 1972, 271–6

Chapter 7

O. Bauernfeind, 'Die Begegnung zwischen Paulus und Kephas Gal. 1.18–20', *Zeitschrift für die neutestamentliche Wissenschaft* 47, 1956, 268–76

O. Betz, 'Die Vision des Paulus im Tempel von Jerusalem', in *Verborum Veritas, Festschrift für G. Stählin*, Wuppertal 1970, 113–23

F. F. Bruce, 'Galatian Problems, 1. Autobiographical Data', *Bulletin of the John Rylands Library* 51, 1968/69, 292–309

——, 'Further Thoughts on Paul's Autobiography, Galatians 1.11–2.14', in *Jesus und Paulus, Festschrift für Werner Georg Kümmel zum 70. Geburtstag*, Göttingen 1975, 21–9

C. Burchard, *Der dreizehnte Zeuge*, Göttingen 1970

J. Dupont, 'The Conversion of Paul, and its Influence on his Understanding of Salvation by Faith', in W. W. Gasque & R. P. Martin (eds), *Apostolic History and the Gospel, Biblical and Historical Essays, presented to F. F. Bruce on his 60th Birthday*, Exeter 1970, 176–94

K. Haacker, 'Die Berufung des Verfolgers und die Rechtfertigung des Gottlosen', *Theologische Beiträge* 6, 1975, 1–19

O. Haas, 'Berufung und Sendung Pauli nach Gal. 1', *Zeitschrift für Missionswissenschaft und Religionswissenschaft* 46, 1962, 81–92

J. Munck, 'La vocation de l'Apôtre Paul', *Studia Theologica* I, 1947, 131–45

A. Oepke, 'Probleme der vorchristlichen Zeit des Paulus', *Theologische Studien und Kritiken* 105, 1933, 387–424

P. Stuhlmacher, *Das paulinische Evangelium, I., Vorgeschichte*, Göttingen 1968

W. C. van Unnik, 'Tarsus or Jerusalem', in id. *Sparsa Collecta* I, Leiden 1973, 259–320

U. Wilckens, 'Die Bekehrung des Paulus als religionsgeschichtliches Problem', *Zeitschrift für Theologie und Kirche* 56, 1959, 273–93

H. G. Wood, 'The Conversion of St Paul', *New Testament Studies* 1, 1954/55, 276–82

Chapter 8

C. K. Barrett, 'Cephas and Corinth', in *Abraham unser Vater, Festschrift für Otto Michel zum 60.Geburtstag*, Leiden-Cologne 1963, 1–12

F. W. Beare, 'The Sequence of Events in Acts 9–15 and the Career of Peter', *Journal of Biblical Literature* 62, 1943, 295–306

O. Cullmann, *Peter: Disciple, Apostle, Martyr*, Philadelphia and London ²1962

W. Dietrich, *Das Petrusbild der lukanischen Schriften*, Stuttgart 1972

J. Dupont, 'Pierre et Paul à Antioche et à Jérusalem', in id. *Études sur les Actes des Apôtres*, Paris 1967, 185–215

H.-M. Féret, *Pierre et Paul à Antioche et à Jérusalem*, Paris 1955

P. Gaechter, 'Petrus in Antiochia (Gal. 2.11–14)', in id., *Petrus und seine Zeit*, Innsbruck 1958, 213–57

D. Gewalt, *Petrus*, Heidelberg dissertation 1966

M. Goguel, 'L'apôtre Pierre a-t-il joué un rôle personnel dans les crises de Grèce et de Galatie?', *Revue d'Histoire et de Philosophie religieuses* 1934, 461–500

W. Grundmann, 'Die Apostel zwischen Jerusalem und Antiochia', *Zeitschrift für die neutestamentliche Wissenschaft* 39, 1940, 110–37

H. Katzenmayer, 'Die Beziehungen des Petrus zur Urkirche von Jerusalem und Antiochia', *Internationale kirchliche Zeitschrift*, Neue Folge 35, 1945, 116–30

G. Schulze-Kadelbach, 'Die Stellung des Petrus in der Urchristenheit', *Theologische Literaturzeitung* 81, 1956, 1–14

Chapter 9

P. Gaechter, 'Jerusalem und Antiochia', in id., *Petrus und seine Zeit*, Innsbruck 1958, 155–212

F. Hahn, *Christologische Hoheitstitel*, Göttingen ²1964

M. Hengel, 'Christologie und neutestamentliche Chronologie', in *Neues Testament und Geschichte, Oscar Cullmann zum 70. Geburtstag*, Zürich 1972, 43–67

——, *The Son of God*, London and Philadelphia 1976

W. Kramer, *Christ, Lord, Son of God*, SBT 50, London and Naperville 1966

See also above, *Books on the Earliest Christian Mission*

Chapter 10

M. Dibelius, 'The Apostolic Council', in *Studies in the Acts of the Apostles*, London 1956, 93–101

T. Fahy, 'The Council of Jerusalem', *The Irish Theological Quarterly* 30, 1963, 232–61

P. Gaechter, 'Jakobus von Jerusalem', in id., *Petrus und seine Zeit*, Innsbruck 1958, 258–310

——, 'Geschichtliches zum Apostelkonzil', *Zeitschrift für katholische Theologie* 85, 1963, 339–54

A. S. Geyser, 'Paul, the Apostolic Decree and the Liberals in Corinth', in *Studia Paulina in honorem Johannis de Zwaan septuagenarii*, Haarlem 1953, 124–38

S. Giet, 'L'Assemblée apostolique et le décret de Jérusalem, Qui était Siméon?', *Recherches de science religieuse* 39, 1951/52, 203–20

H. Katzenmayer, 'Das sogenannte Apostelkonzil von Jerusalem', *Internationale kirchliche Zeitschrift*, Neue Folge 31, 1941, 149–57

G. Klein, 'Galater 2.6–9 und die Geschichte der Jerusalemer Urgemeinde', *Zeitschrift für Theologie und Kirche* 57, 1960, 275–95 (= *Rekonstruktion und Interpretation*, Munich 1969, 99–128, which also contains a supplement)

B. Reicke, 'Der geschichtliche Hintergrund des Apostelkonzils und der Antiochia-Episode, Gal. 2.1–14', in *Studia Paulina in honorem Johannis de Zwaan septuagenarii*, Haarlem 1953, 172–87

W. Schmithals, *Paul and James*, SBT 46, London and Naperville 1965

A. Strobel, 'Das Aposteldekret in Galatien: Zur Situation von Gal I und II', *New Testament Studies* 20, 1974, 177–90

H. Waitz, 'Das Problem des sog. Aposteldekrets und die damit zusammenhängenden literarischen und geschichtlichen Probleme des apostolischen Zeitalters', *Zeitschrift für Kirchengeschichte* 55, 1936, 227–63

G. Zuntz, 'Analysis of the Report about the "Apostolic Council"', in *Opuscula selecta*, 1972, 216–51

Property and Riches in the Early Church

*Aspects of a Social History
of Early Christianity*

1

The Criticism of Property among the Fathers,
Natural Law and Utopia in Antiquity

1 The Criticism of Property among the Fourth-Century Fathers

People today are fond of talking about the 'crisis of private property'. Yet this 'crisis' seems to be as old as mankind itself. One might almost say that it is of the 'essence' of mankind, which is always 'in crisis'. In an early Christian romance, the so-called Pseudo-Clementines (*Hom*.3,25), the name of the first fratricide, Cain, is defined on the basis of a double Hebrew etymology, as 'possession' (from *qana* = acquire) and 'envy' (from *qana'* = be envious). It is explained that as a result Cain became a 'murderer' and a 'liar'. From this follows the terse and radical conclusion: 'For all men, possessions are sins' (*pasi ta ktemata hamartemata*, 15.9). An old Hellenistic-Jewish tradition probably stands behind the connection of Cain with possessions; we shall find it again in Philo the philosopher and Josephus the historian. The latter stresses that in his wickedness Cain 'was only concerned to acquire possessions and was the first to plough the earth', in other words, he was the first to acquire land and do violence to nature (*Antt*.1,52; cf. Philo, *Sac.Ab. et C*.1,2). This idea that private property is a root of human dissension goes through the social admonitions of the fathers of the early church like a scarlet thread. The struggle for individual possessions destroys the original good order of the world, as all had an equal share in God's gifts. The greatest Christian preacher of antiquity, John Chrysostom (354-407), puts this view in a particularly impressive way:

> Mark the wise dispensation of God! That he might put
> mankind to shame, he has made certain things common, as

the sun, air, earth, and water . . . whose benefits are dispensed equally to all as brethren . . . observe, that concerning things that are common there is no contention, but all is peaceable. But when one attempts to possess himself of anything, to make it his own, then contention is introduced, as if nature herself were indignant, that when God brings us together in every way, we are eager to divide and separate ourselves by appropriating things, and by using those cold words 'mine and thine'. Then there is contention and uneasiness. But where this is not, no strife or contention is bred. This state therefore is rather our inheritance, and more agreeable to nature.[1]

The judgment of the rather older monastic father Basil (329-379) was hardly less radical. He himself came from a family of rich landowners in Asia Minor and after his studies distributed all his possessions among the poor, influenced by the radical asceticism of the monks of Egypt (see pp.52f. below). He preached a famous sermon on the rich farmer (Luke 12.18) in which he called the man who could help the needy but keeps his possessions to himself a 'robber and a thief'. At the same time he gives a clear answer to the objection of the hard-hearted man who asks, 'To whom am I doing wrong . . . if I keep my possessions to myself?'

Tell me, what is yours? Where did you get it and bring it into the world? It is as if one has taken a seat in the theatre and then drives out all who come later, thinking that what is for everyone is only for him. Rich people are like that. For having pre-empted what is common to all, they make it their own by virtue of this prior possession. If only each one would take as much as he requires to satisfy his immediate needs, and leave the rest to others who equally needed it, no one would be rich — and no one would be poor (Migne, PG 31, 276f.).

Here the great Cappadocian is taking up imagery which had already been used by Chrysippus, head of the school of Stoic philosophers (*c.*280-207 BC), though he slants it in a polemical direction. The Stoic had wanted to defend 'the right to private property' by reference to a seat at the theatre which is occupied by the first arrival, as. it 'does not militate

against the state or the universe which are common to all'.[2]
Basil holds exactly the opposite view. As Bishop of Caesarea
in Cappadocia, he tried to translate his social demands into
action by setting up a large welfare centre at the gates of the
city for the poor, the old and the sick, together with a
hospice for penniless travellers. Refuges of this kind also
came into being in other cities in his diocese.

His friend and contemporary Gregory Nazianzen gave this
criticism of property and riches a grounding in salvation
history and doctrine: poverty and superfluity, so-called
freedom and slavery are a consequence of the Fall. 'In the
beginning it was not so': God created man 'free and
independent'. He was rich, for the goods of paradise were
freely at his disposal. The 'envy and quarrelsomeness' of the
serpent first destroyed the original harmony and 'shattered
the nobility of nature through covetousness, with the help of
despotic laws'. Works of righteousness and mercy are
therefore an essential step towards the restoration of this lost
state.[3] This thesis that private property came into being as a
result of the Fall had great influence in the history of the
church. We find it later among the Franciscan theologians
and then again in Zwingli and Melanchthon. The later
devaluation of property, the thesis that it has only secondary
character by contrast with an original equality, also in
essentials goes back to this derivation of private property
from the Fall.

2   Natural Law and Utopia in Antiquity

Of course, 'theories of property' like this, which are to be
found in the early church, are not specifically based on the
New Testament. Appeal could be made equally well to
philosophy and natural law for the thesis of Gregory
Nazianzen that private property, riches and poverty are a
consequence of the Fall. Thus we find Ambrose, Bishop of
Milan (339-397), arguing against Cicero (*De off*.1.20ff.) but
agreeing with Stoic teaching:

> Nature has poured forth all things for men for common
> use. God has ordered all things to be produced, so that
> there should be food in common to all, and that the earth

should be a common possession for all. Nature, therefore, has produced a common right for all, but greed (*usurpatio*) had made it a right for a few.[7]

This fundamental idea, that in the 'golden age', i.e. in the primal childhood of the human race, all possessions were held in common — even to the point of sharing wives — and that the moral downfall of man began with the introduction of private property, dominates much of ancient 'philosophy of history' and the utopian states influenced by it. Here ancient natural law, the philosophy of history and the Christian doctrine of man's primal state could join hands. Aristophanes could already present utopias of this kind as feminine wisdom in a comedy about an early agitator for women's liberation. The future and the ideal world will again correspond:

All shall be equal, and equally share
all wealth and enjoyment, nor longer endure
that one should be rich, and another be poor,
that one should have acres, far stretching and wide,
and another not even enough to provide
himself with a grave: that this at his call
should have hundreds of servants and that none at all.
All this I intend to correct and amend:
now all of all blessings shall freely partake,
one life and one system for all men I'll make.[5]

Behind these demands, which sound familiar to us today, stands the romantic regression of 'back to nature', which played an astonishing role in the thought of the intellectuals of antiquity. It was a widely-accepted commonplace that the first men lived in a state of perfect moral innocence, without any external laws, and directed only by 'nature':

Golden was that first age, which, with no one to compel, without a law, of its own will, kept faith and did the right. There was no fear of punishment, no threatening words were to be read on brazen tablets; no suppliant throng gazed fearfully upon its judge's face; but without judges lived secure.[6]

This 'ideal state' was only possible because 'private property' was as unknown as the seductive skills of technology; men lived without any needs whatsoever on what the earth produced generously and without compulsion, acorns, roots and wild fruits:

> Even to mark the field or divide it with bounds was unlawful. Men made gain from the common store, and Earth yielded all, of herself, more freely, when none begged for her gifts.[7]

Obviously, the 'lordship of men over men' was also completely absent, and with it all forms of slavery. This paradisal condition was only destroyed by the introduction of technical means, metal working, agriculture which violated the earth, various forms of craft, voyaging and trade: done violence to by men, nature began to withhold itself. Covetousness, envy, tyranny and war raised their ugly heads and began to darken man's common life.

Still people continued to believe that they would rediscover the lost ideal of the time of paradise, long past, among individual barbarian peoples. Attention was especially fixed on the Scythians, who were regarded as being particularly wild: they were supposed to live almost like animals, but on the other hand supreme moral perfection was attributed to them:

> They are frugal in their ways of living and not money-getters, they not only are orderly towards one another, because they have all things in common (*koina panta echontes*, cf. Acts 2.44, see pp.8f., 31ff. below), their wives, children, the whole of their kin and everything, but also remain invincible and unconquered by others, because they have nothing to be enslaved for.[8]

Another possibility was to tell stories of distant isles of wonder in utopian romances. One instance of this is the famous romance of Euhemerus which tells of the island Panchaea in the Indian Ocean. The whole island was held in common and there was a strict duty to hand over all agricultural products. Fair portions were given 'to each according to his need', though incentives for particular assiduity were not lacking. There was no private property apart from 'house and garden'; the 'intellectual groups', i.e. the wise priests, saw to just laws and distribution. The analogy to Plato's philosophers' state is unmistakable (Diod.5,45,3-5).

It is, of course, striking that the Greeks and Romans hardly thought about a future utopia, the return of the golden age. The agitation in Aristophanes' *Ecclesiazousae* is an exception. Under the influence of the oriental-Jewish Sibyls, that is of apocalyptic, Virgil is the first to proclaim the dawn of future salvation, in his much-discussed fourth Eclogue:

> Every land shall bear all fruits. The earth shall not feel the harrow, nor the vine the pruning hook; the sturdy ploughman, too, shall now loose his oxen from the yoke.[9]

When the earth once again offers its gifts in abundance, and without being violated by man's techniques, there will no longer be any need for private property. The time of the great peace has dawned.

Ideals of this kind gave wing to romantic longing more than to real hope, though at the same time they also inspired the moral preaching of the philosophers. Thus Seneca, the Roman Stoic and Nero's tutor, could already speak in very similar terms to the later church father Gregory Nazianzen:

> (Philosophy) has taught us to worship that which is divine, to love that which is human; she has told us that with the gods lies dominion, and among men, fellowship. This fellowship remained unspoiled for a long time, until avarice tore the community asunder and became the cause of poverty even in the case of those whom she herself had most enriched. For men cease to possess all things the moment they desire all things for their own. But the first men and those who sprang from them, still unspoiled, followed nature (*Epist*.90.3f.).

> But avarice broke in upon a condition so happily ordained, and, by its eagerness to lay something away and to turn it to its own private use, made all things the property of others, and reduced itself from boundless wealth to straitened need. It was avarice that introduced

poverty, and, by craving much, lost all (*Epist*.90.38).[10]

This means that the utopia projected back into primal times, the doctrine of the original state of paradise and the fall that followed, which is said to have consisted not least in the appropriation of private property, is by no means a genuinely Christian doctrine. Rather, it is a mythical speculation about history which was widespread in antiquity.

The connections between the ancient theories of a lofty moral 'primal communism' or of a 'primal catastrophe', allegedly introduced by the division of labour and private possessions, and the modern 'historical myths' of popular Marxism, are evident. Rousseau's 'back to nature', like Proudhon's theory 'property is theft', are not original ideas, but go back to ancient sources.

Even the view that particular people in the South Sea Islands and the primeval Brazilian forest enjoy economic and sexual innocence, or that the 'hunters and collectors' with their primal communism had ideal social conditions, corresponds to a widespread ancient myth about the just laws of the barbarians. In the beginning, a natural, i.e. morally perfect condition is said to have prevailed. A fundamentally religious longing for the 'good old days' underlies these universal ancient doctrines of man's primal state, which can also be found in different variations in Iranian, Babylonian, Indian and indeed Chinese myths.[11] Then, it was believed, the world was whole. Of course, there is no historical proof of this and it is certainly no more rational than hope for an eternal life in the Elysian fields or on the isles of the blessed.

However, these myths of the primal state of man were rarely evaluated in political terms. Pressure for imposing a utopian pattern on the present and future is most likely to be found where one may conjecture a connection with Jewish and oriental apocalyptic (see pp.17ff. below), say in Aristonicus' rebellion in the Pergamene kingdom (133-130 BC). After handing over the country to Rome, he 'quickly assembled a mass of poor people and slaves who were summoned to freedom and whom he named Heliopolitans'. Presumably he was striving for a utopian 'proletarian state', to which he gave the name 'sun state'.[12] The Egyptian Potter's Oracle, which was similarly composed in the second century BC, has many features in common with the Jewish apocalypses. Together with the expulsion of the Greeks from Egypt and the destruction of Alexandria there is also a prophecy of the liberation of the slaves, 'whose masters flee for their life', after the upheaval.[13] The concerns of the ancient social reformers hardly went beyond a demand for the liberation of slaves, remission of debts and a redistribution of agricultural land. Here the strongest social impetus came from the Jewish heritage (see pp.15ff. below). By contrast, the influence of philosophical utopia on political reality was relatively small; the popular philosophical, utopian romance of the state hardly had any concrete effect. There were exceptions, e.g. when the Stoic Sphaerus supported the Spartan king Agis IV in his radical social reform,[14] or when the philosopher Blossius, who was hostile to Rome, fled to Aristonicus at Pergamon. There was no 'ideological' foundation to the great slave revolts of the Hellenistic period between the third and first centuries BC.

3　Greek Influence in Early Christianity?

Early Christianity and the New Testament, the 'documentation of the preaching on which the church was founded' (M. Kähler) and thus the earliest source of Christian history, were only marginally affected by all these theories and utopias, which gave their stamp to later Christian natural law theory about property. A conjunction of the primitive Christian ethos and the universal ideal of antiquity was most likely to come about where a New Testament author — like Luke — introduced his Greek rhetorical training as a writer and stylized certain phenomena of early Christianity in accordance with the tradition in which he had been educated. This is the case, for example, with the account which Luke gives of the so-called communism of the first community in Jerusalem:

> And all who believed were together and had all things in common (Acts 2.44). Now the company of those who believed were of one heart and soul, and no one said that any of the things which he possessed was his own, but they had everything in common (*panta koina*: Acts 4.32).

Here we have the familiar picture of the restoration of the perfect 'primal state' which has analogies, even to the way in which it is formulated, with the sharing of goods among the Scythians (see p.5 above), Plato's doctrine of the state (*Pol.*462, etc.) or the 'primal community' of the Pythagoreans in Southern Italy.[15] The *Sentences of Sextus* which, while Christian, are also fed from popular Pythagorean philosophical sources (see below, pp.56f.), give a theological foundation to this ideal, which both Christians and pagans could accept. 'Those who have in common God as their Father, but do not have possessions in common, are impious.'[16] A still nearer parallel to Luke's account is the 'community of goods' among the Essene groups in Palestine, above all in their centre at Qumran, which we can see particularly well as a result of the discovery of the Dead Sea Scrolls. But even here we must ask whether this 'group communism', with its eschatological stamp, which also made a vivid impression on the educated Graeco-Roman world outside Palestine, was not shaped as much by the ideals of the Hellenistic spirit of the age as by Old Testament patterns. The Essenes wanted to realize here on earth a perfect — one might almost say 'angelic' or 'heavenly' — form of community through the ideal of the sharing of goods. They lived in the awareness that they were in constant contact with the angels of God, and their aim was to regain the original rank and glory of the primal man Adam (1 QS 4.23; 1 QH 17.15). The other side of this exaggerated estimation of themselves was that they regarded the rest of mankind, their Jewish contemporaries and still more the Gentiles, as a 'mass of corruption', as sons of darkness delivered over to annihilation. These people were to be hated eternally until they were completely annihilated in the 'last combat' (1 QS 1.10; 9.21).

There are considerably stronger points of contact between New Testament criticism of property and riches and that of the Graeco-Roman world in the sphere of popular wisdom. Thus in the late I Timothy 6.10 we find a widespread proverb, 'The love of money is the root of all evils', cited in connection with a demand for pious 'self-sufficiency' (*autarkeia*), i.e. the 'favourite virtue of Cynics and Stoics'.[17] This in turn influenced the later Christian tradition. This saying expresses a principal theme of popular philosophical preaching, and an ever-increasing number of variations on it are quoted in ancient sources.[18] An especially favourite version can be found equally in the sage Democritus and in Diogenes, who despised both culture and possessions: 'The love of money is the homeland of all evils'.[19] But the saying is not lacking in Jewish-Hellenistic literature either.[20] Here we have a good example of the way in which popular-philosophical criticism of avarice and riches could be combined with Judaeo-Christian 'social criticism' in the sphere of ethical admonitions.

Finally, an example may be quoted which points forward to the teaching of Jesus.

In the 'Misanthrope' (*Dyskolos*), written by the Attic comedian Menander (born 342/1 BC), the young Sostratus delivers a vigorous moral sermon to his father when the latter is bitter at the thought of a poor cousin marrying into his rich family:

> That's a bit thick!
> I do not want to be father-in-law of
> two penniless children. One is quite enough.

The son rejoins:

> You babble about money, a matter insecure. For if you
> have knowledge that this will abide with you for ever, keep
> it close, share it with none, but be yourself its lord and
> master. Whereas if you possess all this, not as your own
> but Fortune's, why should you, father, begrudge it to
> anyone of these? For she herself perhaps, taking all this
> away from you, will bestow it in turn on someone else
> who is unworthy. Wherefore I say that you yourself, what
> time you are the master, ought to use this nobly, father,
> ought to succour all and through your help effect that as
> many as possible should live in easy circumstances. For
> this is something that will never die, and, if reverses some
> day befall you, from this source you in turn will have the
> self-same help. A visible friend is a better thing by far than
> wealth which you keep buried out of sight.[21]

H. Hommel has pointed to a series of parallels between

these verses and the synoptic gospels and the preaching of
Jesus.[22] The theme that one should exchange the uncertain,
threatened and transitory possession of property for the
permanence of friendship which will recompense good deeds
in future need can be found, for example, in the Lukan
special material as an interpretation of the difficult parable of
the unjust steward: 'And I tell you, make friends for
yourselves by means of unrighteous mammon, so that when
it fails they may receive you into the eternal habitations'
(16.9). There is also a parallel in the favourite theme of
'disappearing riches', which occurs above, to the saying from
the Sermon on the Mount; 'Lay up for yourselves treasures in
heaven, where neither moth nor rust consumes and where
thieves do not break in and steal' (Matt. 6.20 = Luke 12.35).
On the other hand, one should not, of course, overlook the
fact that in the gospel sayings the eschatological reference is
fundamentally different from the naive experiential wisdom
of Greek gnomic thought. Moreover, the whole terminology,
for example the formula about 'unrighteous mammon',
clearly points to a Jewish-Palestinian derivation. Nevertheless,
these more or less chance instances may show how there were
mutual links between the Jewish and early Christian criticism
of riches on the one hand and that of popular Greek
philosophy on the other.

2

Property and Riches in the Old Testament and
Judaism

*1 The Prophetic Criticism of Riches and its Expression in
the Torah*

Before we consider the attitude of Jesus and early Christianity to property and riches, we must take a look at the Old
Testament and Jewish tradition out of which early Christianity grew. Here the message of the prophets and the social
legislation of the Torah had long stimulated criticism of
property. The right to property was in principle subordinated
to the obligation to care for the weaker members of society.
Even the testimony of the first writing prophet, Amos, in the
eighth century BC, leaves nothing to be desired by way of
clarity. With unsurpassable sharpness he attacks the sub-
jection and exploitation of the poor by the rich landowners
and royal officials in the northern kingdom:

They hate him who reproves in the gate,
and they abhor him who speaks the truth.
Therefore:
Because you trample the poor
and take from him exactions of wheat,
you have built houses of hewn stone,
but you shall not dwell in them.
You have planted pleasant vineyards,
but you shall not drink their wine.
For I know how many are your transgressions,
and how great are your sins —
you who afflict the righteous, who take a bribe,
and turn aside the needy in the gate. (Amos 5.10-12)

Hear this,
you who trample upon the needy,
and bring the poor of the land to an end,
saying,
'When will the new moon be over,
that we may sell grain?
And the sabbath,
that we may offer wheat for sale,
that we may make the ephah small and the shekel great,
and deal deceitfully with false balances,
that we may buy the poor for silver
and the needy for a pair of sandals,
and sell the refuse of the wheat?'
The Lord has sworn by the pride of Jacob:
'Surely I will never forget any of their deeds.
Shall not the land tremble on this account,
and every one mourn who dwells in it?' (Amos 8.4-8)

Amos' threats against society are continued a little later by Isaiah, in the southern kingdom. He, too, roughly attacks the dispossession practised by the great landowners, the corruption among the judges and the mercilessness and partiality of officials:

Woe to those who join house to house,
who add field to field,
until there is no more room,
and you are made to dwell alone in the midst of the land.
The Lord of hosts has sworn in my hearing:
'Surely many houses shall be desolate,
large and beautiful houses, without inhabitant.
For ten acres of vineyard shall yield but one bath,
and a homer of seed shall yield but an ephah. . . .'

Woe to those who decree iniquitous decrees,
and the writers who keep writing oppression,
to turn aside the needy from justice
and to rob the poor of my people of their right,
that widows may be their spoil,
and that they may make the fatherless their prey.
What will you do on the day of punishment,

in the storm which will come from afar?
To whom will you flee for help,
and where will you leave your wealth? (Isa.5.8-10; 10.1-3)

Otto Kaiser refers to the third elegy of the great Athenian lawgiver and social reformer Solon, which was written about a century later. Solon is dealing with a similar situation in his native city:

> But the citizens themselves, driven by the desire for money, are blinded and seek the fall of our mighty city.
> For the leaders of the people are wicked and evil-minded, and thereby only bring painful suffering upon themselves. Their greed is insatiable, they do not know how to enjoy with order and sobriety the pleasures of the feast.
> ... The riches they heap up come from violence and wrong; neither what the gods possess nor what belongs to man is spared by their appetite; they are not ashamed of open robbery, have no regard for *dike* (the goddess of righteousness) and her sacred commandment.[1]

At least part of the social message of the prophets was given expression in the Torah, later ascribed to Moses, especially in the book of Deuteronomy, which played a decisive role in king Josiah's reform and in the spiritual renewal of Israel during the exile. Examples of this are the numerous regulations contained in the Torah which protect the weak and underprivileged members of society. In Deut.15.1ff.,12ff., the ordinance of the year of release which takes place every seven years enjoined a universal release of debts and the freeing of all who had been enslaved for debt. The prophet Jeremiah was already protesting against the breach of this practice (34.8ff.). In the fiftieth year, after seven years of release or sabbath years, the 'year of jubilee' was celebrated. In this year all land that had been sold in the meantime was to be returned to its original owner or his heirs (Lev.25.8ff.). The reason given for this 'redistribution' of land was that Yahweh was the real owner of the holy land: 'For the land is mine; for you are strangers and sojourners with me' (Lev.25.23). 'Each of you shall return to his property'(25.13). 'What is called a sale is not really a sale; it is merely a provisional exchange of possessions; for Yahweh alone is the owner of the land. The Israelites are merely hereditary tenants on his property, who have no more ultimate right to dispose of the land which had been assigned to them than the strangers and sojourners whom they have accepted in their midst.'[2] We find the three demands for the remission of debt, the freeing of slaves and the redistribution of land in numerous attempts at social reform in the ancient world: the Jewish law attempted to institutionalize these ever-recurring basic demands of 'ancient social reform', though of course it remains an open question how far the demands were ever realized. Significantly enough, the 'year of jubilee' was later reinterpreted as a symbol of the eschatological liberation of Israel.

On the other side was appropriate and legitimate posses-sion under the protection of the Decalogue, which prohibited envious covetousness of a neighbour's property (Ex.20.15,17 = Deut.5.19,21). The picture of the king's peace in the time of Solomon, when 'Judah and Israel dwelt in safety, every man under his vine and under his fig tree' (I Kings 4.25), became a symbol of the prophetic vision of the time of salvation (Micah 4.4; Zech. 3.10; cf. also II Kings 18.31).

2   Social Tensions in Early Judaism

The contrast between the great landowners and the small peasant farmers or landless tenants had already led to considerable social tensions in the late monarchy (I Kings 21; Isa.5.8ff.; Micah 2.2) and then again in the Persian period under Nehemiah (5.1ff.). The situation became considerably more acute in the Hellenistic period after Alexander, as the Graeco-Macedonian colonizers with their own particular approach to the world went over from the extensive exploitation hitherto usual in the East to an intensive exploitation of their subject territories. The Romans and the rulers appointed by them, like Herod and his successors, continued this form of extreme exploitation of the land. Great estates forced back the free peasant farmers, and the number of landless tenants increased, particularly after the time of Herod. We have a lively picture of the social scene in Palestine from the parables of Jesus with their landowners, tenants, day labourers and slaves; with faithful and unfaithful administrators; with remission of debts and slavery for debts. The social scene has the firm imprint of feudalism upon it. We can understand why the Jewish struggles for freedom — first of all that of the Maccabees against the Macedonian Seleucids and then later that of the 'Zealots' against the Romans — were always also social struggles. When the Jewish rebels plundered Jerusalem in AD 66 from their base in the temple, the first thing that they burnt was the city archive with the land-registers and the accounts of debts (Josephus, *Bell*.2,427). Later, Simon bar Giora, the leader of the Zealots, arranged for a general liberation of slaves (4,508). Josephus particularly stresses that the rebellion was supported above all by the simple people — and the youth — whereas the upper classes sought to maintain peace with Rome.[3]

Thus there was a political and a social division not only in Palestinian Judaism, but also in large areas of the Diaspora, e.g. in Egypt and in Cyrenaica. This rift also goes through many parts of the religious tradition. For example, on the eve of the Hellenistic reform, which led on to the Maccabean revolt (*c*. 180 BC), the wisdom teacher Ben Sira uttered polemic against unscrupulous speculators and against the hectic hunt for riches:

> My son, do not busy yourself with many matters; if you
>   multiply activities you will not go unpunished
> (Sir.11.10).
> He who loves gold will not be justified,
> and he who pursues money will be led astray to it
> (Ecclus.31.5).

Rich and poor act like the wolf and the lamb; the gulf between them is unbridgeable:

> A rich man does wrong, and he even adds reproaches;
>   a poor man suffers wrong and he must add apologies.
> A rich man will exploit you if you can be of use to him,
>   but if you are in need he will forsake you (13.3f.).

> Wild asses in the wilderness are the prey of lions;
>   likewise the poor are pastures for the rich.

Humility is an abomination to a proud man;
  likewise a poor man is an abomination to a rich one.
When a rich man totters, he is steadied by friends,
  but when a humble man falls, he is even pushed away by
  friends (13.19ff.).

Ben Sira's polemic against social injustice at times becomes
even as sharp as the preaching of the prophets:

Like one who kills a son before his father's eyes
  is the man who offers a sacrifice from the property of
  the poor.
The bread of the needy is the life of the poor;
  whoever deprives them of it is a man of blood.
To take away a neighbour's living is to murder him;
  to deprive an employee of his wages is to shed blood
  (34.20-22).

But this is only one side of the coin. On the other side we
find in immediate juxtaposition in Ben Sira the high
estimation of riches which is to be found in traditional
wisdom: riches gained through honest work and God's
blessing guarantee a safe and carefree life, whereas self-
incurred poverty and beggary are hateful to him.[4] It is
certainly no coincidence that Ben Sira praises the just rich
man rather than the poor man:

Blessed is the rich man who is found blameless and who
does not go after mammon (Sir.31.8).

We shall look in vain for direct praise of the poor or of
poverty in Jewish literature: it is first to be found in the
gospel (Luke 6.20, see below, p.25).

The apocalyptic threat of judgment against the unjust rich
is all the sharper. Thus we read in the admonitions of
Ethiopian Enoch:

Woe to those who build unrighteousness and oppression
And lay deceit as a foundation;
For they shall be suddenly overthrown,
And they shall have no peace (cf. Isa.48.22; 57.21).
Woe to those who build their houses with sin;
For from all their foundations shall they be overthrown,

And by the sword they shall fall.
And those who acquire gold and silver in judgment shall
  suddenly perish.
Woe to you, ye rich, for ye have trusted in your riches,
And from your riches shall ye depart,
Because ye have not remembered the Most High in the
  days of your riches.
Ye have committed blasphemy and unrighteousness,
And have become ready for the day of slaughter,
And the day of darkness and the day of the great
  judgment.
Thus I speak and declare unto you:
He who created you will overthrow you,
And for your fall there shall be no compassion,
And your Creator will rejoice at your destruction (94.6-10,
  cf. 96.4ff.).
Woe to you who acquire silver and gold in unrighteousness
  and say:
We have become rich with riches and have possessions;
And have acquired everything we have desired.
And now let us do what we purposed:
For we have gathered silver in our treasuries
And many possessions in our houses . . .
You deceive yourselves, for your riches do not abide
But speedily ascend from you;
For ye have acquired it all in unrighteousness (97.8-10, cf.
  100.6).

God's last judgment brings about the great reversal: the rich,
the powerful and the exploiters are given over to eternal
damnation (102.9ff.; cf. 63.10), whereas the faithful and
righteous poor who have 'toiled laboriously' (103.9) all their
lives receive eternal reward. There is no mistaking the fact
that behind the threats and description of judgment a crude
desire for vengeance on the part of the faithful, who have so
far been suppressed, can also be seen. According to the
Similitudes in Ethiopian Enoch 63.10, 'the mighty and the
kings who possess the earth' must confess: 'Our souls are full
of unrighteous mammon (see Luke 16.9,11), but it does not
prevent us from descending from the midst thereof into the
burden of the flame of Sheol.' There 'they shall be a

spectacle for the righteous and . . . elect; they shall rejoice over them, because the wrath of the Lord of Spirits resteth upon them' (62.12). The tradition which emerges here of the pious feasting their eyes on the torments of hell, can be traced through later Christian apocalyptic down to Dante's Inferno (see below, pp.49f). Behind these threats of judgment there is an earlier Jewish tradition which already appears in the canonical psalms and then is developed by the Essene texts of Qumran and the Pharisaic Psalms of Solomon: the term 'poor' (*'ani* or the related *'anaw* = humble, and *'ebyon*) becomes almost synonymous with 'pious' and 'righteous'. For example, an Essene commentary on Ps.37.10, 'But the humble (*'anawim*) shall possess the land and delight in abundant peace' interprets the text as: '(The congregation of the) Poor (*'ebyonim*) who shall accept the season of penance and shall be delivered from all the snares (of Satan) . . .' In other words, here the Essene community of salvation understands itself to be the 'poor'.[5] According to the War Scroll the hostile nations are conquered 'by the poor', for God himself will 'deliver into the hands of the poor the enemies from all the lands'.[6] Here the eschatological, true Israel is in principle identical with 'the poor'. The term has changed from the designation of a social group to that of a religious group. The early church in Palestine later uses the term 'poor' (*'ebyonim*) to describe itself in a very similar sense (see below, p.34).

3 Poverty and Riches in the Rabbis

Jewish piety which took its stamp from the message of the prophets and the social commandments of the Torah did its utmost to eliminate or at least to alleviate the particularly abrupt contrast between rich and poor in the Hellenistic Roman period. According to a fundamental rule ascribed to the Jewish high priest Simon the Just (200 BC), 'the world stands on three things: on the Torah, and on the Service, and on the doing of kindnesses' (Pirke Aboth 1,2). Later rabbis made a distinction between the so-called 'works of love', like visiting the sick, giving hospitality to strangers, equipping poor betrothed couples, comforting the bereaved, etc., and organized welfare for the poor, but the whole complex could be summed up as 'good works' (cf. Matt.5.16; Bill.4.536,559). The redemption of Jewish slaves, which was particularly important in the Diaspora, must also be included in this complex of 'works of love'. An early rabbinic maxim may clarify the high opinion of these works of mercy, which did much to alleviate social distress:

> Acts of kindness (*gemiloth hasadim*) and charity weigh more than all the commandments. Charity can be given to the living only, acts of kindness can be done to both the living and the dead; charity can be given only to the poor, acts of kindness to the rich and the poor. Charity can be done only with one's money, but acts of kindness can be done with one's person and one's money.[7]

The religious justification of genorisity stressed on the one hand the idea of 'imitating the goodness of God', which was equally favoured by Stoic philosophers and rabbis, and on the other the Old Testament argument, which reappears in Christian parenesis, that all good gifts come from God himself. Thus R. Eleazar b. Judah, about AD 100, remarked:

> Give him (i.e. God) of what is his, for thou and thine are his. And thus (the Scripture) saith, in (the place concerning) David, 'For all things come of thee, and of thine own have we given thee' (Aboth 3,7; Bill.4,541).

Consequently the Jewish communities developed a system of welfare for the poor which was probably unique in antiquity (before the rise of Christianity) and extremely effective. The legal basis for it was the second tithe, the so-called tithe for the poor, commanded in Deut.14.29; 26.12. Of course, at this point we can also see the limitations of this institution. Radical criticism of riches and surrender of one's own resources were taboo among the rabbis; to protect a man from making himself penniless a limit was put on the amount of alms to be given to the poor. The most a man was to give was twenty per cent of his total income; the least, two or three per cent. A rabbinic tradition reports: 'Once a man wanted to give away his property, but his friend did not allow it.'[8] Practical experience underlies this position: the rigorist must not become a burden on the community at a later stage and the resources of the people of Israel may not be squandered. Among the rabbis we increasingly find once again the high estimate put on riches and the despising of the poor which were characteristic of early wisdom. The hasidic, apocalyptic way of poverty had only a very limited influence here. Poverty could be regarded as a curse, and reference could be made to Prov.19.15: 'The days of the poor man are evil.'[9] The judgment was:

'There is nothing harder in the world than poverty; for it is the hardest of all the sufferings in the world.' Consequently Job prayed: 'Lord, I will accept all the suffering in the world, but not poverty' (*ExR* 31.12; Bill.1,818).

In accordance with this attitude, there was widespread praise of riches. The following statement was attributed to the famous teacher Rabbi Johanan in the third century AD:

God makes his Shekinah (i.e. his presence) rest only on a strong man, a *rich man*, a wise man and a humble man . . .

At the same time he is said to have justified it from the Bible:

All the prophets were rich. How do we know that? From Moses, Samuel, Amos (!) and Jonah (*Ned*.38a; Bill.1,826).

Earlier apocalyptic looked for the abolition of poverty in the coming age, and we can understand why:

And they who have died in grief shall arise in joy,
And they who were poor for the Lord's sake shall be made rich,
And they who are put to death for the Lord's sake shall awake to life (Test.Judah 25.4).

But the Babylonian teacher Mar Samuel, head of the school — who was, of course, particularly restrained in his messianic expectation — could refer to Deut.15.11: 'For the poor will never cease out of the land', and assert:

'The only difference between this world and the days of the Messiah is that slavery to governments will cease,' in other words, there will still be poverty and the opportunity for good works. The frequent repetition of this view shows how popular it was (Ber.34b etc.; Bill.1,74).

Here we can see a change in the Jewish attitude to riches. It is connected with the rejection of the Jewish apocalyptic way of poverty which after AD 70 fell more and more under the suspicion of being heresy. At first, the early rabbinic tradition can still report the great poverty of individual teachers between the first century BC and the second century AD. Thus Hillel came from Babylon to Jerusalem as a penurious day-labourer and bought access to the school with half of his scanty earnings. R. Akiba came from equally poor surroundings and was first of all a simple shepherd. However, it is significant that the rabbinic tradition stresses that they achieved not only a great reputation but also prosperity. The riches of the family of the patriarch, the descendants of Hillel, were proverbial after the second century. When R. Akiba declared that 'The poverty of the daughter of Jacob is like a red bridle on the neck of a white horse,'[10] he was not praising poverty as such, but simply saying that Israel was to be brought to repentance by extreme distress. The fearful catastrophes of the Jewish War and the rebellion of Bar Cochba (AD 66-74 and 132-135), which also broke out for social reasons, had brought such profound economic distress on the people that its religious, national and economic existence was threatened. Poverty no longer seemed to be an ideal to be striven for; it was simply God's chastisement. The increasing high estimation of riches and the contempt for poverty among the later teachers is probably connected with the overcoming of this crisis and the strengthening of Judaism towards the end of the second century and in the third century AD. The rabbis had established themselves as the leading religious and political class in Judaism, beyond any question or dispute, and as the acknowledged leaders of the people they had both the possibility and the will to become prosperous. They were opposed to some degree by individual charismatics and miracle workers, whose poverty and extreme asceticism are stressed in legends. Among these were R. Hanina ben Dosa and Abba Hilkiah in the first century, and R. Phinehas b.Jair, the opponent of the immensely rich patriarch Jehuda Hannasi, towards the end of the second century. But these were exceptions which proved the rule.

3

The Preaching of Jesus

What has been said so far indicates that Palestine in the first century AD, at the time of Jesus' ministry and the birth of the early church, was full of acute political, social and religious differences. Evidence for this is provided not least by Josephus and Philo, who report a number of clashes between the Jews and the prefect Pontius Pilate (cf. Luke 13.1f.). The latter was regarded as being particularly avaricious and cruel. The bloody repression of messianic disturbances in Samaria finally led to his dismissal in AD 37 (Josephus, *Antt.* 18,55-64, 85-87; Philo, *Leg. ad C.* 299ff.). This negative picture is supplemented by rabbinic accounts of the avarice and despotism of the leading high-priestly families, among whom pride of place was taken by the house of Annas. This family used their privileged position to exploit those who came to Jerusalem on pilgrimage at festival times and to oppress the more humble ministers of the temple; they often worked hand in hand with the Roman prefects.

1 Jesus' Radical Criticism of Property

We turn first to the synoptic gospels: Mark, Luke and Matthew, which are the main sources about Jesus. In what follows it is impossible to make an exact distinction between what may be supposed to be the authentic tradition about Jesus and its influence on the community tradition of subsequent decades. Cause and effect here are often inextricably fused together.

In contrast to the scriptural learning of the Pharisees, who in their casuistic interpretation of the Torah also concerned themselves intensively with private case law, which to us would seem to belong in the secular sphere, the preaching of Jesus has a quite marked prophetic and religious character. Jesus emerges 'as the one who proclaims and ushers in the coming kingdom of God'.[1] Its dawn is imminent, just about to break, indeed it is already present in a hidden way in the work of Jesus. Thus the demand in the Sermon on the Mount (Matt.6.33) is fundamental to any understanding of his attitude to all earthly goods:

> But seek first the kingdom of God and his righteousness, and all these things shall be yours as well.

For this reason, unlike the scribes, he turns down a request to arbitrate in the case of a disputed legacy:

> Man, who made me a judge or divider over you? (Luke 12.13)

On the contrary, the imminence of the kingdom of God demands freedom over possessions, the renunciation of all care, complete trust in the goodness and providence of the heavenly Father (Matt.6.25-34 = Luke 12.22-32). Service of God and service of mammon are mutually exclusive:

> No one can serve two masters . . . You cannot serve God and mammon (Luke 16.13 = Matt.6.24).

The Aramaic-Phoenician word for possessions or property is clearly used here in a negative sense. Borrowing from contemporary Jewish terminology, the early church could talk directly about 'unrighteous mammon' (Luke 16.19, see above, p.11). Clement of Alexandria supposed that this passage meant that private property was essentially *adikia*, unrighteousness (*Quis dives* 31: GCS 17,180). Perhaps the early church left this Semitic loan-word untranslated because they regarded it almost as the name of an idol: the service of mammon is idolatry. Here possessions acquire a demonic character, because they are a tie to men and close their ears to the summons of the kingdom of God. Jesus' urgent warning against the danger of riches is in accordance with this

fundamental criticism. It should be understood against the
background of his messianic announcement of the imminence
of God, developed in connect with the prophetic pronounce-
ment in Isa.61.1f.:

> The Spirit of the Lord God is upon me,
> because the Lord has anointed me
> to bring good tidings to the poor;
> he has sent me to bind up the broken-hearted,
> to proclaim liberty to the captives
> and the opening of the prison to those who are bound;
> to proclaim the day of the Lord's favour,
> and the day of vengeance of our God;
> to comfort all who mourn;
> to delight those who mourn in Zion.

Luke puts these words in the mouth of Jesus in his first
preaching in his home town of Nazareth (4.16ff.); they recur
in Jesus' reply to John the Baptist (Luke 7.22 = Matt.11.5):
'The poor have the good news preached to them', and above
all in the Beatitudes (Luke 6.20ff.; cf. Polycarp 2.3):

> Blessed are you poor, for yours is the kingdom of God.
> Blessed are you that hunger now, for you shall be satisfied.
> Blessed are you that weep now, for you shall laugh.

Corresponding to the beatitudes on the poor, we find 'woes'
on the rich and those who have plenty (6.24):

> But woe to you that are rich, for you have received your
> consolation.
> Woe to you that are full now, for you shall hunger.
> Woe to you that laugh now, for you shall mourn and weep.

The parable of the rich man and poor Lazarus is similar to
this contrast of beatitudes on the poor and woes on the rich
(Luke 16.19-31). The story of the rich farmer is no less
critical (Luke 12.16-21).

> Fool! This night your soul is required of you; and the
> things you have prepared, whose will they be?

'The deceit of riches' is one of the thorns which choke the

growing seed of the Word and prevent it from bringing forth
fruit (Mark 4.19).

The simile of the needle's eye is even more biting:

> It is easier for a camel to go through the eye of a needle
> than for a rich man to enter the kingdom of God (Mark
> 10.24 par.).

Only God's miracle can save him, 'for all things are possible
with God' (Mark 10.27). It is significant that this uncom-
promising saying was modified in manuscripts at a very early
stage. Also in this context belongs the fact that Jesus himself
had no possessions: 'The Son of man has nowhere to lay his
head' (Matt.8.20 = Luke 9.58), that he required those who
were called to follow him not only to break with their
families (Luke 9.59ff.; 14.26) but also to give up their
possessions (Mark 1.16ff. par.; 10.17ff.,28ff. par.). When he
sends the disciples out he requires extreme poverty of them
(Luke 9.3; 10.4; cf. Mark 6.8f.); he also promises them that
their renunciation of possessions will find recognition with
God (Mark 10.28ff.). Jesus' polemic against concern for
everyday needs (Matt.6.25-34) and his demand to renounce
the use of force and legal proceedings, his requirement of
unconditional generosity, go in the same direction:

> Give to every one who begs from you; and of him who
> takes away your goods, do not ask them again (Luke 6.30;
> cf. Barn.19.11; Did.1.5)

We can understand how at a later date the church father and
ascetic Jerome, who was himself very critical of riches, could
allow the objection to Jesus' demand in Matt.19.29 that 'it is
difficult, harsh and contrary to nature' (*difficile est, durum
est, et contra naturam*). He answers it by the Lord's saying in
Matt.19.12: 'He who is able to receive this, let him receive
it.'[2]

2   *Jesus' Free Attitude to Property*

However, this radical criticism of property and especially of
riches is only one side of Jesus' ministry and preaching. We
should note first that Jesus himself did not come from the

proletariat of day-labourers and landless tenants, but from the middle class of Galilee, the skilled workers. Like his father, he was an artisan, a *tekton*, a Greek word which means mason, carpenter, cartwright and joiner all rolled into one (Mark 6.3). According to Justin Martyr he had 'made yokes and ploughs' (*Dial*.88.8). Two generations later, in the time of Domitian, two of his great-nephews are said to have worked a small piece of land (see below, pp.63f.). As far as we can tell, the disciples whom he called to follow him came from a similar social milieu. Zebedee, the father of James and John, employed day-labourers in his family business as well as his sons (Mark 1.20); another disciple, Levi, was summoned from the seat of custom (Mark 2.14f.) – the first evangelist identifies him with Matthew (Matt.9.9f.; 10.3). Even Jesus' conduct – unlike that of John the Baptist (Matt.11.18; Mark 1.6f.) – was not that of a rigorous ascetic.

Thus Jesus himself took for granted the owning of property in his immediate surroundings. He and his disciples were supported by the means of well-to-do women who followed him (Luke 8.2f.; cf. 10.38f.). In Capernaum he visits the house of his disciple Simon Peter and heals Peter's mother-in-law (Mark 1.29ff.). It is possible that this house served as a base for him during his preaching journeys. Excavations suggest that it perhaps became a house church at a later date; a Byzantine church was then erected on the site. Arguing against Pharisaic casuistry over sacrifice, Jesus enjoins that parents must be supported from their children's possessions, and refers back to the fourth commandment (Mark 7.9f.par.). In the same way, possessions are to be used to help those in need (Mark 12.41ff.; Matt.6.2; 25.40; Luke 10.30-37). In requiring money to be lent without hope of return (Matt.5.42 = Luke 6.30;6.34), Jesus presupposes property that can be lent. The chief publican Zacchaeus is ready to give half his possessions to the poor and to make amends fourfold to those who have been cheated: but he is not required to give up all his possessions (Luke 10.8f.). Jesus did not avoid contact with the rich and the privileged by any means; he was invited to banquets by them (Luke 7.36ff.; 11.37; 14.1,12; Mark 14.3ff.), and particularly by those with the worst reputation, the tax and excise farmers, who collaborated with the foreign occupying power (Mark 2.13-17). He was not an ascetic and was glad to join in festivals (John 2.1ff.); this made him incur the mockery of the pious:

> Behold, a glutton and a drunkard, a friend of tax-collectors and sinners (Matt.11.19 = Luke 7.34).

The one who is fond of celebrations and rejects fasting because it is out of place in the joy of the messianic feast (Mark 2.18ff.) does not look on property with the critical and fanatic eyes of the ascetic rigorist.

He held fellowship meals with his disciples, and for these, as the last supper shows, they relied on the support of well-to-do house-owners (Mark 14.14f.). Finally, it is striking that in his parables he often depicts the social milieu of Galilee with its great landowners, landlords, administrators and slaves, without engaging in any specifically social polemic (apart from the two parables mentioned above). Even servitude for debt and the use of slaves as entrepreneurs and bankers to increase the cash left with them (Matt.25.14ff. = Luke 19.12ff., cf. p.71 below) merely serve as a simile to portray God's demand. In the parable of the labourers in the vineyard those who had worked hard all day complain that they have been paid too little in comparison with those who came later and received the same wages. The employer answers with a classic definition of property which remains valid down to the present day:

> Am I not allowed to do what I choose with what belongs to me? (Matt.20.15)

In his parables Jesus evidently liked to single out unusual, vivid situations and typical situations of injustice; however, he did not use them for the 'social protest' which is so beloved today, but for a positive demonstration of God's will in respect of his coming kingdom.

3 The Imminence of the Rule of God and the Love of the Father

How are we to explain this contradiction? We should certainly not be in too much of a hurry to simplify it and rob it of its acuteness, say by explaining that property was legitimated by Jesus as something entrusted to men by the Creator, who required faithful stewardship of it. Jesus only fights against its misuse. This favourite interpretation of property as a 'loan' entrusted by God, which has played so great a role in modern Christian discussion of property, can certainly be found in the preaching of Jesus or of the early church (Luke 16.13; cf. 16.9, and I Cor.4.7f. in a metaphorical sense), but it is not of central significance. Nor is it a specifically Christian idea. It appears in the Old Testament and Judaism, and even among the Greeks. Thus in the fine verses of Euripides, we find:

What is your profit? Profit but in name.
Enough is quite sufficient for the wise.
We are but stewards of the gifts of heaven.
When gods desire, they take them back again.
Possessions are not ours to call our own (*Phoen.*553ff.).

To understand Jesus' attitude to property we must return to his messianic preaching of the imminence of the kingdom of God which, in contrast to that of his forerunner, John the Baptist, no longer stands under the sign of judgment but under that of the all-victorious love of God. Because men experience forgiveness of their guilt, they themselves can forgive; because they receive the assurance that God's goodness supports and sustains their life, they must no longer fret about their everyday needs, but can pray like children, 'Give us this day our daily bread' (Luke 11.3 = Matt.6.11). Because they themselves have encountered the heavenly Father's boundless love, they must not relapse into anxiety about asserting themselves; they can even dare to love their enemies and can renounce the compulsion of using force in return (Matt.5.38-48; cf. Luke 6.27-36). Anyone who is dependent on his possessions and as a result forgets his neighbour lives in this state of anxious egoistic self-assertion:

he rejects God's commandment to love for the sake of the idol of mammon. God is near to the poor, the despised, the sick, as they stand before him with empty hands, like the prodigal son standing before his generous father. Jesus was not interested in any new theories about the rightness or wrongness of possessions in themselves, about the origin of property or its better distribution; rather he adopted the same scandalously free and untrammelled attitude to property as to the powers of the state, the alien Roman rule and its Jewish confederates. The imminence of the kingdom of God robs all these things of their power *de facto*, for in it 'many that are first will be last, and the last first' (Mark 10.31 = Matt.19.30; 20.16; Luke 13.30). Of course, Jesus attacks mammon with the utmost severity where it has captured men's hearts, because this gives it demonic character by which it blinds men's eyes to God's will — in concrete terms, to their neighbour's needs. Mammon is worshipped wherever men long for riches, are tied to riches, keep on increasing their possessions and want to dominate as a result of them. This radical criticism of riches may be rejected as hopeless enthusiasm, like the demand to renounce force and to love one's enemies, but particularly today, when there is so much talk of a 'definite utopia', one might well ask whether not only Christianity, but the whole of mankind does not need the goad which Jesus' message provides. Such different figures as Leo Tolstoi, Albert Schweitzer, Mahatma Gandhi, Toyohito Kagawa and Martin Luther King may be cited as examples.

The example of Jesus and his closest disciples shows that Jesus' message was also translated into action. Jesus required of his disciples that they should break with their families and renounce their own possessions, so that they could be like him in being completely prepared for serving the cause of the kingdom of God. His scandalous 'social' preaching was certainly one reason why he was condemned and executed by the Romans as a messianic pretender and rebel, though he did not follow the Zealots in demanding change in the system by force. Rather, the power that went out from him was much stronger than all human force.

4

The 'Love Communism' of the Primitive Community

The beginnings of the early community in Jerusalem after the appearances of the risen Jesus show that his message continued to have an effect.

I had already said that Luke has stylized his picture of the early community along the lines of popular philosophical terminology (see pp.8f. above). For example, the repetition of the formula 'they had all things in common' (*panta koina*) is reminiscent of the proverb coined by Aristotle (*Eth.Nic.* 1168b), 'the possession of friends is something held in common' (*koina ta philon*). Aristotle also introduces the term 'one soul', used by Luke in this context (4.32). However, it remains an open question whether primitive Christian sharing of goods, described by Ernst Troeltsch as 'love communism', is simply an idealistic invention of the author, as radical criticism assumes, or has some basis in history. 'Radical criticism' can refer to the fact that Luke makes apparently contradictory statements. At one point he talks about a complete sharing of goods (Acts 2.44; 4.32), but on the other hand it is reported that individuals like Barnabas and Ananias and Sapphira sold their land and brought the proceeds to the apostles. Of course, Ananias and Sapphira are said to have kept back half the proceeds and to have been punished promptly as a result (5.1-11).

It is striking that the atheistic philosopher Ernst Bloch had more confidence in the communism of the early community in Jerusalem than so-called radical criticism:

This community, built up on a communism of love, wants neither rich men nor poor men in a forced or ascetic sense. 'No one said that any of the things which he possessed was his own, but they had everything in common' (Acts 4.32). Their possessions were assembled from gifts, sufficient for the short interval which Jesus had still granted to the old earth. His saying about the lilies of the field and the birds of the air is by no means economically naive, but is deliberately enthusiastic. For if the steps of those who are to bury the world and its care are at the door, economic concern for the day after tomorrow is stupid.[1]

Here Ernst Bloch has a clearer view of the historical conditions than many so-called critical exegetes. This is the case at three points:

1. He bases the sharing of goods in the early community on the strong influence which the eschaton had on them: after the appearances of the risen Christ they expected him soon to come again as their Lord. This point recedes into the background in Luke, so it is easy to misunderstand his account.

2. Bloch stresses the spontaneous and voluntary character of this 'love communism'. It was not organized, nor was it subjected to external compulsion. The decisive thing was *koinonia*, not organization.

By contrast, the sharing of goods among the Essenes was strictly organized and fixed by law. It originally grew out of the protest against the unbounded quest of the Jewish aristocracy for wealth, during the Maccabean rebellion (1 QpHab.8.10ff.), and also had eschatological and utopian motives. Soon, however, it was given a firm legalistic structure. To some degree it became the law for the Jewish way of poverty (see above, p.19). According to the rule of Qumran, every novice who entered the order had to leave his possessions with the overseer. If after a year he was accepted, he had to make them over to the order (1 QS 1.11ff. and Josephus, *Bell*.2,122). All the needs of the members of the community were met from these resources and as a result of their own work in agriculture or crafts. In this way the order seems to have accumulated considerable riches. When Josephus says that the Essenes were 'despisers of riches', he is only talking of individual property. Common possessions were meant to make 'humiliating poverty' and 'inordinate riches' impossible. The rules were strict: anyone who made false statements about his possessions was excluded from the community for a year and had his rations cut by a quarter. The early community certainly did not have so well organized and forcible a 'sharing of goods'.

3. Bloch rightly refers back to the preaching of Jesus with its criticism of 'unrighteous mammon' and of anxiety. Jesus' message and his way of life were still remembered, and it would be quite incomprehensible if they did not continue to have some influence. Here the early church in Jerusalem was simply continuing Jesus' carefree attitude to the goods of this world. In view of the imminence of the coming Son of man, who was identical with Jesus, the barrier of possessions, which had done more than any other power to separate men down the millennia, had been brought down; anything which the individual had was freely put at the disposal of the community, as far as it was needed. The alleged contradiction between the two remarks in Luke, that 'no one said of his possessions that they belonged to him' and that individual landowners like the Levite Barnabas from Cyprus sold their land or houses and put the money at the disposal of the community, is only an apparent one. The mention of Barnabas does not point to a unique and special instance in Jerusalem. Barnabas was mentioned because he was known to the church in Antioch, by whom this piece of tradition was preserved. The church proudly pointed to him as an authority who had himself had a part in the 'love communism' of the Jerusalem church. This note (Acts 4.36) is presumably one of the references to Luke's Antiochene source. A charismatic-enthusiastic community was formed which assembled for daily worship; common meals were held (Acts 2.42); concern over possessions and the future retreated completely into the background; people lived from hand to mouth. The Lord was very near, and he had told people not to worry. The only real concern was missionary preaching among the Jews, including the Greek-speaking

diaspora Jews who had also settled in Jerusalem. The daily needs of the community were met by selling the possessions of those who had such resources; social distinctions were virtually abolished, and there were no longer any poor in the community (Acts 4.34). Yet others put their houses at the disposal of the community as meeting places, like Mary, the mother of John Mark (Acts 12.12). No one bothered with the legal questions connected with property, with entries in land registers or the like. The things of this age had become inessential. Organization was kept to a minimum, and in view of the intensive expectation of the return of Jesus, further forward planning was completely absent. As a result, difficulties in distribution arose, especially as the community grew quickly. Acts 6.1ff. reports how the 'widows' in the Greek-speaking part of the community were neglected at the daily distribution and how disputes arose as a result. In view of the community's glowing expectation of an imminent end and the enthusiasm brought about by the experience of the spirit, people had no interest in economic production organized on community lines, like that among the Essenes of Qumran. The pressure from the Jewish environment and the famine under Claudius during the forties (Acts II.28) also contributed to the considerable economic distress suffered by the community in Jerusalem. As a result the community in Antioch — and probably other mission churches too — had to leap to the rescue. The collections enjoined on Paul and Barnabas at the Apostolic Council at Jerusalem about AD 48, which the apostle was particularly concerned to achieve among his mission communities, must also be understood against this background. Twice he calls the original community in Jerusalem 'the poor' (Gal.2.10 and Rom.15.26). On the one hand this is a religious title of honour, but at the same time it indicates the economic distress in this community. The Jewish Christians in Palestine and Syria who had separated from the mainstream church later called themselves 'Ebionites', in other words 'the poor'.

5

Paul and the Communities of the Gentile Christian Mission

1   The New Situation

In the Pauline mission communities and in the later development of primitive Christianity, we no longer come across the
eschatological and enthusiastic form of sharing goods which
we assume to have been practised by the earliest community
in Jerusalem, on the basis of the reports in Acts. The reason
for this is first, that the tension of the expectation of an
imminent end was relaxed in favour of the task of world-wide
mission, and secondly, that in the long run the form of 'love
communism' practised in Jerusalem was just not possible. It
was impossible to maintain a sharing of goods in a free form,
without the kind of fixed organization and common production which we find, say, at Qumran. Further external
compulsion was indispensable, and it was precisely this that
was felt to be unacceptable. Free, charismatic community
rather than a legalistic idea of order is typical of primitive
Christianity. Even the Pauline communities did not have any
clear organization or strict direction of the community. This
only developed during the second century. The admonition
of the apostle to the members of the community in
Thessalonica that they are to earn their daily bread by
manual labour, so that they do not cause any offence to
outsiders and do not have to endure the lack of anything,
shows that the problem of supporting themselves and owning
possessions in conjunction with an enthusiastic expectation
of the *parousia* still continued to concern at least some of
those within the Pauline mission area (I Thess.4.12; 5.14).
Presumably there were some who simply put their hands in

their pockets and let themselves be looked after by others. II Thessalonians accentuates this admonition (3.7ff.), coming to a climax in a maxim which was taken into the Soviet Russian constitution: 'If any one will not work, let him not eat.'

At least in the genuine letters of Paul, the question of poverty and riches, of possessions and lack of possessions, is left entirely on one side. The term 'rich' (*plousios*) appears only once in Paul, transferred to the pre-existent Christ, and not therefore in a social context (II Cor.8.9), whereas in one passage he refers the word 'poor' to himself ((II Cor.6.10). In so doing he expresses the contradiction in his life as an apostle:

> As poor, yet making many rich;
> as having nothing, and yet possessing everything.

Paul himself had no possessions. During his missionary journeys he earned his keep by hard manual labour as a tentmaker (Acts 18.3). He did not ask the communities to look after him (I Cor.9), but accepted support offered freely with gratitude (Phil. 2.25ff.; 4.15ff.). Accustomed to extreme need, he was glad when he was sufficiently cared for (Phil.4.11f.).

2   The Social Structure of the Gentile Christian Communities

The communities founded by Paul were certainly not well-to-do. Thus he writes to the Christians in Corinth:

> For consider your call, brethren;
> not many of you were wise according to worldly standards, not many were of noble birth (I Cor.1.26).

Of course this much-quoted remark should not be interpreted in the wrong way. Paul says 'not many', not 'none at all'. We cannot infer from this passage that the Pauline mission communities were composed only of the proletariat and slaves, nor may we make Paul an advocate of the Jewish way of poverty. What Pliny the Younger, as governor of Bithynia in Asia Minor, wrote to the emperor Trajan, also applied to the communities founded during the mission of the apostle to the Gentiles: 'many . . . of every class . . . are endangered now and will be endangered in the future' (by the new 'superstition': *multi enim . . . omnis ordinis . . . vocantur in periculum et vocabuntur*). That is, there were members of Christian communities in all strata of the populace, from slaves and freedmen to the local aristocracy, the decurions, and in some circumstances even to the nobility of the Senate. The old dispute whether the nephew of the emperor Domitian, Flavius Clemens and his wife, Flavia Domitilla, because of their Judaizing tendencies — thus Dio Cassius 67,14,1f. — or Flavius Clemens' niece of the same name, because of her conversion to Christianity — thus Eusebius, HE 3,18,4 — were executed or exiled by the emperor, has still not been settled. It shows that we must at least reckon with the possibility that in individual cases the new faith quickly penetrated to the heights of society. Evidence for this increases greatly in the second half of the second century (see below, pp.64f.).

The majority of early Christians will have belonged to the 'middle class' of antiquity from which the 'godfearers' of the Jewish mission were recruited (cf. Acts 13.43,50; 16.14; 17.4,17; 18.7). Women from the upper classes may also have been won over. It should also be noted that the Pauline mission was exclusively limited to the cities, and hardly reached country people. Even the lowest strata of ancient cities had a better social status than the uneducated and downtrodden tenants and peasants in the villages. For Pliny, it was a sign of the dangerous aggressiveness of the new sect that 'the contagion of that superstition has penetrated not the cities only, but the villages and the country' (*Ep*.10,96,9). But until the third century that was the exception. In the footsteps of Paul, the Christian faith, like all the missionary religions in antiquity, remained predominantly a city religion. Of course, Pliny's agitated report could be contrasted with the judgment of the rhetorician Aelius Aristides, written down about a generation later. Comparing the Christians with the Cynics, he stresses 'that they neither worship the gods, nor sit on city councils' (*Or.*46, II,404, ed. Dindorf); but this only says that because of the religious duties bound up with municipal offices they could not undertake posts of this kind. This remains the case down to the third century. The Pauline epistles and even more Luke's Acts of the Apostles (see p.64 below) point to individual Christians from the upper classes. In Corinth they included Erastus, the city treasurer (Rom.16.23), Crispus, the ruler of the synagogue (Acts 18.8), Stephanas and his household (I Cor.1.16; 16.15,17), Prisca and Aquila, who evidently had a business with branches and not only employed Paul in it but also went bail for him (Acts 18.2,18,26; Rom.16.3); in Colossae, Philemon, who not only had the slave Onesimus, but also presided over a 'house church'; in Laodicea, Nymphas (Philemon 2; Col.4.15). The list could be continued, and the role of well-to-do women should not be overlooked. It was probably the rule that not only the 'father of the house' but also the whole household dependent on him, including the slaves, were baptized at the same time. These names are mentioned because prominent Christians of this kind and their households provided bases for mission. At the same time, they stood out because on the whole they were the relatively rare exceptions.

Paul himself says that the communities were predominantly poor and we have no reason for mistrusting him. Thus he speaks of the 'extreme poverty' of the churches in Macedonia (II Cor.8.2), which still did not prevent them from devoting themselves with great self-sacrifice to the decisive collection for the original community in Jerusalem. Nevertheless, the scandals at the eucharist in Corinth (I Cor.11.20ff.) show that at least at the beginning gross differences could exist between the relatively well-to-do and the poor. Individual members of the church evidently confused it with a Dionysian festival and behaved accordingly, whereas others 'went hungry'. Newly-converted Hellenistic Gentile Christians from the Greek metropolis and port first had to learn to take social responsibility for their poorer fellow-members, since Hellenistic religions — which were very strongly oriented on class lines — hardly knew them. The lawyer Apuleius had to pay dearly in Corinth for the mysteries of Isis and later incurred additional expense in Rome at the mysteries of Osiris. He emerged from all this on the verge of financial ruin (Apuleius, *Met.* 11,22,2; 23,1;

24,6; 28.1ff.) The missionary expansion of a new religion was not least suspect because of practices of this kind; similar insinuations were made about Paul (II Cor.2.17; 4.2; 11.13). This was probably one of the reasons why, in contrast to the Jerusalem missionaries, the apostle refused support from the communities and supported himself by his own manual labour (I Cor.9.6,13ff., see above, p.36). In his ethical admonitions he did not require complete abolition of differences in means, but looked for active and effective brotherly love (II Cor.8.13ff.). This means that the 'abundance' of some is to supply the 'want' of the brethren – e.g. in Jerusalem – 'that there may be equality (*isotes*)'. Similarly, in the paraenetic parts of his letters and elsewhere one can find the appeal to generosity and hospitality which was also already traditional in Judaism (Rom.12.13), for 'he who sows sparingly will also reap sparingly, and he who sows bountifully will also reap bountifully' (II Cor.9.6f.). The gifts of love not only supply the needs of the brethren, but also lead to grateful praise of God among those who receive them (II Cor.9.12). Conversely, in the so-called catalogue of vices he warns against avarice and cupidity (Rom.1.29; I Cor.5.10f.; 6.10; II Cor.9.5f.). The later epistle to the Colossians identifies these vices directly with idolatry (3.5).

3   The Eschatological Relativization of Property

Paul shares with Jesus and the first community in Jerusalem the view that the imminence of the *parousia* makes the possession of property a relative matter: 'The appointed time has grown very short' (I Cor.7.29). Even if the task of extending his mission to the ends of the then known world, as far as Spain, lies between the present and the *parousia*, the end is nevertheless near:

> The night is far gone, the day is at hand;
> Let us then cast off the works of darkness and put on the armour of light (Rom.13.12).

His summons to obedience to the state powers, which comes to a climax in his admonition to obedience (13.7), must also be seen in this eschatological perspective. Certainly, through

Christ all believers are freed and reconciled with God and their neighbour. The limits set by nation, race, class and — one may also add — property no longer stand. In the community the believer has restored to him the lost image of God, so that there is no longer

> Greek and Jew, circumcised and uncircumcised, barbarian, Scythian (the allegedly sub-human race in antiquity, see above p.5), slave, free man, but Christ is all and in all (Col.3.11; cf. Gal. 3.28).

The revolutionary force of statements like this, which founded a new community in antiquity, can hardly be measured. Boundaries were overcome here which hitherto had been regarded as impassable throughout antiquity. But precisely because in reality they are already free, slaves are now not to seek to become freemen quickly, nor are Gentiles to go over to Judaism and vice versa. Were they to do this, they would be giving recognition to the old forces of this world, which have been robbed of their power and whose end is imminent. Paul admonishes the Corinthians: 'Do not become slaves of men. So, brethren, in whatever state each was called, there let him remain with God'(I Cor.7.23f.). This also applies to the question of property:

> Further, that those . . . who buy be as though they had no goods, and those who deal with the world as though they had no dealings with it. For the form of this world is passing away (7.29ff.).

Here we have a revolution in the standard of values previously taken for granted, the gaining of freedom on the basis of a 'detachment' of the believer, motivated by the nearness of the Lord and the end of the world. What is accepted or takes place here and now is neither what ultimately matters, nor is it the power that determines men. Here we have to some degree Paul's equivalent to the commandment 'Do not be anxious' in the preaching of Jesus (cf. I Cor.7.32ff.; Matt.6.25ff. = Luke 12.22ff.). Paul automatically follows the promise 'The Lord is at hand!' with the admonition 'Do not be anxious' (Phil.4.5f.)

This freedom following from the 'detachment' achieved by

the believer continued when the imminent expectation of the *parousia* died down and people began to reckon with a — relatively — long duration of history. It gave the small 'sect' of Christians the strength to bear all the insults, oppression and persecution from the Roman state authorities which came during the first three centuries and to overcome them. Without any external force, but simply through the inner power of the words and actions of love, Christians succeeded in conquering the Roman empire.

Paul already found the basis for this detachment in the presence of salvation: 'For our citizenship is in heaven' (Phil.3.20). It will only be made manifest through the *parousia*: 'from where we await a saviour, the Lord Jesus Christ...' Colossians 3.3f is very similar: 'Your life is hid with Christ in God. When Christ who is our life appears, then you also will appear with him in glory.' In concrete terms, that means that concern for property and possessions had become a quite secondary matter. At the same time, it also means that the first Christians simply were not aware of the question which concerns us so much today: 'How can we make a better future for our threatened world?' They cannot give us a practicable programme of social ethics to solve the question of possessions, which has become so acute today as a result of industrialization. Not only is it that our world-wide industrial society, with all its technology, can only to a very limited degree be compared with the predominantly social structure of late antiquity; since the first Christians were a tiny minority, who were also politically suspect, they could not strive in their ethical action for the social reform of the Roman empire of the time. They had to limit themselves to the construction of a community ethics within an unfriendly, indeed hostile world, sustained by true love and humanity — but at the same time quite 'transitory' (I Cor.13.10). The best to be expected from the political authorities was tolerance, and this was only granted in AD 311; as a rule people believed that they would fall into the hands of anti-Christ, who would mount a last attack on the church and would then be vanquished at the *parousia* of Christ.

6

Attempts at Solving the Question of Property in the Community Ethics of Early Christianity

It follows from what has been said that the ethics of the early church was exclusively community ethics, binding on the community of believers. This is also the case with the question of property. Like the question of slavery, within the Christian community it seemed largely to have been solved. True, Paul sends the runaway slave Onesimus back to his Christian master Philemon, but he asks Philemon to accept the fugitive as a brother with equal rights. The requirement of the Didache, which was written in Syria at the beginning of the second century, is simple:

> Do not turn away the needy, but share everything with your brother, and do not say that it is your own (Did.4.8).

This attitude created a new structure within the Christian communities which is unique in antiquity. Travellers found a hospitable welcome (Heb.13.2; I Clem.10-12). Those who were capable of work had a right to work, and the disabled were adequately supported. The Christian 'philosopher' Aristides, who sent the first Apologia that we have to the emperor Hadrian about AD 125, sums up this new social attitude of the Christians in a few moving words:

> They walk in all humility and kindness, and falsehood is not found among them, and they love one another. They despise not the widow, and grieve not the orphan. He that hath distributeth liberally to him that hath not. If they see a stranger, they bring him under their roof, and rejoice over him, as it were their own brother: for they call

themselves brethren, not after the flesh, but after the spirit and in God; but when one of their poor passes away from the world, and any of them see him, then he provides for his burial according to his ability; and if they hear that any of their number is imprisoned or oppressed for the name of their Messiah, all of them provide for his needs, and if it is possible that he may be delivered, they deliver him. And if there is among them a man that is poor and needy, and they have not an abundance of necessaries, they fast two or three days that they may supply the needy with their necessary food.(15.7f.).

The Pseudo-Clementine romance cited above (p.1), puts forward what virtually amounts to a social programme for the community:

> Give the unskilled an opportunity to earn their daily bread; give work to those who can do it, take care to look after those who are unable to work (*Ep.Clem.*8,6: GCS 42,12).

For Cyprian, the bishop and martyr in Carthage (died AD 258), it went without saying that the community should support at its own expense, in case of emergency, an actor who had given up his profession when he became a Christian and was also prohibited from teaching acting, bound up as it was with pagan mythology. There was, however, a significant qualification:

> He must be content with frugal but innocent food. And let him not think that he is redeemed by an allowance to cease from sinning, since this is an advantage not to us, but to himself. What more he may wish he may seek thence, from such gain as takes men away from the banquet of Abraham, and Isaac, and Jacob, and leads them down, sadly and perniciously fattened in this world, to the eternal torments of hunger and thirst . . . If the church with you is not sufficient for this, to afford support for those in need, he may transfer himself to us (in Carthage), and here receive what may be necessary to him for food and clothing.[1]

By about AD 250, the Roman community was looking after about 1500 people in distress regularly, with only about 100 clergy. About eighty years earlier, Bishop Dionysius of Corinth had confirmed that this generosity of the Roman church was not limited to its own poor, but extended far beyond the boundaries of Rome:

> For this has been your custom from the beginning: to do good in divers ways to all the brethren, and to send supplies to many churches in every city: now relieving the poverty of the needy, now making provision, by the supplies which you have been sending from the beginning, for brethren in the mines (forced labour imposed by the state).[2]

Ignatius (about AD 116) is probably already alluding to this Roman custom when he describes the Roman community as 'leading in love' (*Rom.*, proem.) This tradition of many-sided and effective readiness to help among Roman Christians in the second and third centuries cannot simply be explained in terms of ecclesiastical or secular politics. Behind it stood a real solidarity of Christian faith. The lack of demands made by the clergy corresponds to this readiness to help. Thus while Origen can appeal to I Cor.9.14 and stress the right of the clergy to receive support, at the same time he adds that they should only ask for basic necessities, i.e. no more than the poor receive, so that the latter are not deprived of anything.[3]

In cases of catastrophe, readiness to help knew no bounds. When barbarian nomads laid waste Numidia in AD 253 and made many Christians homeless, Cyprian collected a spontaneous contribution of 100,000 sesterces for those who had been affected. This was from the relatively small community in Carthage — Cyprian claimed that he still knew all its members (*Ep.*62). We hear of similar generous help — even towards pagans — in epidemics of plague in Carthage, Alexandria and elsewhere.[4] This selfless, widespread care was all the more effective since from the second half of the second century the Roman empire was involved in an increasingly severe political and social crisis, which came to a climax in the middle of the third century. Even in the fourth century the emperor Julian the Apostate (361-363), an enemy of the Christians, told the pagan high priest Arsacius of Galatia 'that the godless Galileans feed not only their (poor) but ours also', whereas the pagan cult, in the revival of which the ruler was so interested, was a complete failure in the welfare of the poor (*Ep.* 84; p.430d, ed.Bidez). In this way the early Christian communities abolished complete penury among their own members and at the same time made a very good impression on outsiders, since such comprehensive care was alien to the pagan world.

However, real communism of goods no longer played a decisive part among the communities. As has already been said, it was hardly possible without some organized pressure. A radical demand for it was only made by outsiders, like the Gnostic Epiphanes, son of Carpocrates who founded the Carpocratians. He referred both to the philosophical doctrine of natural law and to Pauline freedom in his demand for complete equality of possessions:·

'The righteousness of God is a kind of fellowship on the basis of equality . . . For he makes no distinction between rich and poor.' On the other hand, the individual human laws contradict the divine command: 'As the laws could not punish human ignorance, they taught men to transgress the law (of God)', a thesis which the author bases on Rom.7.7 (Clem. Alex., *Strom*.III,6,1).

Faithful to ancient utopian pictures, he also argued for the sharing of wives: property becomes theft, exclusive possession of one wife becomes adultery. But this Gnostic Paulinism of an Alexandrian intellectual who is said to have died at the age of seventeen remained completely ineffectual. It was only of interest to fathers hostile to the Gnostics. Community of goods appeared on quite another basis among the Coenobitic monks of Egypt in the first half of the fourth century. Here the gospels' radical criticism of 'unrighteous mammon' comes to life again. Whether other influences — say the recollection of the Jewish sect of the Therapeutae, the Egyptian counterpart to the Essenes in Palestine — also play their part remains questionable. It is significant that such community was only possible because the individual subjected himself in complete obedience to the 'abbot' or to the monastery.

Christian communities may have attempted to solve the social 'problem' in their own sphere in a way unique in antiquity, but the question of the justice or injustice of property in excess of basic needs, i.e. of the possibility of reconciling riches with Christian life, remained an open question.

The answer to it was not a clear one, but took a variety of directions. We shall limit ourselves to three aspects: the radical criticism of property, the philosophical and ascetic motive of self-sufficiency and the compromise of effective compensation.

The Criticism of Property in Apocalyptic Christianity and its Tradition

1 The Influence of Crude Apocalyptic Polemic

These communities which continued the tradition of Palestinian Jewish Christianity, with its apocalyptic stamp, condemned riches in a form which was often quite crude. Thus the Epistle of James sharply attacks the way in which the rich and well-to-do have pride of place over the poor when the church is gathered together, for

> Has not God chosen those who are poor in the world to be rich in faith and heirs of the kingdom which he has promised to those who love him? . . . Is it not the rich who oppress you, is it not they who drag you into court? Is it not they who blaspheme that honourable name by which you are called? (James 2.1-7)

Similarly, the author utters a lament on the rich which is reminiscent of the polemic of the Jewish prophets and apocalyptic writers:

> Come now, you rich, weep and howl for the miseries that are coming upon you. Your riches have rotted and your garments are moth-eaten. Your gold and silver have rusted, and their rust will be evidence against you and will eat up your flesh like fire . . .
> Behold, the wages of the labourers who mowed your fields, which you kept back by fraud, cry out; and the cries of the harvesters have reached the ears of the Lord of hosts. You have lived on the earth in luxury and in pleasure; you have fattened your hearts in a day of

slaughter. You have condemned, you have killed the righteous man; he does not resist you (James 5.1-6).

These verses express equally both the oppression and also the revolt of the simple people in agricultural Palestine. It can be seen here that primitive Christianity was also a movement that was critical of society — even if it did not resort to revolutionary expedients, but delivered over the oppressors to God's judgment.

We find similar tones in the Revelation of John. Here the visionary exiled to Patmos 'on account of the word of God and the testimony of Jesus' (1.9) sees the final climax of the godlessness of the Roman empire in the rule of the anti-Christ, who persecutes the community mercilessly to the point of economic boycott (13.16f.). In glowing colours he depicts the fall of the whore of Babylon who is enthroned on the seven hills, i.e. the world city of Rome. At the same time its fall represents the end of inconceivable riches, and the writer's scorn for the consumption of luxuries can clearly be heard in his words:

> And the merchants of the earth weep and mourn for her, since no one buys their cargo any more, cargo of gold, silver, jewels and pearls, fine linen, purple, silk and scarlet, all kinds of scented wood, all articles of ivory, all articles of costly wood, bronze, iron and marble, cinnamon, spice, incense, myrrh, frankincense, wine, oil, fine flour and wheat, cattle and sheep, horses and chariots, and slaves . . .
>
> The merchants of these wares, who gained wealth from her, will stand far off, in fear of her torment, weeping and mourning aloud, 'Alas, alas, for the great city . . . in one hour all this wealth has been laid waste.'

God's judgment brings the annihilation of the luxurious civilization of this metropolis which dominated the whole world:

> For thy merchants were the great men of the earth, and all nations were deceived by thy sorcery. And in her was found the blood of prophets and of saints, and of all who have been slain on earth (18.23f.).

Here the bitter rejection of riches and luxury is associated with crude opposition to the world power which wants to force Christians to acknowledge its pseudo-religious ruler-ideology through bloody persecution: 'A death sentence is pronounced on the world of Roman capitalism and its state.'[1] The aggressive, zealous undertone, the joy at the expected annihilation of the enemy, cannot of course be overlooked. At this point the popular hope of early Christianity was still closely bound up with the expectations of Jewish apocalyptic, which expressed its hope for the fall of 'godless rule' even in official Jewish prayers. There was also delight in depicting the torments of the godless and unmerciful rich in the apocalyptic accounts of hell (Apoc. Pet.30; Act.Thom.56; Sib.2,252ff.; cf. also already Luke 16.23ff.). The counterpart, the picture of the Christians' own hope, had quite realistic paradisal features. This can be seen from the Jewish-Christian Sibyllines, where apocalyptic themes are combined with the dream of the golden age (see pp.4f. above):

> And there are threefold springs of wine and milk and
>   honey.
> Earth the same for all, not divided by walls
> And fences, will then bear fruits more abundant
> Of its own accord; livelihood held in common, wealth
>   unapportioned.
> No pauper is there, no rich man, nor any tyrant,
> No slave, nor again any great, nor shall any be small,
> No kings, no rulers; but all share in common.[2]

Even the dream of 'freedom from rule' is not a modern invention.

2   Thorough-going Criticism of Riches in the Community

Even within the community, however, immoderate possessions remained a stumbling block. In the apocalypse of Hermas (*Vis.*III 6,5-7), composed in Rome during the first half of the second century, the author compares the rich men in the community to round stones which are not suitable for building the church:

> 'When persecution comes, because of their wealth and

because of business they deny their Lord.' Hermas asks, 'Then when will they be useful for the building?' He is given the answer: 'When their wealth, which leads their soul astray, shall be cut off from them, then they will be useful to God. For just as the round stone cannot become spare, unless something be cut off and taken from it, so too they who have riches in this world cannot be useful to the Lord unless their wealth be cut away from them.'

Even the author, a small businessman living in Rome who perhaps also had some land to call his own, is regarded as 'rich'; his business separated him from God (*Vis*.II 3,1; cf. III 6,7). For 'riches make a man blind and blunt him towards the truth', even if they do not necessarily lead to his complete downfall (*Sim*.IX 30,4-31,2).

In the apocryphal writing *The Acts of Peter and the Twelve Apostles*, found at Nag Hammadi and only recently published,[3] Peter and the Twelve are sent out to heal the poor, but they are to have nothing at all to do with 'the rich of the city', who do not ask after Christ, 'but delight in their riches and their contempt for men'. For giving preference to the rich in the communities only brings about sin and transgression.[4]

Critical remarks of this kind can be multiplied at will, for example from the rigorist Tertullian, who could describe God as one who 'despises the rich and pleads the cause of the poor' (*Adv.Marc*.4,15). Christ, who himself was utterly poor, 'always justifies the poor and condemns the rich' (*De Patientia* 7,2f.). To the rich, luxury-loving matrons the churches seem small and contemptible: 'It is difficult to find a rich man in the house of God.' But even Tertullian cannot deny that they are there (*Ad Uxorem* 2,8,3, see pp.60f. below). The apologist Tertullian's Christian consciousness corresponds to his social criticism:

> Whereas among pagan families, 'as a rule brotherliness ceases' when it is a question of family wealth, 'one in mind and soul, we do not hesitate to share our earthly goods with one another. All things are common among us but our wives.'[5]

However, the collections at worship described below (p.67)

show that even in Tertullian we may no longer presuppose a real 'sharing of goods'. The sharpness with which he attacks luxury and the search for pleasure and finery shows that these vices could already be found in the Christian community in Carthage about AD 200.

A little later the apologist Minucius Felix sounds almost like a Cynic philosopher in explaining why Christians despise riches:

> All of which things, if we do not lust after, we possess. Therefore, as he who treads a road is the happier the lighter he walks, so happier is he in this journey of life who lifts himself along in poverty, and does not breathe heavily under the burden of riches. And yet even if we thought wealth useful to us, we should ask it of God. Assuredly he might be able to indulge us in some measure, whose is the whole; but we would rather despise riches than possess them; we desire rather innocency, we rather entreat for patience, we prefer being good to being prodigal.[6]

3   The Motive of Asceticism

At this point the motive of asceticism comes very clearly to the fore in the rejection of riches; it is to gain increasing significance for the further development of the church. Eusebius reports that even one of the greatest theologians of the church, Origen, lived in extreme personal poverty (HE 6,3). There were wandering ascetics in Syria as early as the second century AD who had no possessions; we meet them in the Didache (11.5ff.). The ascetic stamp of the ideal of poverty to be found in the apocryphal Acts of Thomas, coming from the Syrian church at the beginning of the third century, is even more marked.

> Thomas, the twin brother of Jesus, 'eats only bread with salt, and his drink is water, and he wears (only) one garment . . . and takes.nothing from anyone, and what he has he gives to others'.[7] God has 'brought him into the poverty of the world, and invited him to true riches'. At God's command he becomes 'poor and needy and a stranger and a slave, despised and a prisoner and hungry

and thirsty and naked and weary'.[8] The theme of the radical *imitatio Christi* here is evident. For Christ himself deceived the demons 'by his form most unsightly and by his poverty and need'.[9] Thomas's preaching against covetousness, riches and gluttony is very much oriented on the preaching of Jesus, particularly the command not to be anxious. But at the same time it has a feature which does not occur in the message of Jesus. 'The wealth which is left here, and the possession which (comes) of the earth (and) grows old . . . support the body itself', that is, they bind men to transitory matter.[10] Thus sexual abstinence occupies the foreground of the apostle's preaching even more. In reality he does not require complete renunciation of property in principle,[11] but works of mercy.[12] Only the apostle himself is absolutely without possessions. In the newly-founded communities he institutes, among other things, social welfare for the poor, which is administered by deacons.[13] It is explicitly stressed 'that many believed him, and even some of the leading people'.[14] It is no coincidence that the official of highest rank to be converted, the commander Siphor, who put his house at the apostle's disposal, became presbyter and leader of a community.[15]

This remarkable work thus shows a division in the communities. The preachers, or a few 'perfect', who are practising the imitation of Christ, renounce possessions radically, whereas the community, which includes a number of well-to-do people, is summoned to have little regard for riches and to be generous towards the poor. By this they show that they no longer belong to the transitory material world, but to the invisible rule of Christ. Jesus' demand, understood in radical terms and interpreted dualistically, is no longer applied to all Christians, but transferred to individual ascetics, who have been singled out from the rest.

From the beginning of the third century we find a Christian monasticism in Egypt; the first actual monasteries, communities of monks, came into being a little later, not least under the influence of Pachomius. Here there were new possibilities of putting the renunciation of possessions and the sharing of goods into practice: in addition to the old ascetic ideal of a 'life like the angels', which follows Essene models (see p.9 above), there was also the social motive of helping the poor and the sick.[16] At almost the precise time when state and church were entering into an increasingly close alliance — probably out of some historical necessity, but not entirely for the good of Christianity — monasticism was creating a new form of life. Here the critical detachment from the world required by faith and particularly detachment from possessions could be realized in, and in some circumstances even over against, the 'imperial church' which was now coming into being. Without the new ascetic ideal of monasticism, the social-critical preaching of the great church fathers Basil, Gregory Nazianzen, John Chrysostom and Ambrose of Milan, with their stress on the obligations to the community of those with possessions, would hardly have been conceivable.

8

The Ideal of 'Self-sufficiency' in Popular Philosophy

1   Paul and the Influence of Popular Philosophy

The reference to asceticism introduces a further theme from the early Christian criticism of private property, namely, the demand for inner freedom. Paul was already putting forward this thesis:

> All things are lawful for me, but not all things are helpful. All things are lawful for me, but I will not be enslaved by anything(I Cor.6.12).

For this reason he stresses his self-sufficiency almost like an itinerant Cynic philosopher:

> I have learned, in whatever state I am, to be content. I know how to be abased, and I know how to abound; in any and all circumstances I have learned the secret of facing plenty and hunger, abundance and want (Phil.4.11f.)

In this stress on self-sufficiency (*autarkeia*, see above, p.9), we presumably have the combination of an ideal from Jewish wisdom with ideas from Greek popular philosophy. According to Pirke Aboth 4.1, Simeon ben Zoma (*c.*AD 100) gave the following definitions:

> Who is mighty? He who controls his disposition (*yezer*) ... Who is rich? He who rejoices in his portion; as it is said (Ps.128.2): 'When you eat of the labour of your hands, happy are you and it shall be well with you.' Rabbinic legend put these words into the mouth of the

elders of the South in their dialogue with Alexander the Great (*Tamid* 32a); it may be compared with the famous answer of the first cynic Diogenes to the same ruler's offer: 'Ask of me whatever you will.' 'Get out of my light' (Diog.Laert.6,38).

Yet there is an essential difference between Paul and the philosophical ideal. It was a pupil of Socrates, Antisthenes, the teacher of Diogenes, who was the first to formulate the maxim that 'the wise man is self-sufficient (*autarkes*)' (Diog.Laert.6,11). A later Cynic, Crates, is said to have followed in his footsteps. Using a formula for freeing slaves, he renounced his own possessions and gave them away.[1] This ascetic ideal of complete self-sufficiency was essentially derived from Socrates. Xenophon, the conservative, well-to-do country nobleman, praised his master because 'he was living on very little, and yet was wholly independent (*autarkestata*); he was strictly moderate (*enkratestaton*) in all his pleasures (*hedonai*)' (*Mem.*1,2,14). He also puts this confession on the lips of Socrates: 'My belief is that to have no wants is divine; to have as few as possible comes next to the divine' (1,6,10). A similar remark could come from one of the monastic fathers of the fourth century AD. The radical break with all possessions which is becoming visible here also served the philosopher guided by reason alone in his attempt to realize his autonomy. However, for Paul and early Christianity, to gain freedom was not an end in itself but a matter of gaining freedom to serve God's cause, to proclaim the gospel and to serve neighbours.

> Of course, it is quite possible that the 'historical Socrates' came nearer to the Pauline 'freedom for service' than the philosophical ideal. In Plato's *Apology* he confesses that the God of Delphi had bidden him bring men to the insight that they are not wise: 'And by reason of this occupation I have no leisure to attend to any of the affairs of the state worth mentioning, or of my own, but am in vast poverty on account of my service to the god'(236/c).

Tatian, the Christian apologist and valiant ascetic, seems quite consistent in his standpoint when he abruptly challenges the pagan philosophers' claim to 'self-sufficiency':

'Who of your most eminent men has been free from vain boasting? Diogenes, who made such a parade of his independence with his tub, was seized with a bowel complaint through eating a raw polypus and lost his life by gluttony. Aristippus, walking about in a purple robe, led a profligate life, in accordance with his professed opinions. Plato, a philosopher, was sold by Dionysius for his gormandizing propensities' (*Or. ad Graec.* 2,1ff.). 'But do you, who have not the perception of these things, be instructed by us who know them; though you do profess to despise death, and to be sufficient of yourselves for everything. But this is a discipline in which philosophers are so greatly deficient, that some of them receive from the king of the Romans 600 aurei yearly, for no useful purpose they perform, but that they may not even wear a long beard without being paid for it'(19.1f.).

From the watch-tower of Tatian's rigorism, even the great Aristotle, 'who made happiness to consist in the things which give pleasure', and therefore consistently questions the felicity of those 'who have neither beauty, nor wealth, nor bodily strength, nor high birth', simply appears to be a fool: 'And these are the people who are supposed to do philosophy!' (2.5,9). He probably incorporated in his harmony of the gospels, the Diatessaron, an apocryphal saying of Jesus which was popular in the Syrian church: 'Accept nothing from anyone, and do not acquire anything in the world.'[2]

But the marriage with traditional philosophy could not be postponed, precisely in the sphere of ethics. The foundations for it had already been laid too long. A fine example of this is provided by the *Sentences of Sextus*, composed towards the end of the second century, the purpose of which was 'to bring the moral wisdom of the Greek sages under the wing of the church to whom all truth belongs'.[3] In them we find the lapidary admonition: 'Be content with a sufficiency' (*autarkeian askei*). Another saying gives the reason: 'The wise man without possessions is like God', for, 'God does not need anything, and the believer only needs God' (Sayings 98, 18, 49). The ideal of 'becoming like God' which appears here (fundamentally Socratic and Platonic) is matched by a wisdom-saying attributed to the Pythagoreans:

The man who is self-sufficient, without possessions, and wise, truly lives like God. He holds it to be the greatest riches not to require anything, not even for his natural needs. For in the acquisition of possessions, desire never rests. Rather, renunciation of injustice is enough for a good life.[4]

Here the idea of 'becoming like God' is connected with demands from the Sermon on the Mount (cf. Matt.5.48), like 'Give to him who begs from you' (5.42). On this, Sextus says:

Do not complain if someone robs you of your worldly goods. Hand over everything but freedom to the man who would rob you (Sayings 15,17).

2 Bourgeois Influence on the Ideal

The theme of self-sufficiency similarly appears in the deutero-Pauline Pastoral Epistles, which were written about the turn of the century, albeit in a rather different 'unascetic' form. It occurs in the context of controversy with Gnostic heresies, put forward by those who are 'bereft of the truth, imagining that godliness is a means of gain'.

The author then continues:

There is great gain in godliness with contentment (*autarkeian*); for we brought nothing into the world and we cannot take anything out of the world; but if we have food and clothing, with these we shall be content. But those who desire to be rich fall into temptation, into a snare, into many senseless and hurtful desires that plunge men into ruin and destruction (I Tim.6.6-9).

Here too the popular-philosophical background is obvious. However, freedom towards possessions, which is shown by contentment, does not so much serve a positive purpose, say the service of the gospel, as ward off harmful desires of the kind that are to be found among the Gnostic opponents of the author. Stoics and Cynics here would talk of 'passions'. But there is no ascetic rigorism. The individual is allowed possessions to a modest degree, necessary to support life.

This amounts to a deliberate rejection of radical asceticism and points to the entry of a bourgeois element into the early Christian community, a development which was historically inevitable. Although the word 'bourgeois' often has negative connotations nowadays, it should certainly not be taken in a derogatory sense. We might continue to ask today whether the 'bourgeois' phase of our history has not produced a far greater move towards learning tolerance and humanity, and has alleviated the tensions of class warfare. From the beginning, early Christianity was essentially a petty bourgeois movement. This was its strength. For in the historical form which it attained as a result, the Christian community found inner constancy, missionary strength and a sense of social responsibility which extended beyond its own ranks and courage to withstand state persecution. It is certainly no coincidence that in the Shepherd of Hermas, which in many ways is related to the Pastoral Epistles, the demand constantly recurs for Christians to be aliens in the world and to be content with 'a sufficient competence' (*autarkeia, Sim*.I,6 cf. *Mand*. VI,2,3). Riches, on the other hand, are given by God to be used in the service of the poor (*Sim*. I,6,8ff.). At the same time, this produces a fair exchange. The rich man, who is a poor man in God's eyes and whose prayer has no effect, supports the poor man with all that he has; in turn, the poor man prays for him:

> Therefore the two together complete the work . . . Blessed are they who are wealthy and understand that their riches are from the Lord, for he who understands this will also be able to do some good service (*Sim*.II,5-10).

These very simple remarks indicate the solution that the problems of poverty and riches was to find in the communities of the second century. It was a compromise. On the one hand, the traditional outright condemnation of the rich was maintained, but they were allowed a chance of salvation if they lived modestly and distributed their possessions generously to the poor. The solution which Clement of Alexandria — who had a much better philosophical and theological education — sought in his writing on 'The Rich Man's Salvation' was also along these lines. Clement, too, values *autarkeia* highly as a 'nurse of righteousness', since it is 'an attitude which is content with necessities and acquires by its own efforts those things which produce a happy life'.[5]

9

The Compromise of Effective Compensation

The way forward for the future was therefore neither a condemnation of possessions in principle (especially as the borderlines between poverty, a modest sufficiency and relative 'riches' were variable), nor the individualistic *autarkeia* of the wise man, but an attempt at constant, effective compensation. Anyone who did not want to involve himself in such a 'compromise with unrighteous mammon' always had the possibility of choosing the course of rigorous asceticism. Three viewpoints should be noted here.

1 The Positive Evaluation of Manual Labour and the Moderate Acquisition of Possessions

Recruits to early Christianity certainly did not come primarily from the lowest ranks of the proletariat of antiquity, without work and living on occasional earnings, nor from the slaves, who were restricted by law — it was not a slave religion. The early Christians were petty bourgeois: manual workers and craftsmen, small businessmen and workers on the land, all of whom had a great respect for honest labour (see pp.36ff. above). In his polemic, Celsus speaks contemptuously of 'wool-workers, shoemakers and clothmakers . . . quite uneducated and boorish men' who want to instruct others (*C.Cels*.3,55); this is the voice of the intellectual of antiquity, who despised manual labour. Even the rigorist Tertullian, who would most have liked to forbid all occupations which had even the slightest connection with pagan cults, asserts in his defence of Christianity:

We live among you, eating the same food, wearing the same attire, having the same habits, under the same necessities of existence. We are not Indian Brahmins or Gymnosophists, who dwell in woods and exile themselves from ordinary life. We do not forget the debt of gratitude we owe to God our Lord and Creator; we reject no creature of his hands, though certainly we exercise restraint upon ourselves, lest of any gift of his we make an immoderate or sinful use. So we live with you in the world, abjuring neither forum, nor shambles, nor bath, nor booth, nor workshop, nor inn, nor weekly market, nor any other places of commerce. We sail with you, and fight with you, and till the ground with you; and in like manner we unite with you in your business — even in the various arts we make public property of our works for your benefit (*Apol.* 43).

In his writing on idolatry he enumerates the occupations which he feels to be inappropriate for a Christian. He forbids Christians to be artists of any kind, engaged in making idols or building temples; magicians and astrologers, and also teachers and men of learning, since these communicate knowledge of pagan mythology in one form or another. Even the merchant who deals in the requisites of idolatry and at the same time hunts for deceitful gold, falls under suspicion (*De Idol.* 8-11). Here we can see something of that 'great refusal' which was typical of early Christianity. At the same time, however, the practical common-sense of the lawyer from Carthage also has its say. He deals with the objection that artists must earn a living in some way or another:

The plasterer knows both how to mend roofs, and lay on stuccos, and polish a cistern, and trace ogees, and draw in relief on party-walls many other ornaments beside like-nesses. The painter too, and the marble mason, and the bronze worker, and every graver whatever, knows expansions of his own art, of course much easier of execution. For how much more easily does he who delineates a statue overlay a sideboard! How much sooner does he who carves a Mars out of a lime-tree fasten together a chest! . . There is only a difference in wages and rewards. But smaller wages are compensated by more frequent earnings. How many are the party walls which require statues? How many the temples and shrines which are built for idols? But houses, and official residences, and baths, and tenements, how many are they? (*De idol.* 8,2-4; cf; *De Cult.Fem.* 1,6,1).

This means that the honest craftsman will still obtain the remuneration he deserves, provided he has nothing to do with idols and their temples. We find the same sober common sense in Tertullian's advice to well-endowed daughters of the Christian community to marry a poor fellow-Christian rather than a pagan of the same social status. We find once again the theme of compensation, which has already been noted:

> For if it is the poor, not the rich, whose are the kingdoms of the heavens, the rich will find more in the poor. She will be dowered with an ampler dowry from the goods of him who is rich in God. Let her be on an equality with him on earth, who in the heavens will perhaps not be so (*Ad Uxor.* 2,8,4f.).

Even Tertullian knew how to adapt his teaching to the social reality of the community. For all his forthright polemic against riches, he too stresses that God also has the right 'to grant riches', since 'with them many works of righteousness and philanthropy can be achieved' (*Adv.Marc.* 4,15,8).

This positive attitude towards respectable manual labour is also to be found in an earlier period. Paul followed a good rabbinic precedent in earning his living by manual work, and enjoined the Thessalonians to work as energetically (see pp.00 above). Even when attention was exclusively focused on the coming kingdom of God, it was impossible to avoid the 'pressure of work' which is now indissolubly bound up with human existence (Gen.3.17ff.). Idlers were therefore given short shrift by the communities. The Didache is generally well-disposed towards the poor, but it advises that while anyone who comes 'in the name of the Lord' is to be received as a guest, he must also be carefully investigated. Presumably there have been some unfortunate experiences.

> If he who comes is a traveller, help him as much as you can, but he shall not remain with you more than two days,

or, if need be, three. And if he wishes to settle among you and has a craft, let him work for his bread. But if he has no craft, provide for him according to your understanding, so that no man shall live among you in idleness because he is a Christian. But if he will not do so, he is making traffic of Christ; beware of such! (Did.12).

The satirist Lucian of Samosata has a long account of the way in which the Christians of Syria allowed themselves to be taken in and exploited by Peregrinus Proteus, a travelling philosopher and good-for-nothing, who gave himself out to be a Christian teacher and believer:

So if any charlatan and trickster, able to profit by occasions, comes among them, he quickly acquires sudden wealth by imposing upon simple folk.[1]

Certainly this is a caricature and an exaggeration, but Lucian is nevertheless indicating an acute problem among the Syrian communities, and probably not only there. This is clear from the Didache's mistrust of travelling prophets who allow the community to look after them. The *Didascalia apostolorum* follows in its footsteps:

Do you the faithful, therefore, all of you, daily and hourly, whenever you are not in the church, devote yourselves to your work; so that in all the conduct of your life you may either be occupied in the things of the Lord or engaged upon your work, and may never be idle . . .

Therefore, be always working, for idleness is a blot for which there is no cure. But if any man among you will not work, let him not eat; for the Lord God also hates sluggards: for it is not possible for a sluggard to be a believer.[2]

Industrious and frugal people, who also supported each other, in time acquired modest possessions, whether they deliberately sought them or not. Hegesippus tells how two great-nephews of Jesus administered a small estate of 39 plethra which was rated for tax at 9000 denarii. When they were brought before the emperor Domitian because of their Davidic descent,

They showed him their hands and the hardness of their skin and the calluses on their hands which came from hard work, to show that they were manual workers.

Despising them as 'common people', the emperor sent them home, where they were held in great respect as 'confessors' (Eusebius, HE 4.20). The Epistle to the Hebrews, which also comes from the time of Domitian, shows that the Christians in the community to which the letter is sent — probably in Rome — not only 'serve the saints (probably the communities in Palestine)' (6.20), but also 'joyfully accepted the plundering of your property (by the state)' (10.34). So they cannot have been completely without means.

2   *The Increase in Members from the Upper Strata in the Communities*

In time, more and more members of the upper classes came into contact with the church, and Christians neither could nor wanted to exclude them. We can already see how ambiguous the situation was from Luke. On the one hand, his gospel sets out an explicit 'theology of the poor', so that in the interpretation of the parable in 14.33, which is probably redactional, he can make Jesus say: 'Whoever of you does not renounce all that he has cannot be my disciple.' Nevertheless, he did not feel it a contradiction that he should dedicate his two-volume work to the well-born (*kratistos* = *egregius*, 1.3) Theophilus and take a special pleasure in enumerating prominent people who joined Jesus and his community. The list of such people extends from Joanna the wife of Chusa, one of the financial administrators of Herod Antipas, through the centurion Cornelius; the Athenian assessor, Dionysius; Menahem, the boyhood friend of Herod Antipas and so on, to Sergius Paulus, governor of Cyprus. A particular source of upper-class members for the early church was the group of godfearers on whom the Gentile-Christian mission concentrated its attention (see above, p.37); perhaps Luke himself came from this milieu. This development, the penetration of the Christian message into the ranks of the upper classes, which is already indicated — with a certain degree of pride — by the *auctor ad Theophilum*, continued in the second century, even if the overwhelming majority of Christians came from the simple people. According to Eusebius (HE 5,21,1), in the time of Commodus (180-192),

> Large numbers even of those at Rome, highly distinguished for wealth and birth, were advancing towards their own salvation with all their households and kindred.

Even the emperor's mistress, Marcia, came close to Christianity. She received Victor, bishop of Rome, and brought about the release of Christians condemned to forced labour in the quarries of Sardinia (see below, p.71). At about the same time the client king Abgar IX of Adiabene (AD 174-214) on the Parthian border was converted to Christianity. The strongly ascetic Acts of Thomas (pp.51f. above) probably reflects these events. Here kings, members of royal families, high officials and — not least — well-to-do women are converted to Christianity. At the same time we hear from Tertullian that Gentiles of 'every status' (*omnem dignitatem; Ad Nat.*1,1,2; *Apol.*1,7) come over to Christianity (see above, pp.36f.). Indeed Christians even enter the ranks of the senators (*Apol.*37,4; cf. *Ad Scap.*4,5f.). This development, once begun, could not be stopped. The mission had either to address all classes, or it had to close its ranks and become an ascetic sect, hostile to the world, or even a revolutionary movement. The decision in favour of social universalism had, in fact, already been taken by Paul. It is striking that the pagan opponents of Christianity, from Celsus to Julian, nevertheless regarded it as a subversive and hostile sect, although the course of negative regression had in fact been ruled out.

3   Comprehensive Care of the Poor and its Basis

We have already referred to the care for the poor in the early Christian communities, which was unique in antiquity. By this means an attempt was made to achieve a relative balance between rich and poor (see above, pp.42ff.). This meant that the communities had to have considerable means at their disposal. These came from free gifts which were collected at services, or even from particular settlements. This custom already began among the Pauline communities and can be traced onwards from there. Such intensive care of the poor and charitable activity did, however, presuppose that the majority of members of the community had a regular income. This is how we are to understand the admonition which appears in the instruction to newly-converted Christians contained in the Epistle to the Ephesians, a work which probably comes from one of Paul's pupils (4.28; cf.Act. Thom.58):

> Let the thief no longer steal, but rather let him labour, doing honest work with his hands, so that he may be able to give to those in need.

Only those who are themselves earning can be prepared to offer help to others. What is said of the former thief of course also applies to the rich. They are not to set their hope proudly on uncertain riches,

> but on God who richly furnishes us with everything to enjoy. They are to do good, to be rich in good deeds, liberal and generous, thus laying up for themselves a good foundation for the future, so that they may take hold of the life which is life indeed (I Tim.6.17ff.).

Elsewhere the verdict on riches is strict (see above, pp.47ff.), but here it is relatively mild; the rich have a chance of good works; the idea of merit which derives from the Jewish tradition is not to be left out of account. The argument of I Clement goes in a similar direction, also introducing the theme of the unity of the body of Christ:

> Let, therefore, our whole body (the church) be preserved in Christ Jesus, and let each be subject to his neighbour, according to the position granted to him. Let the strong care for the weak and let the weak reverence the strong.(!) Let the rich man bestow help on the poor and let the poor give thanks to God, that he gave him one to supply his needs ... (38.1f.).

The proximity of the ideas here to those of Jewish wisdom teaching, which had a strong influence on the practice of the early Christian communities, is unmistakable in all three passages. The way to the mutual exchange between poor and rich that we found in Hermas has ceased to be a long one (see p.58 above). While we may have theological hesitations about statements of this kind, in view of the situation of the community at the beginning of the second century they were practical and effective.

Paul could already put forward a similar argument over the collection for the 'poor' in Jerusalem:

> He who sows sparingly will also reap sparingly, and he who sows bountifully will also reap bountifully . . . for God loves a cheerful giver (II Cor.9.6f.).

He gives the very practical instruction that each Christian in Corinth should put something aside on the first day of the week, i.e. on Sunday (I Cor.16.2). Both Justin (*c*.150) and Tertullian (*c*.200) give a similar picture of the custom of the communities in Rome and Carthage at their services:

> And those who are well to do, and willing, give what each thinks fit, and what is collected is deposited with the president, who succours the orphans and widows, and those who through sickness or any other cause are in want, and those who are in bonds, and the strangers among us, and in a word takes care of all who are in need (Justin, *Apol*.67,6).

> Though we have our treasure-chest, it is not made up of purchase money, as of a religion that has its price. On the monthly collection day, if he likes, each puts in a small donation; but only if it be his pleasure, and only if he be able: for there is no compulsion; all is voluntary. These gifts are, as it were, piety's deposit fund. For they are not taken thence and spent on feasts, and drinking-bouts, and eating-houses, but to support and bury poor people, to supply the wants of boys and girls destitute of means and parents, and of old persons confined now to the house; such, too, as have suffered shipwreck; and if there happen to be any in the mines, or banished to the islands, or shut up in the prisons, for nothing but their fidelity to the cause of God's church, they become the nurslings of their confession. But it is mainly the deeds of a love so noble that lead many to put a brand upon us. See, they say, how

they love one another, for themselves are animated by mutual hatred; how they are ready even to die for one another, for they themselves will sooner put to death (Tertullian, *Apol.* 39, 5-7).

Another contributory factor to this readiness for sacrifice was the idea, common in antiquity, that God is the owner and giver of all good gifts (cf. James 1.17). Thus generosity could be interpreted as an 'imitation of God'; for God gives everyone what is necessary out of his inexhaustible riches, because of his 'benevolence to men' (*philanthropia*) (see above, pp.1f.). When there are anxious complaints about his regulations for eating, Paul quotes a saying from the Psalms which could also be applied to all other goods: 'The earth is the Lord's and the fullness thereof' (I Cor.10.26 = Ps.24.1). There is a similar thought in Hermas, that in the last resort all riches are ultimately the possession and the gift of God (see p.58 above). This theme constantly recurs in the later fathers, whether they are recalling the 'primal communism' of paradise when all had everything in common, or whether they derive from it the idea that possessions are a 'loan' made to man by God for which he will demand a reckoning (see p.29 above). The latter notion is much more common. A late collection made by John of Damascus contains a quotation from an apocryphal 'Teaching of Peter', which is typical of this early Christian verdict on riches:

> Rich is that man who has compassion on many and who in imitation of God gives of what he has. For God has given to all all of that which he has made. Understand then (ye) rich men that ye must serve since ye have received more than ye yourselves need. Learn that others lack what ye have in abundance. Be ashamed to retain other people's property. Imitate God's equity, and no one will be poor.[3]

God's goodness enlists the believer in its service and compels him to ward off poverty with the aid of his possessions. The rich man is the one who can give richly (cf. already Mark 12.41ff. = Luke 21.1ff.). From this there automatically follows the principle that the man with possessions who closes his heart and his hand to those in need shuts himself off from the love of God and thus from salvation:

But if any one has the world's goods and sees his brother in need, yet closes his heart against him, how does God's love abide in him? (I John 3.17)

Modern commentators are fond of quoting Mandaean parallels to this well-known saying from I John. In reality, however, we have here a basic theme of early Christian ethics which has its roots in Judaism, though its real point comes through its application to the love of God in the person and work of Christ (John 3.16; 17.26; I John 4.7ff.). In the end, the appeal to God as the giver of all good gifts and the theme of the 'imitation of God' in early Christianity must be seen from the perspective of christology.

4 Three Examples from the Roman Community

For the communities of the second and third centuries with their often well-organized, generous care for the poor and social concern, which called for a constant stream of money and responsible administration of it, this 'compromise', which did not reject the rich but laid extra financial demands on them, was the only practicable expedient. As a result, possessions acquired a contradictory aspect. They were regarded simultaneously as a dangerous threat and a supreme obligation. This tension could only be removed by specific action. Suspicion of riches largely continued in the communities, but abundant giving was nevertheless sought and appreciation of it also reflected in part on the giver.

Here are three instances, which all come from the Roman community, as we are best informed about it in the second and at the beginning of the third century:

1. Marcion, son of the Bishop of Sinope, a well-to-do shipowner from Asia Minor, gave the considerable sum of 200,000 sesterces on entering the Roman community (c.AD 139). It is uncertain whether this was all his wealth, or only part of it. One thing is certain, that he earned his fortune as a Christian, despite his ascetic tendencies (though of course he had been excommunicated in the East before his arrival in Rome). Five years later, when he was expelled from the Roman community, this great sum was immediately returned

to him.[4] The community therefore seems constantly to have had considerable liquid means at its disposal.

2. The apocryphal acts of the apostles also reflect this changed attitude towards members of the upper classes and their riches. Their primitively didactic, romance-like narratives, interspersed with crude miracles, correspond to the expectations of the simple members of the community. It would be possible to construct something like an 'ideal' social history of Christianity on the basis of them.

The earliest acts of Peter, composed towards the end of the second century, are particularly fond of telling of the conversion of rich and well-to-do people. The matron Eubula is helped by Peter in a miraculous way to regain money stolen from her by Simon Magus. When she becomes a believer, 'having recovered all her property, she gave it for the care of the poor'.[5] The Roman senator Marcellus, who is led astray by Simon and rescued by Peter, gives over his house to widows and Christian virgins: 'For the things that are called mine, to whom do they belong but you?'[6] As the result of a vision, the rich Chryse, who 'since her birth has never used a silver or glass vessel, but only golden ones', bestows 10,000 gold denarii on Peter. He accepts these, despite the objection that 'she is notorious all over Rome for fornication'. The apostle confidently replies: 'She was bringing it as a debtor to Christ, and is giving it to Christ's servants; for he himself has provided for them.'[7] The story of the woman who was a sinner in Luke 7.36-50 may have served as a model here, but at the same time it is possible to see an indication that there was not too much narrow-mindedness over the acceptance of gifts in view of the great social tasks of the community. According to Harnack's calculations the Roman church had to provide between 500,000 and 1,000,000 sesterces a year in the middle of the third century for the support of the 1500 needy people who have already been mentioned.[8] Such a financial burden could only be supported if there was a regular financial influx into the community and an administration which functioned well.

3. The third example gives us a glimpse of the development

of this administration and the human problems involved in it. The evidence adduced so far is predominantly of an idealistic literary character, with little specific biographical detail; the foreground is often occupied by the ideal demand or the apologetic description rather than human reality and its conflicts. Hippolytus' *Refutation of all Heresies*, rediscovered in 1842, contains a brief biography of Hippolytus' opponent and counter-bishop, Callistus of Rome. It is, of course, polemical and is extremely distorted. Here we have a view of the chequered personal fate of a bishop of the Roman church, whose work was also dominated by social problems (*Ref. Her.* 9,12). H. Gülzow has recently clarified the historical and sociological background of this *Vita* in exemplary fashion.[9] Callistus was originally a slave of the Christian imperial 'official' Carpophorus, who was himself either a slave or a freedman, but nevertheless enjoyed considerable respect because of his position. Callistus, who probably grew up as a Christian, was involved by his master Carpophorus in some rather risky banking on his own account. 'As time passed, not a few deposits were entrusted to him by widows and brethren thanks to the reputation of Carpophorus'(12,1). However, possibly because of constant devaluation, his banking ran into difficulties and he attempted to abscond. The attempt misfired, and his master put him in a slaves' prison. He was released from it through the pleas of his fellow Christians. Carpophorus' unscrupulous self-interest and his obligations as a Christian were clearly in conflict here. Released from prison, Callistus, seeking to call in some of the debts outstanding to him, rushed into the synagogue on a sabbath, hoping to meet some of those who owed him money. A tumult arose, the Jews dragged him before the prefect of the city, Fuscian, and charged him with disturbing their worship and being a Christian.

Fuscian had him scourged and deported to the lead mines in Sardinia (AD 188), where a considerable number of Christians were already working as state slaves. A little later bishop Victor, with the help of Marcia, the concubine of the emperor Commodus, managed to achieve the release of the Christian prisoners in Sardinia (see p.65 above); an imperial eunuch and Christian priest Hyacinthus brought the letter of emancipation to the governor of Sardinia. Callistus was among those freed; as a 'confessor' who had been deported for his faith he was accepted into the clergy. His former master no longer had any claim on the freeman. Possibly to avoid conflicts, bishop Victor sent Callistus to live in Antium and paid him a monthly allowance for food. We may also see in this treatment of the former slave a tendency to mistrust his earlier master. Victor's successor in the bishopric, Zephyrinus, made Callistus his closest 'collaborator in organizing the clergy' and 'assigned him the supervision of the *coemeterium*' (12,14). In other words, Callistus was entrusted with the supervision of the burial places of the Roman community. Anxiety about an honourable burial was a special problem to simple people in antiquity, including slaves, and led to numerous burial clubs. As the evidence of Aristides shows (see p.43 above), this area was also included in Christian social welfare from the beginning, following Jewish tradition. The first burial places of the Roman church depended on gifts of money made by rich Christians; the former slave Callistus seems to have done sterling work in this area, by making the support of the cemeteries the immediate task of the communities.

If the archaeologists are right in unanimously putting the development of the cemeteries in the time between Caracalla (211-217) and Severus Alexander (222-235), then the success of Callistus, who was responsible for the cemeteries for twenty years during this period, is obvious.[10]

The former slave now occupied the most influential office at the bishop's disposal: the entire administration of community finances, including care for the poor, was in his hands. The community were so satisfied with his performance of this difficult task that after the death of Zephyrinus in AD 217 he was elected bishop, despite his lowly origin. The well-to-do and theologically well-educated Hippolytus, who had the best of connections with the imperial household, went away empty and was chosen as counter-bishop by a minority. The community of 'intellectuals' who gathered round him soon sank to the level of a school. The man from the ordinary people, the former slave who effectively represented the interests of broad areas of the community, seemed to be more trustworthy. He proved his good sense not only in rejecting rigorism in the question of repentance, but also in allowing the unions of well-to-do Christian women with Christian slaves or freedmen to be fully valid marriages — against traditional Roman legal thinking. In this way he solved an ethical emergency (Hippolytus, *Ref.Her.*9,12,24). According to Gülzow, this is the 'first clear acknowledgment after the New Testament period of the equal rights of slaves, outside worship and the arena'.[11]

Clement of Alexandria: The Rich Man's Salvation

The development sketched out so far was also written down in theological form. Clement of Alexandria (died before 215) wrote a treatise on the theme with which we are concerned, the title of which, *The Rich Man's Salvation* has already been mentioned. This writing simply sets out to give a theological foundation to the compromise which had already been put into practice, but still involved a good deal of tension. Drawing abundantly on his philosophical learning, Clement sets out his thought in the form of a sermon on the rich man and Jesus (Mark 10.17-31). He rejects the literal interpretation put forward by radical asceticism and seeks to 'internalize' Jesus' demand. The heart must be cleansed of its desire for riches. Voluntary poverty is not yet completely identical with the freedom of man's disposition from damaging passions, which is what Jesus requires. The Stoic influence is unmistakable: 'He who casts away worldly wealth can still be rich in the passions . . . We must therefore renounce those possessions that are injurious, not those that are capable of being serviceable, if one knows the right use of them'(15,2,4). This means two things: first, riches are not evil 'in themselves'. They are neutral, an 'intermediate matter'. Everything depends on the right use of them. This is a good Stoic way of putting things. Secondly, the rich man is not excluded from the kingdom of heaven for being rich, but as a sinner who refuses repentance. Extreme need 'bends the thought' and keeps it from divine things (12,5; cf.18,5); moderate means not only drive away care but also offer the possibility of doing works of love (13,1). The positive side of possessions is also noted here: used moderately and responsibly, they can also give a man freedom, though this freedom must always, of course, include the freedom of his neighbour. Thus possessions, rightly understood, are an instrument given by God (14,1ff.), indeed they are God's gift, which we receive for our brother's sake and not for our own (16,3). Everything depends on using riches to supply the need of one's fellow-men:

> For he who holds possessions . . . and houses, as the gifts of God; and ministers from them to the God who gives them for the salvation of men; and knows that he possesses them more for the sake of the brethren than his own; and is superior to the possession of them, not the slave of the things he possesses; and does not carry them about in his soul, nor bind and circumscribe his life with them, but is ever labouring at some good and divine work, even should he be necessarily some time or other deprived of them, is able with cheerful mind to bear their removal equally with their abundance. This is he who is blessed by the Lord, and called poor in spirit, a meet heir of the kingdom of heaven, not one who could not live rich (16.3).

The only unjust thing is to be greedy in seeking possessions for one's own sole use. As in I Tim. and in Hermas, the motive of exchange appears: 'By giving the perishing things of the world, he receives in exchange for these an eternal mansion in the heavens'(32.1).

For all Clement's concern to find a 'liberal' way between radical asceticism and a clear-cut justification of riches, compared with the preaching of Jesus his solution remains unsatisfactory, because in part it twists the gospel sayings. On the other hand, a positive evaluation must be made: he stresses energetically the absolute religious and social obligations which go with property. Property is the gift of God and in all cases is there to meet the needs of others.

Thus this short, sermon-like writing marks a revolution in the spiritual and sociological situation of the church. At that time Alexandria was not only the largest city of the Greek-speaking East, but at the same time also the richest in the whole empire, the trade centre for India, the Orient and the Mediterranean, a city which had both a unique educational tradition and a luxurious style of life second to none. A spurious letter of Hadrian's, though only coming from the fourth century, gives a satirical description of it:

> The city is well-to-do, rich, luxurious; no one in it is inactive. Some are glass-blowers, others make paper, yet others weave linen; all are engaged in some work or other . . . The only God they have is money (*unus illis deus nummus est*); this deity is worshipped by Christians, Jews and pagans alike.[1]

Leaving aside the last sentence, which is part of the anti-Christian polemic of the post-Constantine period, the description also fits the earlier period. Evidently Clement was seeking a hearing among educated and well-to-do groups in his writing on the rich young man. He also addresses them in his larger work 'The Teacher' (*Paedagogus*). In Books 2 and 3 he attacks the unbridled luxury of the upper classes of Alexandrian society with inexorable sharpness. For example, at the end of Book 2 he attacks the desire of prominent women to adorn themselves with gold and precious stones. Evidently there were about 200 of these Christian matrons in Alexandria, whose argument was as follows:

> 'Why may I not use what God has made? I have it by me, why may I not enjoy it? For whom were these things made, then, if not for us?'

According to Clement, people who talk like this do not know God's will:

> For first necessaries, such as water and air, he supplies free to all; and what is not necessary, he has hid in the earth and water . . . Behold, the whole heaven is lighted up and you do not seek God; but gold which is hidden, and jewels, are dug up by those among us who are condemned to death.

This argument from natural law is followed by Clement's own theological observations, which indeed form the beginning of a Christian argument:

But if all things have been conferred on you, and all things allowed you, and 'if all things are lawful, yet all things are not expedient', says the apostle (I Cor.10.23). God brought our race into communion by first imparting what was his own, when he gave his own word, common to all, and made all things for all (John 1.1ff.). All things therefore are common, and not for the rich to appropriate an undue share. That expression, therefore, 'I possess, and possess in abundance: why then should I not enjoy?', is suitable neither to the man, nor to society. But more worthy of love is that: 'I have: why should I not give to those who need?' For this is the true luxury – the treasured wealth. But that which is squandered on foolish lusts is to be reckoned waste, not expenditure. For God has given us ... the liberty of use, but only so far as necessary; and he has determined that the use should be common. And it is monstrous for one to live in luxury, while many are in want.[2]

Thus Clement counters the extravagance of the well-to-do neither with the threat of the horrors of Jewish-Christian apocalyptic nor with the rigorous ascetic ideal of the later Egyptian monks, but with reasonable, disciplined moderation, which is guided by the 'Logos' (the 'Word' of John 1.1) and gives a full share to the neighbour in need. The aim of this instruction by the Logos is not a flight from the world, but a reasonable, moderate and at the same time generous use of worldly goods. Steadfast mastery of self leads to inner detachment from them. Riches are like a serpent which administers a fatal bite to those who are inexperienced, 'unless one, despising them, use them skilfully, so as to crush the creature by the charm of the Word, and himself escape unscathed' (*Paed*.3,35,1). Of course, anyone who has such mastery over his desires by virtue of the Logos knows that in reality 'only those (i.e. the Christians) are rich'; independently of their external situation they dispose of 'the best possession to its possessor, rendering man truly blessed' (3,36,1,12).

Thus in Clement traditions of Jewish wisdom, Stoic ethics and the message of the New Testament. combine with the specific situation of the Alexandrian church in a new synthesis which is to point the way forward for the later church. The generally expressed radical and rigorist criticism of property was toned down and made more inward, though the possibility of completely renouncing possessions remained open. Riches were judged critically, but were no longer ruled out in principle; stress was laid, rather, on strict obligations to the community and the right use of them. Inner freedom in the detachment of faith had to prove itself in generosity and the renunciation of avarice and luxury.

11

Cyprian of Carthage : On Good Works and Almsgiving

For a Western counterpart to Clement's writing, coming from the Latin-speaking church, one might turn to the treatise of Cyprian, Bishop of Carthage, *On Good Works and Almsgiving*. It was written about fifty or sixty years later, between 253 and 256. Cyprian came from a prominent family, presumably part of the nobility of the city. According to the account of his biographer, Pontius, even while he was a catechumen he 'sold his property and distributed almost all the proceedings to provide sustenance for countless people who were in need' (*Vita* 2). That is, he seems to have distributed his personal possessions and made over his estates to the church. When persecution became imminent, however, he took back the estates as private or family property, to prevent their being requisitioned by the imperial authorities.[1] This rigorously ascetic, but also sovereign attitude is typical of the author of the brief work in which — in contrast to that of Clement of Alexandria — philosophical features fade into the background in the face of influence from the Old Testament and Judaism, and the theme of merit is developed much more powerfully. The author's attention is concentrated especially on the final decision at the last judgment (chs.23 and 26). Readiness for sacrifice is seen in the light of a competitive ideal, and the purple crown of martyrdom — which is not achieved by everyone — is contrasted with the white crown of good works, which anyone can attain. Like Tertullian and Clement of Alexandria before him, Cyprian rejects the 'love communism' of the early apostolic period, 'when ... in the first beginnings the heart still proved to be alive in greater virtues and the faith of believers still glowed in a new warmth'. By holding goods in common, the first Christians imitated

> the equity of God the Father. For whatever is of God is common in our use,[2] nor is any one excluded from his benefits and his gifts, so as to prevent the whole human race from enjoying equally the divine goodness and liberality ... In which example of equality, he who, as a possessor in the earth, shares his returns and his fruits with the fraternity, while he is common and just in his gratutitous bounties, is an imitator of God the Father (*De Op. et El.*25).

Paul had already stressed the ideal of 'equality' (see p.39 above). Cyprian now bases it on God's attitude and demands 'imitation of God'. This idea — partly nourished from philosophical sources and partly from biblical sources — is to become especially significant with the great fathers of the fourth century (see above, pp.67f.). Cyprian does not question the legitimacy of private property any more than Clement and the later fathers, but he vigorously attacks the general misuse of it. Immediately after his baptism he is already depicting the great African property-owners with their insatiable desire for riches in a way which imitates Roman satire and his teacher Tertullian:

> They add forests to forests and, excluding the poor from their neighbourhood, stretch out their fields far and wide into space without any limits, possess immense heaps of silver and gold and mighty sums of money, either in built-up heaps or in buried stores, — even in the midst of their riches those are torn to pieces by the anxiety of vague thought, lest the robber should spoil, lest the murderer should attack, lest the envy of some wealthier neighbour should become hostile, and harass them with malicious lawsuits ... From him there is no liberality to dependents, no communication to the poor. And yet such people call that their own money, which they guard with zealous labour, shut up at home as if it were another's ...

Their possession amounts to this only, that they can keep others from possessing it: and oh, what a marvellous perversion of names! they call those things goods which they absolutely put to none but bad uses (*Ad Donat.*12).

This polemic against the anxiety and care which tempt men to accumulate riches and hope for everything from their possessions is also a constantly recurring theme of his later writing on good works:

If you dread and fear, lest, if you begin to act thus abundantly, your patrimony being exhausted with your liberal dealing, you may perchance be reduced to poverty: be of good courage in this respect, be free from care: that cannot be exhausted whence the service of Christ is supplied, whence the heavenly work is celebrated. Neither do I vouch for this on my own authority but I promise it on the faith of the Holy Scriptures and on the authority of the divine promise (*De Op. et El.*9).

Anyone who is so anxious about the way in which he is going to sustain his life that he does not trust this promise, 'that those who feed Christ are also in turn fed by Christ', is like those covetous Pharisees who mocked Jesus' parable of the unjust steward (Luke 16.1ff.,14). The claim to be concerned about children and family, or about the generations to come, is not a sufficient reason for not being generous. On the contrary,

the state neither takes away the property entrusted to God, nor does the exchequer intrude on it, nor does any forensic calumny overthrow it. That inheritance is placed in security which is kept under the guardianship of God . . . You . . . are sinning twice, both in not providing for your children the aid of God their Father, and in teaching your children to love their property more than Christ (ch.19, cf. 10.16-18).[3]

At a later date, Basil the Great (see above pp.2f.) laid special stress on the responsibility of those with property to abolish social injustice. He himself even sacrificed his own possessions to this end. He then brings up the influential idea of redistributing private property by means of legacies. The testator or the heir should make over a fixed part – Basil himself suggests half, on the basis of Luke 19.8 – to the poor. 'Strictly speaking, this conception of the "soul part" leads to a kind of church tax, a social tax for the struggle against poverty.'⁴ Here too we find in the background the basic idea that God is the real master and owner of all possessions.

And so we come to a conclusion. The argument over the question of property, which already emerged in a radical way in the preaching of Jesus, was not settled in the early church, nor was there any clear and comfortable solution. The social demands associated with it introduced new stimuli to the ancient world which can be described without exaggeration as revolutionary. Of course the possibility of developing this new social ethic of agape and mutual equality was at first limited to Christian communities. The state was outside its range. Its sources were on the one hand Greek natural-law thinking and the ascetic ideal of self-sufficiency, and on the other the tradition of Old Testament prophecy and Jewish wisdom, though pride of place was of course taken by the impetus of the early Christian message itself. Even where the compromises demanded by historical circumstances were made, the intention of the early Christian message to act as a ferment continued to be effective. As a rule its foundation was explicitly theocentric. Even the natural-law arguments were drawn into this christologically determined 'theocentricity' and were changed as a result: God's graciousness, which takes shape in the work of Christ, liberates believers to do good with open hands, to overcome social barriers and to work for a just order.

The idea of merit, taken over from Judaism and to be found above all in Hermas, Tertullian or Cyprian, may be seen as a theological regression, but it was this that provided a strong motive for concrete social and philanthropic action. We may have had to subject this point to criticism, but we should not overlook the seriousness of its demands. Unlike some modern anthropologies, the fathers had no utopian, ideal picture of man; they knew that as a fallen creature man was selfish and a sinner by nature.

In many respects, an abyss separates us from the early church. But for that very reason we must try to see those things that still link us together, with the aim of making its spiritual and social life fruitful for our crisis-torn time.

Ten Concluding Theses

I shall attempt to indicate the possibilities of building the kind of bridge indicated in the previous chapter in ten theses:

1. We cannot extract a well-defined 'Christian doctrine of property' either from the New Testament or from the history of the early church. Right down to most recent times, views which have claimed to possess this character owe more to natural law than to Christianity. Where the beginnings of natural-law theories have been offered in the early church, whether for the purpose of radical criticism or to provide a relative justification for property, they have usually been borrowed from Graeco-Roman philosophical discussion. Of course they were closely associated with the biblical doctrine of creation.

2. By contrast, primitive Christianity contains a radical criticism of riches, a demand for detachment from the goods of this world and a conquest of the barriers between rich and poor through the fellowship of agape. All this comes about under the shadow of the imminent coming of the kingdom of God. It robs 'unrighteous mammon' of its force. In the further course of the history of early Christianity this stimulus leads to a tense controversy over injustice and the limitations and relative necessity of property.

3. Because they come from such a different situation, the various statements made in early Christianity can only be applied with many qualifications to our industrial society and the problems of possessions which so oppress us today. These

problems arise on the one hand from the progressive accumulation of productive capital and the concentration of economic power in the hands of relatively few people — including the state — and on the other from the irresistible transference to public corporations of the functions of care and protection hitherto bound up with possessions. Quite independently of the different and apparently antagonistic social systems, we find today that all over the world economic power and control is concentrated in the hands of a few 'functionaries' or élite groups.

4. By contrast, for the first Christians the question of property was a problem of personal ethics or at most the problem of relatively small groups. Their ethic was a theonomous community ethic, born of 'faith working through love'(Gal.5.6). The possibility of better social legislation by the state was no more within their scope than the limitation of the economic omnipotence of the state. A 'theocracy' which imposes the ideal of an allegedly divine will in the sphere of the state by means of political force is no more specifically Christian that the totalitarian 'philosophers' state', which seeks to justify itself on the basis of the sole rule of 'reason'.

5. As a result, early Christian ethics cannot provide us with any system of generally binding norms for today's society, nor does it set out to do so. However, we can gain certain insights from it which may hope to gain acceptance beyond the bounds of Christianity even today, especially as we can find some analogous notions in antiquity, sometimes even outside Christianity. One example is the idea that in some circumstances property leads man astray and puts him in danger, and that it can even seduce him into the misuse of power. Further, that for this very reason the misuse of power must be prevented by public controls and that those who own it must be obliged to use it also for the well-being of their fellow-men, or that a man's status and value in no way depend on his capacity to accumulate means of wealth. Readiness to refuse to become a consumer and to renounce luxury in a world in which extravagance and poverty often stand side by side can also very well be motivated by the Christian tradition.

6. Principles of this kind can have a considerable effect on the ethical conduct of both individuals and groups, and the perspicacious will gladly acknowledge their correctness. However, as a social ethic they will not make sufficient impact on society as a whole to solve the problems that face us to day. For § 14,2 of the Basic Law, 'Property confers obligations. Its use should at the same time serve the general good', is more the expression of a wish than of a norm proven in civic practice. In the Federal Republic, charitable foundations are still underdeveloped, tax evasion is partly regarded as a peccadillo, the placing of productive capacity in the hands of the workers is making all too slow process and public prestige is largely bound up with possessions. An egotistic private interest, oriented one-sidedly on consuming goods and increasing possessions, is holding back under-standing of the urgent tasks which face the community: educational policies, protection of the environment, the improvement of the social structure for those who vegetate on the borders of our affluent society, and still more, of course, understanding of the problems of the Third World, and the poverty which is often increasing there rather than decreasing. This 'egotistic private interest' is to be found not only among individuals but in groups, associations, parties, trades unions and states, whose spheres of influence the individual can hardly avoid.

7. Here we can see a dilemma which we have already met in part, although in another form, in the discussion in early Christianity: the crisis of property also proves to be the crisis of man, his selfish desire to assert himself, his struggle for power and his mercilessness. Here we can see what the fathers called original sin. It may sound old-fashioned today, but it is very real.

8. Knowledge of man's selfish heart prevents the Christian from having an uncritical and utopian faith in the possibility of an ultimately perfect society, an infallibly political orthopraxy, a realizable ideal 'kingdom of freedom' which in some circumstances would have to be introduced by an act of force and whose goal would be the equality of all individuals and the end of 'man's rule over men'. Such 'equality' can

only be achieved through total manipulation and the utmost use of force. Like almost all philosophical utopian states, it leads to something very near to insect states. Moreover, as a rule what happens is that even more repressive ruling hierarchies take over the old structures. Man is not really equal, either in disposition and endowment, or in his wishes and needs. Equality must therefore be understood in the first place as real equality of opportunities, of the satisfaction of basic human needs. This equality is certainly progressing today in many democratic, free states with a concern for social justice, but in other parts of the world it is still far from being realized. The goal would be to grant each individual the chance of personal development in accordance with his capabilities and wishes, for the well-being of and in responsibility for the whole of society. The old opposition between freedom and righteousness can never be 'solved' except through a compromise.

9. This knowledge of man's selfish heart should not just lead to a resigned attitude which simply confirms and fixes existing social conditions. Precisely because man is entangled in his 'boundless' egotism both as an individual and as a group, we are called to constant reform, to progress towards the better. Eberhard Jüngel defines so-called 'progress' in history 'as progress in the reduction of an infinite series of ills'.[1] This also applies to the question of property. Because land and soil, pure air, water, energy and raw materials can no longer be 'produced' at will and thus there is a limit to industrial growth, new solutions must be found to the question. Of course we do not need new dualistic theories of society, but a readiness to prove what we have in social and economic reality, in which, in some circumstances, compromises may be required. Not least among these 'progressive' compromises is assent to the restriction of one-sided individual and collective 'rights' or 'privileges' in favour of the 'underprivileged' and the common good.

10. Finally, as an example of faith, we may remind ourselves of the attempt of the first Christian communities to resolve the tension which destroys fellowship between poor and rich, freemen and slaves, and to do away with opposi-

tions. This moves between the 'love communism' of the early community — which to our eyes seems unrealistic — and the more effective — but still endangered — compromise of the communities of the later period. This equalization created a healthy detachment from external goods, and at the same time overcame the barriers of status and class. The church, even today, could again become the place where mistrust and old prejudices are overcome and new forms of life and community are created on the basis of faith, love and hope. Furthermore, it is our duty as Christians and citizens to be ready to make sacrifices of our own and by pressure for better legislation break down social barriers, help minorities to achieve justice, and bring complexes of arbitrary power under better, democratic control. In this way we shall rob the 'demonic' nature of property of its force.

Bibliography

Chapter 1

In comparison with literature on the history of doctrine, relatively little has been written on the question of property or on the question of the social work of the early church. There is clear evidence here of the one-sidedness of Protestant patristic scholarship over the last decades. A brief survey of literature can now be found in W.-D. Hauschild, 'Christentum und Eigentum. Zum Problem eines altkirchlichen "Sozialismus" ', *ZEE* 16, 1972, 34-49 (34 n.2). Some earlier Catholic investigations are important, though of course they have a strongly apologetic character: I. Seipel, *Die wirtschaftsethischen Lehren der Kirchenväter* (Theologische Studien der Leo-Gesellschaft 18), Wien 1907; O. Schilling, *Reichtum und Eigentum in der altkirchlichen Literatur*, Diss., Tübingen/Freiburg 1908; id., 'Der Kollektivismus der Kirchenväter', *TQ* 114, 1933, 481-92; A. Bigelmair, 'Zur Frage des Sozialismus und Kommunismus der ersten drei Jahrhunderte', in *Festgabe Adolf Ehrhard*, Bonn 1922. The brief study by the Swiss Marxist Konrad Farner, *Christentum und Eigentum bis Thomas von Aquin*, Bern 1947, reprinted in the same author's *Theologie der Kommunismus*, Frankfurt 1969, 9-90, but without the detailed notes, is an idiosyncratic survey, but full of material. The penetrating study by S. Giet, *Les Idées et l'Action sociale de Saint Basile*, Paris 1941, 84ff., 96ff., 400ff. is specifically devoted to Basil the Great. In addition to the literature cited in Hauschild, mention should be made of: J. Leipoldt, *Der soziale Gedanke in der altchristlichen Kirche*, Leipzig 1950, reprinted 1972; K. Beyschlag, 'Christentum und Veränderung in der alten Kirche', *Kerygma und Dogma* 18, 1972, 26-55, esp.35ff.; H. Diessner, *Studien zur Gesellschaftslehre und sozialen Haltung Augustins*, Halle 1954; P. Christophe, *L'usage Chrétien du droit de Propriété dans l'Ecriture et la Tradition Patristique*, Paris 1963.

For early Christian charity and the social history of early Christianity, G. Uhlhorn, *Die christliche Liebestätigkeit in der alten Kirche*, Stuttgart 1882 (with indications of source material), and id., *Die christliche Liebestätigkeit*, Stuttgart [2]1895 (reprinted Neukirchen 1959, without source material), are still indispensable; also A.von Harnack, *The Mission and Expansion of Christianity*, London 1908, reprinted New York 1961; E. Troeltsch, *The Social Teaching of the Christian Churches*, London 1931, two vols., reprinted New York 1960. C. Schneider, *Geistesgeschichte des antiken Christentums* I, Munich 1954, 504ff., 517ff.; W. Schwer, 'Armenpflege', in *Reallexikon für Antike und Christentum* I, 1950, 689ff. There is an urgent need for a social history of early Christianity. A very brief introduction is offered by E.A. Judge, *Christliche Gruppen in nichtchristlicher Gesellschaft*, 1964. An important study by H. Gülzow, 'Die sozialen Gegebenheiten der altchristlichen Mission', will soon appear in G. Kretschmar and H.-G. Frohnes (eds.), *Kirchengeschichte als Missionsgeschichte*.

For the social question in Graeco-Roman antiquity see the dated but still indispensable standard work R. v. Pöhlmann, *Geschichte der sozialen Frage und des Sozialismus in der antiken Welt*, revised and with an appendix by F. Oertel, Vols I and II, Munich [3]1925. Vol. II, 464ff., also deals with the early church. For criticism see J. v. Hasebroek, *Gnomon* 3, 1927, 257-66; also H. Bolkestein, *Wöhltätigkeit und Armenpflege im vorchristlichen Altertum*, Utrecht 1939 (reprinted Groningen 1967); J. Gagé, *Les Classes sociales dans l'Empire Romain*, Paris 1964; A. R. Hands, *Charities and Social Aid in Greece and Rome*, Ithaca, NY 1968. Unfortunately there is too brief a treatment of the Hellenistic period and of late antiquity, and the influence of Christianity is only mentioned on the periphery; N. Brockmeyer, *Socialgeschichte der Antike*, Urban-Taschenbücher 153, 1972. Quite essential for the whole economic and cultural background are the two standard works by M. Rostovtzeff, *The Social and Economic History of the Hellenistic World*, Vols. I-III, Oxford 1941, and *The Social and Economic History of the Roman Empire*, I and II, ed. P. M. Fraser, Oxford [2]1957.

For utopia in antiquity see, in addition to R. v. Pöhlmann (above), E. Salin, *Platon und die griechische Utopie*, Munich/Leipzig 1921; E. Nestle, *Vom Mythos zum Logos*, Stuttgart[2] 1942 (reprinted 1966), 462ff.; H. Braunert, *Utopia. Antworten griechischen Denkens auf die Herausforderung durch soziale Verhältnisse*, (Veröffentliehungen der schlesw.-holst. Universitätsgesellschaft, NF 51), Kiel 1969. A recent basic study is B. Gatz, *Weltalter, goldene Zeit und sinnverwandte Vorstellungen*, Hildesheim 1967. For the question of slavery see especially J. Vogt, *Sklaverei und Humanität*, [2]1972, esp. 20ff., 131ff.; C. Despotopoulos, 'La "Cité Parfaite" de Platon et l'Esclavage', *Revue des Etudes Grecques* 83, 1970, 26-37.

Chapter 2

For social order in the Old Testament see N. Peters, *Die soziale Fürsorge im Alten Testament*, 1935; F. Horst, *Das Eigentum nach dem AT* (1949), in id., *Gottes Recht*, Munich 1961; H. Donner, 'Die soziale Botschaft der Propheten im Lichte der Gesellschaftsordnung in Israel', *Oriens Antiquus* 2, 1963, 229-45; R. de Vaux, *Ancient Israel*, London 1961, 68ff., 80ff, 164ff.; H. H. Schmid, *Gerechtigkeit als Weltordnung*, Tübingen 1968; W. Zimmerli, *Man and his Hope in the Old Testament*, London 1971; M. Fendler, 'Zur Sozialkritik des Amos', *EvTh* 33, 1973, 32-53.

For Judaism see E. Bammel, 'Ptochos', *TDNT* VI, 894ff.; M. Hengel, *Judaism and Hellenism*, I London 1974, 6-57, 131ff., 175ff.; id., *Die Zeloten* (AGSU 1), Leiden 1961; A. Schalit, *König Herodes* (Studia Judaica 4), Berlin 1969, 256ff., 483.; H. Kreissig, *Die sozialen Zusammenhänge des judäischen Krieges* (Schriften zur Geschichte und Kultur der Antike 1), Berlin 1970.

For communal goods among the Essenes and in antiquity see W. Bauer, 'Essener', *Pauly-Wissowa*, Suppl. IV, 1924, 386-430 = *Aufsätze und kleine Schriften*, Tübingen 1967, 1-59 (esp. 19f., 33ff.); M. Hengel, *Judaism and Hellenism*, vol. I, 243ff.

For the social situation at the time of Jesus see E. Lohmeyer, *Soziale Fragen im Urchristentum*, 1921 (reprinted 1973); J. Jeremias, *Jerusalem in the Time of Jesus*, London 1969; M. Hengel, 'Das Gleichnis von den Weingärtnern Mc.12,1-12 im Lichte der Zenonpapyri und der rabbinischen Gleichnisse', *ZNW* 59, 1968, 1-39; id., *Victory over Violence*, Philadelphia 1973; M. Rostovtzeff, *Roman Empire* I, 261-73.

For rabbinic Judaism see H. Strack/P. Billerbeck, *Kommentar zum NT aus Talmud und Midrasch*, I, 1922, 817-28; IV, 1928, 536-610 (= Bill.).

Chapter 3

Jesus (and the NT): E. Lohmeyer, *Soziale Fragen im Urchristentum*; W. G. Kümmel, 'Der Begriff des Eigentums im Neuen Testament', *Heilsgeschehen und Geschichte*, (Marburger theologische Studien 3), 1965, 271-77; H.-J. Degenhardt, *Lukas, Evangelist der Armen, Besitz und Besitzverzicht in den lukanischen Schriften*, Stuttgart 1965; M. Hengel, *Was Jesus a Revolutionist?*, Philadelphia 1971; J. Jeremias, *New Testament Theology Vol. 1, The Proclamation of Jesus*, London 1971, 228f.; G. Breidenstein, *Das Eigentum und seine Verteilung*, Stuttgart/Berlin 1968, 288ff., lit.

Chapter 4

The early church: for Hellenistic style in Acts 2.22f. and 4.32 see E. Plumacher, *Lukas als hellenistischer Schriftsteller* (SUNT 9), Göttingen 1972, 17ff.; K. Lake, 'The Communism of Acts II and IV-VI . . .', in F.J. Foakes Jackson/Kirsopp Lake, *The Beginnings of Christianity*, V, London 1932 (reprinted Grand Rapids 1966), 140-51; E. Haenchen, *The Acts of the Apostles*, Oxford 1971; H. Conzelmann, *Die Apostelgeschichte* (HNT 7), Tübingen 1963, 31, 38f.; E. Bloch, *Das Prinzip Hoffnung*, III, Stuttgart 1959, 1482-93; cf. also Seipel, *Der soziale Gedanke*, 107ff.; Lohmeyer, *Soziale Fragen in Urchristentum*, 79ff.

Chapter 5

Paul: Kümmel, 'Der Begriff des Eigentums'; W. Schrage, *Die konkreten Einzelgebote in der paulinischen Paränese*, Gütersloh 1961; id., 'Die Stellung zur Welt bei Paulus, Epiktet und in der Apokalyptik. Ein Beitrag zu I Kor.7.29-31', *ZThK* 61, 1964, 125-54; D. Georgi, *Die Geschichte der Kollekte des Paulus für Jerusalem.* (Theol.Forschung 38), Hamburg-Bergstedt 1965; O. Merk, *Handeln aus Glauben* (Marburger theol.Studien 5), 1968.

For the question of slavery in early Christianity see F. Bömer, *Untersuchungen zur Religion des Sklaven in Griechenland und Rom*, I-IV, Abh.Ak.Mainz 1957, 7; 1960, 4; 1961, 4; 1963, 10; H. Gülzow, *Christentum und Sklaverei*, Bonn 1969; J. Vogt, *Sklaverei und Humanität.* (Historia Einzelschriften 8), 1972.

Chapter 6

For the question of work and professions and organized social welfare see A. v. Harnack, *The Mission and Expansion of Christianity*, London 1908 (reprinted New York 1961), 147-98; Leipoldt, *Der soziale Gedanke*, 161ff.; Carl Schneider, *Geistesgeschichte* I, 693ff.; H. Holzapfel, *Die sittliche Wertung der körperlichen Arbeit im christlichen Altertum*, 1941.

Chapter 7

For the ascetic rejection of property see H. von Campenhausen, 'Early Christian Asceticism', in id., *Tradition and Life in the Church*, London 1968, 90-122; G. Kretschmar, 'Ein Beitrag zur Frage nach dem Ursprung der frühchristlichen Askese', *ZThK* 61, 1964, 27-67; P. Nagel, *Die Motivierung der Askese und der Ursprung des Mönchtums*, (TU 95), Berlin 1966; F. von Lilienfeld, 'Basilius der Grosse und die Mönchsväter der Wüste', *ZDMG* Suppl. I, 2, 1969, 418-31. See also the popular account of ancient monasticism and its rigorous asceticism in J. Lacarrière, *The God-Possessed*, London 1963.

Chapter 8

For 'self-sufficiency' see P. Wilpert, 'Autarkie', *RAC* I, 1950, 1039-50. Cf. R. Nickel, *Hermes* 100, 1972, 42-7. For the ideal of similarity to God see H. Merki, *Homoiosis Theo*, Freiburg (Schweiz) 1952.

For the penetration of Christianity into the upper classes, A. von Harnack, *Die Mission und Ausbreitung des Christentums*, Leipzig [4]1924, II, 559ff.; W. Eck, 'Das Eindringen des Christentums in den Senatorenstand', *Chiron* I, 1971, 381-406. For the imitation of God see A. Heitmann, *Imitatio Dei*, Rome 1940. For the Acts of Peter see E. Hennecke—W. Schneemelcher—R. McL. Wilson, *New Testament Apocrypha* II, London 1965, 259-321.

Chapter 9

For Marcion see A. von Harnack, *Marcion* [2]1924, reprinted Darmstadt 1960.

Chapter 10

For Clement of Alexandria see H. von Campenhausen, *The Fathers of the Greek Church*, London 1963, 25-36; H. Kraft, *Die Kirchenväter*, Bremen 1966, 136-65; H. Lietzmann, *The Founding of the Church Universal*, London [3]1953, 277-94.

Chapter 11

For Cyprian see H. von Campenhausen, *The Fathers of the Latin Church*, London 1964, 36-60; H. Kraft, *Die Kirchenväter*, 359-436; H. Lietzmann, *The Founding of the Church Universal*, 225-38.

Abbreviations

AGSU	Arbeiten zur Geschichte des Spätjudentums und Urchristentums
ANF	The Ante-Nicene Fathers, ed. Alexander Roberts and James Donaldson, Edinburgh
BZNW	Beiheft zur *Zeitschrift für neutestamentliche Wissenschaft*
ET	English Translation
EvTh	*Evangelische Theologie*
HAT	Handbuch zum Alten Testament
HNT	Handbuch zum Neuen Testament
LCL	Loeb Classical Library, London
NPNF	The Nicene and Post-Nicene Fathers of the Christian Church, ed. Philip Schaff and H. Wace, London and New York
PG	Migne, *Patrologia Craeca*, Paris
PL	Migne, *Patrologia Latina*, Paris
RAC	*Reallexikon für Antike und Christentum*
SUNT	Studien zur Umwelt des Neuen Testaments
TDNT	*Theological Dictionary of the New Testament*, ed. G. Kittel
TQ	*Theologische Quartalschrift*
TU	Texte und Untersuchungen
ZDMG	*Zeitschrift der Deutschen Morgenländischen Gesellschaft*
ZEE	*Zeitschrift für evangelische Ethik*
ZNW	*Zeitschrift für die neutestamentliche Wissenschaft*
ZPapEp	*Zeitschrift für Papyrologie und Epigraphik*
ZThK	*Zeitschrift für Theologie und Kirche*

Notes

Chapter 1

1. John Chrystostom, *Hom.XII on I Tim.4*: Migne, PG 62,563f.; ET from NPNF, vol.XII, by Philip Schaff.

2. Cicero, *De Finibus*, 3,67; ET from LCL, by H. Rackham.

3. Gregory Nazianzen, *Hom.XIV,25*; Migne, PG 35, 892; cf. O. Schilling, *Reichtum und Eigentum in der altkirchlichen Literatur*, Diss., Tübingen/Freiburg 1908.

4. Jerome, *De Officiis* I, 28: Migne, PL 16,67; ET from NPNF, by H. de Romestin.

5. Aristophanes, *Ecclesiazousae* 590-4; ET from LCL, by B.B. Rogers.

6. Ovid, *Metamorphoses* I, 89ff.; ET from LCL, by Frank Justus Miller.

7. Virgil, *Georgics* 1, 126ff.; ET from LCL, by H. Rushton Fairclough.

8. Strabo, *Geography* 7, 3, 9; ET from LCL, by Horace Leonard Jones.

9.   Virgil, *Eclogues* 4, 39ff.; ET from LCL, by H. Rushton Fairclough.

10.   Seneca, *Ad Lucilium Epistulae Morales*; ET from LCL, by R.M. Gummere.

11.   Cf. B. Gatz, *Weltalter, goldene Zeit und sinnverwandte Vorstellungen*, Hildesheim 1967; cf. also F. Engels, *Der Ursprung der Familie, des Privateigentums und des Staats*, [4] 1891.

12.   Strabo, *Geography* 14,1,38; J. Vogt, *Sklaverei und Humanität*, [2] 1972, 31ff., 41ff.

13.   L. Koenen, *ZPapEp* 2, 1968, 205 line 44.

14.   W.W. Tarn, *Cambridge Ancient History* VII, 741ff.

15.   E. Plumacher, *Lukas als hellenistischer Schriftsteller*, SUNT 9, Göttingen 1972, 17f.

16.   H. Chadwick, *The Sentences of Sextus*, Cambridge University Press 1959, no.278.

17.   M. Dibelius and H. Conzelmann, *The Pastoral Epistles*, Philadelphia 1972, 85f.; see below, p.000.

18.   See Polycarp 4; Tertullian, *De Patientia* 7,5; Clement of Alexandria, *Paedagogus* 2,39,3, cf. 38,5.

19.   Cf. C. Spicq, *Les Epîtres Pastorales* I, Paris [4] 1969, 564; W.F. Arndt − F.W. Gingrich − W. Bauer, *A Greek-English Lexicon of the New Testament*, Chicago 1957, 866.

20.   Pseudo-Phocylides 41; Sib.3,235f., 642f.; 8,17f. and often in Philo.

21.   Menander, *Dyskolos*, frag.; ET from LCL by Francis G. Allinson, 345f.

22.   H. Hommel, in *Festschrift zum 65. Geburtstag Walter Mönch*, Heidelberg 1971, 20ff.

Chapter 2

1.   Otto Kaiser, *Isaiah 1-12*, OTL, London and Philadelphia 1972, 70.

2.   K. Elliger, *Leviticus*, HAT 4, Tübingen 1966, 356.

3.   M. Hengel, *Victory over Violence*, Philadelphia 1973, 32; id., *Die Zeloten* (AGSU 1), Leiden 1961, 341f.

4.   M. Hengel, *Judaism and Hellenism*, Vol. I, London and Philadelphia 1974, 036ff.

5.   4QpPs 37 II, 9ff.; ET from G. Vermes, *The Dead Sea Scrolls in English*, Harmondsworth [2] 1965, 243f.

6.   1 QM 11.8f., 13; ET from Vermes, op.cit., 138.

7.   Tos.Pea 4,19 = Sukka 49b; Bill.4,537, cf. 541.

8.   Bab. Keth.50a; Bill.4,550f.

9.   Keth.110b; Sanh.100b; cf. E. Bammel, *TDNT* VI, 901.

10.   Pes.R.Kah. 1,241f., ed. Mandelbaum; Hag. 9b, etc.

Chapter 3

1.   W.G. Kümmel, 'Der Begriff des Eigentums im Neuen Testa-

ment', *Heilsgeschehen und Geschichte*, Marburger Theologische Studien 3, 1965, 271-7.

2.   Jerome, *Ep.*120,1,11: Migne, PL 22, 985; cf. R. von Pöhlmann, *Geschichte der Sozialen Frage und des Sozialismus in der antiken Welt* II, Munich ³ 1925, 470.

Chapter 4

1.   Ernst Bloch, *Das Prinzip Hoffnung* III, Stuttgart 1959, 1488.

Chapter 6

1.   Cyprian, *Ep.*2.2; ET from ANF, by A. Cleveland Coxe, Vol.V, 356, where it is numbered *Ep.*60.
2.   Eusebius, HE 4,23,10; ET from H.J. Lawlor and J.E.L. Oulton, *Eusebius: The Ecclesiastical History*, SPCK 1927, 130.
3.   A. von Harnack, *The Mission and Expansion of Christianity in the First Three Centuries* I, Williams and Norgate 1908, 158f.
4.   Harnack, op.cit., 171ff.

Chapter 7

1.   R. von Pöhlmann, *Geschichte der Sozialen Frage* I³ , 492.
2.   'Christian Sibyllines', in: E. Hennecke — W. Schneemelcher — R. McL. Wilson, *New Testament Apocrypha* II, Lutterworth Press 1965, 718, translated by R. McL. Wilson. The passage is Sib.2,318-24.
3.   M. Krause and P. Labib, *Gnostische und Hermetische Schriften aus Cod.II and Cod. VI*, 107ff., cf. *ThLZ* 98, 1973, 13ff.
4.   Op.cit., 11f.
5.   Tertullian, *Apologia* 39.10f., cf. *Ep.Diogn.*5.7f.
6.   Minucius Felix, *Octavius* 36,5; ET from ANF, by A. Cleveland Coxe.
7.   Acts of Thomas 20, in *New Testament Apocrypha* II, 453; cf. chs.62,96,136, pp.477,493,514.
8.   Ibid., chs.144f., p.519.
9.   Ibid., ch.45, p.468; ch.47, p.469.
10.   Ibid., ch.37, pp.463f.; cf. ch.117, p.505.
11.   Ibid., chs 60,100, pp.476,494.
12.   Ibid., ch.66, p.479; cf. chs.83-85, pp.487f.
13.   Ibid., ch.59, p.475.
14.   Ibid., ch.164, p.522.
15.   Ibid., chs. 131,170, pp.512,531.
16.   P. Nagel, *Die Motivierung der Askese und der Ursprung des Mönchtums*, (TU 95), Berlin 1966, 34ff., 75ff.

Chapter 8

1.   M. Hengel, *Nachfolge und Charisma* (BZNW 34), Göttingen 1968, 32.
2.   A. Resch, *Agrapha, Aussercanonische Schriftfragmente gesam-*

melt und untersucht, Leipzig ²1906, no.171, pp.198f.; cf. above, p.5ll
   3.   H. Chadwick, *The Sentences of Sextus*, 160.
   4.   Ibid., 87.
   5.   Clement of Alexandria, *Paedagogus* 2,128,2; cf. 1,98,4; *Strom.* 3,89'; 6,24,8, and below pp.74ff.

Chapter 9

   1.   Lucian, *Peregrinus* 13; ET from LCL V, by A.M. Harmon.
   2.   *Didascalia Apostolorum* 13; ET from ibid., *The Syriac Version translated and accompanied by the Verona Fragments* by R. Hugh Connolly, Clarendon Press 1929. Cf. Harnack, *The Mission and Expansion*, 177ff.
   3.   *New Testament Apocrypha* II, 98,
   4.   A. von Harnack, *Marcion*, Berlin 1921, 24ff.
   5.   Ch.18, *New Testament Apocrypha* II, 300.
   6.   Ch.22, ibid., 304.
   7.   Ch.30, ibid., 314.
   8.   Harnack, *The Mission and Expansion*, 157f.
   9.   H. Gülzow, *Christentum und Sklaverei*, Bonn 1969, 142-72; there is an English text of the relevant part of the Refutation in J. Stevenson, *A New Eusebius*, SPCK 1957, 160ff.
  10.   Gülzow, op.cit., 165.
  11.   Ibid., 172.

Chapter 10

   1.   *Hist.Aug.*29,85f. = Fl.Vopiscus, *Vita Sat.*
   2.   Clement of Alexandria, *Paedagogus* 2,119,2-120,5; cf. *Protrept.* 122,3; ET from ANF, by A. Cleveland Coxe, which is also used for the other extracts from Clement.

Chapter 11

   1.   Cf. *Vita* 15, and H. Kraft, *Die Kirchenväter*, Bremen 1966, 362f.
   2.   *Quodcumque enim Dei est in nostra usurpatione commune est*, cf. Ambrose and Cicero, above, pp.3f.
   3.   ET here and in this chapter from ANF, by A. Cleveland Coxe.
   4.   W.-D. Hauschild, *ZEE* 16, 1972, 45.

Chapter 12

   1.   Eberhard Jüngel, *Unterwegs zur Sache*, Tübingen 1972,272.